Reinterpreting the Constitution

Reinterpreting the Constitution

How the Supreme Court Changes the Law

Edward F. Mannino

LEXINGTON BOOKS
Lanham • Boulder • New York • London

Published by Lexington Books
An imprint of The Rowman & Littlefield Publishing Group, Inc.
4501 Forbes Boulevard, Suite 200, Lanham, Maryland 20706
www.rowman.com

86-90 Paul Street, London EC2A 4NE

British Library Cataloguing in Publication Information Available

Library of Congress Cataloging-in-Publication Data Available

ISBN 978-1-66693-830-2 (cloth)
ISBN 978-1-66693-831-9 (electronic)

For Toni, my wife and my muse
and
For Bruce K, friend and mentor

Contents

Acknowledgments

I owe special thanks to Sara Noakes, my editor, for her gracious assistance and highly professional editing and shepherding of this manuscript to publication. I also thank the anonymous peer reviewer for his/her helpful comments, which improved the quality of this book. Thanks also to Bruce Kuklick, my long-term friend and mentor, who provided sage advice regarding preparation and publication of this manuscript. Most especially, I thank Toni, my wife and resident muse, for her consistent encouragement and support during the many years over which this book was written.

Introduction

The Supreme Court in the twenty-first century has often changed its prior rulings on constitutional law. During the first quarter of this century, the Supreme Court has been called upon to decide many issues of great importance to the American people. In resolving those issues, the court has created new rights, while expanding or limiting others. Those issues have included the following:

- Is there a constitutional right to have an abortion?
- Do same-sex couples have a constitutional right to marry?
- How far do Congress' powers under the Commerce Clause extend?
- Can a church or a religious school receive direct governmental benefits?
- Is it permissible to open a town hall meeting with a prayer?
- Can states maintain a war memorial that features a cross?
- What, if any, limitations can be imposed on free speech?
- Can unions compel nonunion members to pay agency fees?
- Can restrictions be placed on access to social media?
- Do corporations have a right to free speech sufficient to invalidate contribution limits for elections?
- Does the right to keep and bear arms extend to individuals not serving in a militia?
- Can cell phone records be searched without first obtaining a warrant?
- Does it constitute cruel and unusual punishment to impose a life sentence without the possibility of parole?
- Are limitations imposed upon Southern states and certain other political subdivisions in the Voting Rights Act of 1965 constitutionally valid?
- Is it permissible to consider race as a factor in state university admissions?
- Can the voters of a state ban the use of affirmative action in state university admissions?
- Can states compel pro-life pregnancy centers to inform women where to obtain an abortion?
- Can state legislators draw congressional districting maps to unduly favor their own party?

In this book, we review the most recent decisions on those issues, as well as on many others. We will examine the composition of the current court under Chief Justice John Roberts. Prior to Roberts assuming that position, the Supreme Court had not experienced any changes in its membership between 1994, when Justice Stephen Breyer began his service on the court, and September of 2005, when Chief Justice Roberts took the oath of office. Beginning in 2005, the identity of the justices changed dramatically, with seven new associate justices joining the new chief justice by 2022. Since these are the justices (as of the end of the Court's Term in 2022) who will decide these and other new issues, and further extend or contract existing precedent, we review their backgrounds, writings, and legal views, as well as their judicial opinions, both before and during their tenures on the Supreme Court.

We review the constitutional decisions of the Supreme Court, first summarizing the precedents as they existed through the end of the twentieth century. These older cases provide a base against which the more recent rulings in the twenty-first century may be assessed. What emerges from this analysis is a recognition that the current court has, on various constitutional issues, extended, limited, or overruled prior precedent; created new rights; adjudicated many novel issues; and affected the lives of ordinary Americans in many new ways. In the course of this analysis, we also document the historical, political, and social contexts that serve as a backdrop to the court's decision-making.

The current court has extended prior precedents in many ways. Chief among these decisions are its rulings on the First and Eighth Amendments. The guarantee of free speech has been broadened to include many additional areas of political, religious, and commercial discourse. Similarly, the protection of free exercise of religion has been expanded, while the prohibitions of the Establishment Clause have been narrowed. The Eighth Amendment prohibition against cruel and unusual punishments has been broadened to include many areas of criminal sentencing, with the court increasingly applying its own standards regarding which punishments are cruel and unusual.

In other rulings, prior precedents have been limited, including the protections accorded to voting rights as well as the congressional power to legislate under the Commerce Clause. In addition, the Second Amendment right to bear arms was extended to recognize a personal right despite an earlier ruling relating it to the militia.

The current court has also created new constitutional rights, most notably by recognizing a constitutional right to same-sex marriage, overruling prior precedent to the contrary.

And, most notably, the court overruled *Roe v. Wade*, a nearly fifty-year-old precedent, returning the issue of permissible restrictions on abortion to the states.

In reviewing these decisions, our analysis will let the justices speak for themselves by quoting the language of the justices in the majority, as well as those who concur or dissent from the various rulings. Finally, we will examine the implications of each ruling and, where available, how these new decisions have been applied or interpreted in practice.

Chapter 1

Free Speech

The First Amendment explicitly prohibits the government from making any law that, among other things, "abridg[es] the freedom of speech, or of the press; or the right of the people peaceably to assemble, and to petition the Government for a redress of grievances." The Roberts Court has been particularly active in interpreting the protections accorded to free speech, deciding more than fifty cases presenting this issue and extending the protections of the Free Speech Clause to many types of speech. These decisions come at a time when public officials at the federal and state level, as well as universities and much of the media, call for limits on what they consider to be "hateful" speech, particularly when such speech involves perceived slights to people of color or who identify as LBGT+.

The issue of protection of free speech under the First Amendment came late to the Supreme Court. Until 1925, free speech was only protected against federal intrusion. As such, the earliest cases involved federal legislation that inhibited free speech. The first important Supreme Court cases involved criminal sanctions imposed under the Espionage and Sedition Acts enacted during World War I. These statutes criminalized both conduct and writings that opposed the war effort.

The first Supreme Court case involving free speech under the First Amendment was *Schenck v. United States* (1919). That decision in that case upheld criminal penalties against individuals who had circulated leaflets urging workers to resist being conscripted into the armed forces. In an opinion written by Justice Oliver Wendell Holmes, the court applied a "clear and present danger" test, with Holmes analogizing the leaflets' effect to that of a person "falsely shouting fire in a theater and causing a panic."

In the same year, in *Abrams v. United States*, the court upheld the imposition of twenty-year jail sentences for five individuals who circulated leaflets urging workers in munitions plants to go on a general strike. This time, however, Justices Holmes and Brandeis dissented, suggesting a test examining whether the activity in question presented a "present danger of immediate evil."

In a second set of cases, the court years later considered the penalties imposed by the Smith Act of 1940, which criminalized advocating forcible overthrow of the United States government. All twelve members of the Communist Party USA's executive board were indicted and participated in a trial that was the longest criminal trial in the history of United States up to that time. The court struggled with reconciling the First Amendment protection of free speech against attacks against the government. While upholding convictions of five years in jail for ten of the eleven defendants, *Dennis v. United States* (1956) did not deliver a majority opinion. The lead opinion by Chief Justice Fred Vinson adopted a formula under which the courts are required to ask "whether the gravity of the 'evil' discounted by its improbability justifies such an invasion of free speech as is necessary to avoid the danger." There were two dissenting opinions by Justices Hugo Black and William Douglas, and two concurring opinions by Justices Félix Frankfurter and Robert Jackson. No approach to the issue was accepted by more than four members of the court.

A second case, *Yates v. United States* (1957), reversed the convictions of the leaders of the Communist Party of the United States in California. Again, there was no majority opinion. Justice John Harlan's lead opinion avoided the constitutional issue by reading the Smith Act as not criminalizing "advocacy and teaching of forcible overthrow as an abstract principle, divorced from any effort to instigate action to that end." In Harlan's view, "The essential distinction is that those to whom the advocacy is addressed must be urged to *do* something, now or in the future, rather than merely to *believe* in something." Harlan's opinion was joined only by two other justices. Justices Black and Douglas took an absolutist position, with Black writing that "the First Amendment forbids Congress to punish people for talking about public affairs, whether or not such discussion incites to action, legal or illegal." With two other justices not participating, the remaining Justice, Tom Clark, dissented, contending that the *Yates* case was no different than that presented in *Dennis*.

The failure to articulate a uniform standard as to the limits of the First Amendment's protection of free speech continued to plague the court for several more years. Finally, in *Brandenburg v. Ohio* (1969), the court ruled that the First Amendment "do[es] not permit a state to forbid or proscribe advocacy of the use of force or law violation except where such advocacy is directed to inciting or producing imminent lawless action and is likely to incite or produce such action." In that case, the court reversed the conviction of the leader of the Ohio Ku Klux Klan for making a speech attacking African

Americans and Jews. The speech was attended only by a single newsperson and several participants from the Klan.

While these and other early cases principally involved core political speech, the more recent decisions of the Supreme Court, particularly since 2010, have expansively interpreted the protections of the First Amendment in the area of free speech for both individuals and corporations, extending protections to political, religious, and many other areas of speech, including campaign financing, commercial speech, trademark registration, access to the internet, and even compelled speech of nonunion members of public employee unions. This expanded protection of varied forms of speech comes at a time when, as noted above, many call for limitations on politically incorrect and otherwise disfavored speech. Indeed, in a May 2017, commencement speech to the graduates of a Catholic seminary in Philadelphia, Justice Alito cautioned that "The idea that speech can be banned if it expresses an idea that is offensive is spreading around the country." He again spoke to the issue in a 2020 speech to the Federalist Society, noting that "We should all welcome rational civil speech on important subjects, even if we do not agree with what the speaker has to say. Unfortunately, tolerance for opposing views is now in short supply in many law schools, and in the broader academic community. When I speak with recent law school graduates, what I hear over and over is that they face harassment and retaliation if they say anything that departs from the law school orthodoxy."

The current court has served as a sign of contradiction to multiple efforts to limit free speech. As such, it has strongly and increasingly validated Professor Richard Garnett's observation that "it is crystal-clear that this is a free-speech court."[1]

Not all the justices have approved of all of these extensions of the First Amendment's protection of free speech. Indeed, in her dissenting opinion for four justices in *Janus v. American Federation of State, County & Municipal Employees* (2018), a case involving the right of nonunion public employees to refuse to pay "agency fees" to the union, Justice Kagan accused the majority of "weaponizing the First Amendment," and acting as "black-robed rulers overriding citizens' choices."[2]

Federal and state executives and legislatures have begun to push back on efforts by state universities to limit speech they deem objectionable. On March 21, 2019, President Trump issued an Executive Order "to promote free and open debate on college and university campuses," encouraging these institutions "to avoid creating environments that stifle competing perspectives, thereby potentially impeding beneficial research and undermining learning." The order directed federal agencies to take "appropriate steps" consistent with the First Amendment and applicable laws "to ensure institutions that receive Federal research or education grants promote free inquiry, including through compliance with all applicable Federal laws, regulations and policies."

The Trump Executive Order followed by one day the enactment by the South Dakota Legislature of HB No. 1087, which required the boards of each of South Dakota's six public universities to "require each institution under [their] control to maintain a commitment to the principles of free expression and encourage the timely and rational discussion of topics in an environment that is intellectually and ideologically diverse." The boards of these universities were prohibited from attempting "to shield individuals from constitutionally protected speech, including ideas and opinions they find offensive, unwise, immoral, indecent, disagreeable, conservative, liberal, traditional, radical, or wrong-headed."

We review below a great variety of recent opinions by the Supreme Court upholding the right of free speech. They are discussed to demonstrate how broadly the current membership of the Supreme Court has extended the protections of the First Amendment to speech and activities well beyond core political speech. These rulings have been delivered in most cases by large majorities, including members of both the liberal and conservative wings of the court.

VIDEOS DEPICTING ANIMAL CRUELTY

Millions of people in the United States are fortunate enough to have animals as pets. Pet owners do their best to protect their animals, and this has fueled the rise of several outspoken animal rights groups. These groups and many other organizations and individuals strenuously object to videos that portray the killing or barbarous treatment of animals. Thus, the question arises as to what extent the First Amendment may protect the right of video makers to film and distribute videos that depict cruelty to animals. *United States v. Stevens* (2010) addressed this issue, striking down as "substantially overbroad" a federal statute that prohibited the creation, sale, or possession of any "depiction of animal cruelty," defined as "any visual or auditory depiction" of any conduct in which a living animal was, among other things, "wounded" or "killed." The coverage of the Act also extended to animals that were "maimed, mutilated, [or] tortured," but was not limited to those categories. While the statute provided an exception for depictions that were of "serious religious, political, scientific, educational, journalistic, historical, or artistic value," eight members of the court held that this exception was insufficient to save the Act. Thus, while the other words of the statute such as "maimed" or "tortured" conveyed cruelty, "wounded" and "killed" did not do so, and a substantial number of legitimate depictions of such animals, as in hunting magazines and various videos, could potentially have been prosecuted under the Act.

Chief Justice Roberts's opinion of the court explained that the First Amendment only permits "restrictions on the content of speech in a few limited areas," including obscenity, defamation, fraud, and "speech integral to criminal conduct." In addition, "Our Constitution forecloses any attempt to revise that judgment simply on the basis that some speech is not worth it," and "we decline to carve out from the First Amendment any novel exception" for this Act.

In a solitary dissenting opinion, Justice Alito focused on the fact that the case in question involved videos depicting dogfights, which are illegal in all fifty states, and participation in promoting such fights constitutes a felony under federal law, as football star Michael Vick discovered to his dismay when he served twenty-two months in prison for his financing of, and participation in, such fights and related animal abuse.

The majority found the fact that Stevens had been involved in videos depicting dog fighting to be irrelevant since the appeal made a facial challenge to the Act, and therefore the court was not required to consider the particular videos in question. By contrast, Justice Alito argued that court had a "duty to interpret [the Act] so as to avoid serious constitutional concerns." As such, the statute should have been interpreted in his view not to apply to hunting, which was the principal example relied upon the majority in ruling that the Act was constitutionally overbroad under the First Amendment. Looking at the congressional debates, Justice Alito pointed out that proponents of the law expressly stated that it did not apply to ordinary hunting and fishing activities. Moreover, he contended that a reasonable construction of the Act would limit its prohibitions to "depictions involving acts of animal cruelty as defined by applicable state or federal law. . . . " He found that dogfight videos met this definition because they have no "appreciable social value," encourage the illegal act of dog fighting, and enable gambling on the outcome by those who fear prosecution if they attend the live event.

Various interest groups had different reactions to the *Stevens* decision. The Humane Society of the United States had pushed for Stevens's prosecution, and the animal rights activist group PETA, in a blog posting, saw the announcement of the decision as "Sad, Bad News From U.S. Supreme Court." By contrast, various publishers' groups and the NRA praised the majority opinion for upholding the right of vigorous free speech. Congress, in turn, passed new legislation at the end of 2010 to specifically prohibit so-called crush videos, which the Government had argued in *Stevens* were the actual target of the original legislation. In this area, therefore, statutes seeking to limit the rights of video makers will be closely examined by courts, and will require more careful drafting than that which characterizes the work of most legislatures, both state and federal.

RELIGIOUS PROTESTS AT SOLDIERS' FUNERALS

Funerals represent a sacred time to friends and relatives of the deceased. To what extent, then, can protesters at funerals be subjected to civil or criminal judgments for disrupting the final rites or burial ceremonies of people who are despised by some group? In this sensitive area, the Supreme Court opted for according First Amendment protection against imposition of a civil damages judgment on protesters who invoked religious beliefs to justify their actions. Thus, in *Snyder v. Phelps* (2011), eight justices agreed that members of the Westboro Baptist Church had First Amendment protection for their extremely hateful speech during picketing near a Catholic Church, which was the site of the funeral of an American marine killed in the line of duty in Iraq.

Snyder differed from many First Amendment cases because it arose in a civil, rather than a criminal, context. The Westboro congregation had been sued civilly for intentional infliction of emotional distress and other tort causes of action by the soldier's father, who had seen only the tops of the signs held by the picketers while he was driving to the funeral, but did not learn what the signs actually said until after the funeral. The jury returned a verdict for both compensatory and punitive damages, totaling some $10,900,000.

The Westboro congregation was protesting both the toleration of homosexuality by the military and scandals in the Catholic Church. Their signs carried such messages as "Thank God for dead soldiers," "Thank God for 9/11," "Fags doom nations," "Semper Fi Fags," "America is doomed," "Priests rape Boys," and "Pope in Hell." Members of the Westboro church had participated in such picketing at almost six hundred funerals over a twenty-year period.

In the opinion of the court, Chief Justice Roberts noted that the key question was whether the picketing involved a matter of public concern. The majority concluded that it did, because the picketers were highlighting such issues as "the political and moral conduct of the United States and its citizens, the fate of our Nation, homosexuality in the military, and scandals involving the Catholic clergy." In addition, Roberts saw the fact that the Westboro church had previously participated in hundreds of such protests for two decades as demonstrating that their actions were not directed at the soldier and his family personally.

While the majority held that the speech was subject to "reasonable time, place, or manner restrictions," it noted that the congregants had complied with the applicable laws, and "the church members had the right to be where they were." That the speech was hurtful and reprehensible, particularly in the context of a funeral, was not relevant. Chief Justice Roberts stated that "we cannot react to that pain by punishing the speaker," and that the speech in question "cannot be restricted simply because it is upsetting or arouses contempt." As such, the congregation was "shield[ed] . . . from tort liability for its picketing in this case."

Justice Samuel Alito dissented in *Snyder*, as he had in *Stevens*. His dissenting opinion described the picketing as a "vicious verbal assault" that interfered with the father's right "to bury his son in peace," thereby "brutaliz[ing]" him. Alito saw the picketing as lending "no contribution to public debate," but rather as intentionally inflicting "grave injury" legitimately punishable by an award of civil damages.

Justice Alito found evidence that the picketing was directed at the soldier and his family, rather than at issues of public import. He noted that the signs could be read to state that the soldier was gay and/or was damned. Moreover, in an online posting after the funeral, the church attacked the parents for having been divorced, and for raising the soldier as a Catholic, which gave support to "satanic Catholicism" and "the largest pedophile machine in the history of the entire world, the Roman Catholic monstrosity." In light of this evidence, Justice Alito concluded that "While commentary on the Catholic Church or the United States military constitutes speech on matters of public concern, speech regarding [the soldier's] private conduct does not."

Snyder v. Phelps has occasioned much commentary. One point that has been stressed is that speech of the type involved in the case would not be protected, and indeed would be criminally prosecuted, in many countries, including Canada and several countries in Europe. Former federal Circuit Judge Michael McConnell has said that "we should be grateful that our courts are standing up against the international trend toward punishing speech on the ground that it is offensive to protected minority groups. That is part of what makes America unique." McConnell also questioned whether *Snyder* might affect prohibitions on "hate speech" imposed on many college campuses and at workplaces, or on harassment laws generally.[3] This has become an increasingly important issue as universities across the nation have vigorously promulgated speech codes that ban certain phrases or characterize as disfavored "racial microaggressions," including such comments as "America is a melting pot," "I believe the most qualified person should get the job," or "You are a credit to your race."

ABORTION "BUFFER ZONES"

One familiar sight outside many clinics that perform abortions is the presence of pro-life advocates who attempt to persuade women not to undergo an abortion. These efforts have often met with success, and therefore are vigorously opposed by pro-abortion groups such as Planned Parenthood. These latter groups have often been successful in convincing state and local governments to enact legislation banning pro-life advocates from coming closer than a specified number of feet to an abortion clinic. By relegating opponents of abortion to the back of the areas where the clinics are located, these laws have reduced the effectiveness of the pro-life groups in persuading women not to undergo an abortion.

In another important First Amendment case, the Supreme Court struck down a Massachusetts statute that barred all individuals, except for certain municipal agents and facility workers "acting within the scope of their employment," from approaching closer than thirty-five feet to any abortion clinic entrance, exit, or driveway. Violations of the statute could be punished by criminal penalties ranging from three months' imprisonment for a first offense to a maximum of two and a half years for subsequent offenses. In *McCullen v. Coakley* (2014), the Supreme Court unanimously struck down the statute as violative of the First Amendment. Previously, a very different Supreme Court in *Hill v. Colorado* (2000) had upheld, by a six-to-three vote, an eight-foot ban on approaching a person without her consent within one hundred feet of an entrance to any healthcare facility. There, Justice John Paul Stevens concluded that the ban did not regulate speech, but only where speech might occur, and that it did not single out abortion-related communications because it applied to all demonstrators, no matter what their message or cause. He also opined that the eight-foot restriction was not wide enough to preclude communications through verbal or visual speech.

The legal context in which *McCullen* was decided is important to an understanding of its significance. Thus, for nearly fifty years, in the wake of its controversial decision in *Roe v. Wade* (1973), the Supreme Court persistently upheld the right of a woman to choose to have an abortion. This judicially created right was subjected to very few restrictions, and many state laws that attempted to limit abortion were declared unconstitutional by the Supreme Court. For example, in a decision discussed later in this book, the court struck down Texas state laws that attempted to require that abortion doctors have admitting privileges at hospitals located within thirty miles of their facility, and that the facilities themselves satisfy minimum standards for ambulatory surgical centers previously enacted under state law (*Whole Woman's Health v. Hellerstedt* [2016]). Until the decision in *Dobbs v. Jackson Women's Health Organization* (2022), which overruled *Roe v. Wade*, limitations on abortion were rarely upheld. One limitation that was upheld was that prohibiting partial-birth abortions. In *Gonzales v. Carhart* (2007), in the early days of the Roberts Court, a five-member majority upheld this ban on a procedure used only in late-term abortions, finding that Congress could legislate against its use because of what Congress characterized as the procedure's "similarity to the killing of a newborn infant."

Given the court's pre-2022 refusal to overrule *Roe v. Wade*, and its striking down of many different attempts by state legislatures to limit or prohibit abortions in certain cases, those opposing abortions have decided to appear at abortion facilities to attempt to counsel women visiting those facilities to choose an option other than abortion, such as putting their infant up for adoption. Justice Scalia, dissenting in *Hill v. Colorado*, noted that the court's previous abortion decisions had left individuals opposing abortion as the taking of a human life "no option but to persuade women, one by one, not to make that choice. And as a general matter, the most effective place, if not the only place, where that persuasion can occur is outside the entrances to abortion facilities. By upholding the restrictions on speech in this place the Court ratifies the State's attempt to make even that task an impossible one."

Other jurisdictions than Colorado, at both the state and local level, have also attempted to limit anti-abortion counseling near abortion clinics by prohibiting, under criminal penalties, approaching women near abortion clinics for the purpose of counseling, whether done orally or in writing, as by the distribution of pro-life literature.

McCullen established that there are some limits on these attempts to ban counseling near abortion facilities. The result in *McCullen* was unanimous in striking down the thirty-five-foot "buffer zone" around abortion facilities, but the justices split five to four on why the statute was unconstitutional. In an opinion written by Chief Justice Roberts, and joined by Justices Ginsburg, Breyer, Sotomayor, and Kagan, the majority ruled that the statute was neither content- nor viewpoint-based, and thus was not subject to heightened strict scrutiny review. Nevertheless, they held the statute unconstitutional because it was not narrowly enough tailored, and it burdened the free-speech rights of the pro-life petitioners to express their opposition to abortion and to have conversations with women seeking to enter the clinics regarding alternatives to abortion. By contrast, Justice Scalia, joined by Justices Kennedy, Thomas, and Alito, saw the statute as content-based, aimed at anti-abortion speech, and would have held it unconstitutional as such under strict scrutiny review. Indeed, Justice Scalia chided the majority for continuing to abridge the free-speech rights of pro-life speakers under what he termed an "abortion-speech-only jurisprudence" because of its refusal to adopt the strict scrutiny standard in abortion-related cases.

The unanimous result was foreshadowed at the oral argument, when several of the justices questioned whether a thirty-five-foot buffer zone was narrowly enough tailored to address the problems actually experienced by Massachusetts clinics, and the majority opinion pointed out that other federal and state laws were sufficient to address any significant problems that the clinics might experience in the future. In addition, there was significant evidence that the buffer zones had had a significant impact on the effectiveness of the advocacy being pursued by pro-life groups. The majority opinion noted that the pro-life leaders had experienced success in persuading women not to undergo an abortion before the establishment of the buffer zones, but that their successes had experienced a "precipitous decline" thereafter, and the efforts of the pro-life groups to distribute literature had become "substantially more difficult."

It was also significant that the majority opinion refused to classify the pro-life speakers as protesters. Instead, that opinion concluded that "Petitioners are not protesters. They seek not merely to express their opposition to abortion, but to inform women of various alternatives and to provide help in pursuing them. Petitioners believe that they can accomplish this objective only through personal, caring, consensual conversations." The majority opinion further cited earlier precedent, echoing Justice Scalia's dissenting opinion in *Hill*, for the proposition that "'one-on-one communication' is 'the most effective, fundamental, and perhaps economical avenue of political discourse.'"

While three of the four dissenters would have overruled *Hill v. Colorado*, the majority opinion mentioned that decision only in passing, and did nothing to affect its precedential status.

Several pro-choice groups assailed the decision as infringing upon the rights of women to seek an abortion, and Massachusetts officials promptly called for and enacted new legislation in July 2014 to limit pro-life advocacy near abortion clinics in that state, changing the buffer zone to twenty-five feet but increasing the criminal penalties for violation of the law.

Given the unanimous decision in *McCullen*, pro-choice groups attempting to limit pro-life groups from approaching abortion clinics that are still allowed to operate after the *Dobbs* decision are unlikely to succeed in the courts in any future litigation over buffer zones similar to that mandated by the original (and perhaps by the revised) Massachusetts law because the opinion was narrowly drawn to emphasize protection for the free-speech rights of peaceful pro-life advocates who counsel women to seek alternatives to abortion. Thus, so long as their advocacy remains peaceful, it likely will be protected by the Supreme Court. Indeed, attempts to single out such advocacy legislatively may trigger strict scrutiny review of any such laws directed at pro-life advocacy at abortion clinics. Thus, such laws may lead to challenges that will raise the issues of singling out pro-life advocacy, the use of strict scrutiny review, and the continued status of *Hill v. Colorado* as a viable precedent, particularly in light of the decisions in *Reed v. Town of*

Gilbert and *National Institute of Family & Life Advocates v. Becerra*, both of which are discussed in this chapter.

COMPELLING INFORMING WOMEN WHERE THEY CAN OBTAIN AN ABORTION

In *National Institute of Family & Life Advocates v. Becerra* (2018), the Supreme Court was again presented with a First Amendment issue relating to the rights of pro-life groups to challenge laws regulating their activities. In that case, a California law required clinics that mostly served pregnant women to provide certain notices to those women. If the clinic was licensed, it was required to inform women in a government-drafted notice of the availability of free or low-cost services, including abortions, and to supply a telephone number the women could call to obtain an abortion. In the case of unlicensed clinics, they were required to inform women that they were not licensed to provide medical services. Two pro-life clinics, one licensed and the other unlicensed, challenged the regulations, but were unsuccessful in obtaining a preliminary injunction against their enforcement.

On appeal, the Supreme Court, in a five-to-four decision, found that both notice requirements violated the First Amendment, and that the plaintiffs were likely to succeed in their constitutional challenge. With respect to the licensed clinics, the court held, in an opinion by Justice Thomas, that the notice was a content-based regulation. "By compelling individuals to speak a particular message," such notices "alte[r] the content of [their] speech." As such, the notices are judged under a strict scrutiny standard, and are presumptively unconstitutional unless narrowly tailored to serve a compelling state interest.

It made no difference, in the majority's view, that "professional speech" was involved. The court held that such speech is only afforded lesser protection under two circumstances. The first circumstance is where "factual, uncontroversial" information is required to be disclosed by professionals. Here, however, "abortion [is] anything but an 'uncontroversial' topic." The second instance in which professional speech is afforded lesser protection is where the law regulates professional conduct that only incidentally involves speech. Such was not the case here.

The court concluded that even if the state had a substantial interest in informing women of the availability of the state-sponsored services, the notice it required was "wildly underinclusive." This was because it applied only to clinics whose primary purpose was to provide family planning for pregnancy-related services. In addition, even some otherwise eligible clinics, such as those that were federally designated community health centers, were exempted from the requirement of providing the government notice. The court also noted that California itself could provide a government notice to inform women of the availability of the services in question, rather than burden the licensed clinics to go against their religious beliefs by steering women to abortion centers.

The court also held that the notice required to be given by the unlicensed centers likewise violated the First Amendment. First, the state offered a purely hypothetical justification for requiring the notice, contending that women did not know these clinics were staffed by unlicensed medical professionals. Thus, "It imposes a government-scripted, speaker-based disclosure requirement that is wholly disconnected from the State's informational interest." Second, the required notice was a "speaker-based law" and applied only to a narrow group of speakers. As such, "It targets speakers, not speech, and imposes an unduly burdensome disclosure requirement that will chill their protected speech."

Although it reversed the Ninth Circuit, it did not end the case, but instead remanded it to go forward on the centers' motion for preliminary injunction. In a footnote to the majority opinion, Justice Thomas noted that "Nothing in our opinion should be read to foreclose the possibility that California will gather enough evidence in later stages of this litigation."

In an important concurring opinion written by Justice Kennedy, and joined by Chief Justice Roberts and Justices Alito and Gorsuch, these justices noted that "It does appear that viewpoint discrimination is inherent in the design and structure of the Act" because it was targeted primarily at pro-life pregnancy centers. Indeed, the "apparent viewpoint discrimination here is a matter of serious constitutional concern" because it "imperils [the] liberties" of "freedom of thought and belief." Nevertheless, these justices concluded that the issue was not properly reached in the case at the current time, since the point was not developed in the preliminary injunction record in the lower court.

Justice Breyer wrote a dissenting opinion, which was joined by Justices Ginsburg, Sotomajor, and Kagan. He wrote that he would not have granted the pro-life clinics' motion for preliminary injunction because the California law was not unconstitutional on its face. Returning to a point he had made in his concurring opinion in *Reed v. Town of Gilbert* (2015) (discussed immediately below), Justice Breyer argued that the content-based approach taken by the majority threatens all disclosure laws, such as those imposed in securities regulation. He noted that the majority attempted to respond to this point with a general, but in his view unclear, disclaimer that its approach would not endanger traditional health and safety warnings. Justice Breyer concluded that "in suggesting that heightened scrutiny applies to much economic and social legislation, the majority pays . . . First Amendment goals a serious disservice through dilution."

The dissenters also contended that courts have traditionally deferred to "state legislative judgments concerning the medical profession." Moreover, referring to earlier Supreme Court decisions on regulation of abortion providers, Justice Breyer stated that "If the State can lawfully require a doctor to tell a woman seeking an abortion about adoption services, why should it not be able . . . to require a medical counselor to tell a woman seeking prenatal care or other reproductive health care about childbirth and abortion services?"

With respect to California's regulation of the unlicensed clinics, the dissenters argued that the state's interest was not hypothetical, and that it is "self-evident" that patients might think they are receiving qualified medical care when they visit a clinic. In addition, there is no invidious discrimination against pro-life centers on the face of the legislation since no distinction is made between them and pro-choice clinics.

Perhaps the most important future impact of the various opinions in this case is contained in the concurring opinion, which argued there was a "serious constitutional concern" raised by California's "apparent viewpoint discrimination." While the four dissenting justices saw no distinction drawn between pro-life and pro-choice centers on the face of the law, the concurring justices were clearly warning California not to target pro-life institutions based on their opposition to abortion. It is particularly significant that Justice Thomas, who wrote the majority opinion, had previously joined in the concurring opinion in the *McCullen* case, which called for strict scrutiny to be applied in adjudicating the constitutionality of regulations imposed on pro-life individuals and institutions, while the majority in that case chose not to decide that issue. Thus, a majority of the court may now be prepared to apply a stricter standard when reviewing laws that have a disparate impact on pro-life institutions. This possibility is enhanced by the court's decisions in such cases as *Trinity Lutheran*, *Espinoza v. Montana Department of Revenue*, and *Masterpiece Cakeshop* (all of which are discussed later in this book), where it ruled, respectively, that it was impermissible to exclude religious institutions from otherwise available benefits, or to treat religious objectors differently than others when providing goods or services. That possibility is even stronger given the recent appointments of Justices Kavanaugh and Barrett.

OUTDOOR SIGN CODES AND RESTRICTIONS ON ROBOCALLS

Most Americans would find it hard to believe that the protections of the First Amendment could be extended to the restrictions announced by outdoor sign codes erected by local governments. Nevertheless, in *Reed v. Town of Gilbert*

(2015), the Supreme Court unanimously struck down a municipal sign code that established permissible parameters for the display of outdoor signs. The code discriminated among various categories of signs. Ideological signs were permitted to be twenty square feet in area, and could be displayed without any time limit; political signs could be between sixteen and thirty-two square feet in area, and be displayed up to sixty days before, and until fifteen days after, an election; temporary directional signs, by contrast, could only be six square feet in area, and could remain in place only for twelve hours before, and one hour after, the event. The restrictions on temporary directional signs were challenged by a small church group that was required to advertise the time and location of its Sunday services because it had no permanent home. Despite its requests for accommodation, the church group received two citations for, among other things, exceeding the time limits for displaying its signs.

The majority opinion by Justice Thomas, which was joined by five other justices, held that "these provisions [of the municipal sign code] are content-based regulations of speech that cannot survive strict scrutiny." Justice Thomas further explained that "Government regulation of speech is content-based if a law applies to particular speech because of the topic discussed or the idea or message expressed." Such content-based regulations are subject to strict scrutiny review regardless of motive; there is no need to demonstrate an animus toward a particular idea or message implicated.

Under strict scrutiny review, the government must demonstrate a compelling interest for the regulation, and the regulation must be narrowly tailored to achieve that particular interest. In the case of the sign code, the town claimed two interests—aesthetics and traffic safety. All the justices agreed that these interests were insufficient, and that there was no reason to treat signs in the three different categories differently with regard to size or the permissible time limits during which they might be displayed. Justice Thomas observed that the distinctions made were "hopelessly underinclusive."

Finally, the majority opinion indicated that not all sign codes were impermissible. Many restrictions could be imposed so long as they were content-neutral. This issue of permissible signage in the wake of the *Reed* decision generated a concurring opinion by three of the justices who joined the majority opinion, and two opinions that simply concurred in the judgment and read more like dissents.

Justice Alito's concurring opinion listed nine categories of signs that would be permitted, ranging from those uniformly governing size to those imposing time restrictions for all onetime events. By contrast, Justice Breyer and Justice Kagan, the latter joined by Justices Ginsburg and Breyer, protested the use of the strict scrutiny standard of review for all sign codes, pointing to the confusion that will result as to what is, and what is not, permitted in the realm of signage regulations. This led Justice Kagan to warn that "This Court may soon find itself a veritable Supreme Board of Sign Review."

The most significant potential results of the *Reed* majority opinion go well beyond directional signs. There are two principal concerns. First, what might have motivated Justices Breyer, Kagan, and Ginsburg is the impact of the opinion's broad use of the strict scrutiny standard on restrictions to access to abortion clinics, and the continuing viability of *Hill v. Colorado* (2000) on that issue. Thus, Justice Thomas's opinion cited the dissenting opinions of both Justices Kennedy and Scalia in *Hill*; three justices had previously called for the reversal of *Hill* in *McCullen v. Coakley*, as noted above; and Chief Justice Roberts and Justice Sotomayor (neither of whom was on the court when *Hill* was decided) joined the majority opinion in *Gilbert*. Second, some academics and constitutional lawyers have suggested that federal and state regulatory legislation may be subject to attack under a strict scrutiny standard because of the approach taken by *Reed*. First Amendment expert Floyd Abrams, for example, has observed that *Reed* will require "a second look at the constitutionality of aspects of federal and state securities laws, the Federal Communications Act and many others."[4] This is because regulatory legislation may operate by singling out a particular topic for regulation, and then discriminate based on content.

The court confronted that issue in a confusing mix of opinions in *Barr v. American Association of Political Consultants, Inc.* (2020). That case took a second look at a provision of the Telephone Consumer Protection Act in light of the teachings of *Reed*. That Act originally prohibited almost all robocalls to cell phones but it was amended to provide a new exception for robocalls made to collect a debt owed to, or guaranteed by, the United States. While a plurality of the court noted that a prohibition against robocalls made to cell phones was constitutional because of the interest of preserving consumer privacy, a majority of the court concluded that the exception for calls made to collect government debt was not. That was because "the law favors speech made for collecting government debt over political and other speech," and therefore is "a content-based restriction on speech" that did not survive strict scrutiny.

By contrast, the court limited the reach of *Reed* in *City of Austin v. Reagan National Advertising of Austin, LLC* (2022), a case involving off-premises signs. The City of Austin prohibited construction of new off-premises signs but did not mandate the same for on-premises signs. Justice Sotomayor's majority opinion upheld the disparate treatment because it was content neutral on its face and no impermissible purpose or justification was demonstrated. The majority also declined to apply *Reed*'s strict scrutiny standard, and Justice Breyer agreed in a concurring opinion.

Justice Thomas dissented, joined by Justices Gorsuch and Barrett, and Justice Alito dissented in part. Justice Thomas contended that the law was unconstitutional because "It discriminates against certain signs based on the message they convey—*e.g.*, whether they promote an on- or off-site event, activity, or service." Once again, his opinion attacked the decision in *Hill v. Colorado*, which he characterized as "an aberration in our case law" that applied a "long-discredited approach."

Despite the dissents, it is clear that six members of the court felt a need to rein in the reach of *Reed*'s strict scrutiny approach principally for signage, but also with an undercurrent, as noted above, of the fear of some justices that a similar standard would be applied to abortion cases.

SPECIALTY LICENSE PLATES

Many people pay extra money to their state for the privilege of obtaining a vanity or specialty license plate that announces their support of some belief or a favored organization, ranging from the local zoo to a professional or university football team. To what extent may governmental authorities choose not to permit a willing buyer to obtain such a license plate that displays a message with which the governmental authority disagrees, or feels it is too controversial to be permitted?

The Supreme Court retreated from its generally full-throated defense of the First Amendment in *Walker v. Texas Div., Sons of Confederate Veterans, Inc.* (2015). By a five-to-four vote, it held that the Texas Department of Motor Vehicles could reject a specialty license plate that featured the Confederate flag and the name and logo of the Sons of Confederate Veterans based on public comments indicating that "many members of the general public find the design offensive."

Justice Breyer's majority opinion characterized specialty license plates as government speech. This made the rejection permissible because "[w]hen government speaks, it is not barred by the Free Speech Clause from determining what it says." If citizens object to governmental action of this type, "It is the democratic electoral process that first and foremost provides a check on government speech."

Issuance of a specialty license plate was found to be government speech because the government sends messages through such plates; the designs on such plates are identified by the populace with the state; the state controls the messages conveyed; and the name "TEXAS" appears in all capital letters on the license plates. Since such plates constitute government speech, the Sons of Confederate Veterans "cannot force Texas to include a Confederate battle flag on its specialty license plates."

In a strong dissenting opinion by Justice Alito, four members of the court contended that specialty license plates contain a message of the motorist, not one from the state. In a particularly compelling point, Justice Alito suggested a "test" based on the views of passing motorists: "Would you really think that the sentiments reflected in the specialty plates are the views of the State of Texas and not those of the owners of the cars?" Pointing out that the State of Texas has authorized some 350 license plates containing particularized messages, the dissenters pointed to plates extolling the virtues of golf or bowling; of out-of-state football teams; and of a specific NASCAR driver, contending that a passing motorist would not conclude that the State wished to encourage any sport or individual, or favor Notre Dame in a football contest against a Texas university.

The dissenters criticized the majority's conclusion that specialty license plates constituted government speech, concluding that "This capacious understanding of government speech takes a large and painful bite out of the First Amendment." Justice Alito invoked the example of Texas' approval of a specialty license plate honoring African American "Buffalo Soldiers," who began their combat experience in the Indian Wars of the nineteenth century, as an example of governmental favoritism based on the viewpoint expressed. The Buffalo Soldiers license plate was approved despite the opposition of Native Americans, who expressed the view that they felt "'the same way about the Buffalo Soldiers,' as African-Americans felt about the Confederate flag," further noting that "When we see the U.S. Cavalry uniform, we are forced to relive an American holocaust." Thus, controversy alone did not dictate which group was awarded a specialty plate, and the viewpoint expressed seemed to have been controlling in the eyes of the government decision-makers.

The dissenters also concluded that specialty license plates constituted limited public fora. As such, the controlling case law provides that such a forum "cannot discriminate on the basis of viewpoint." In the dissenters' view, that is exactly what happened in the case of the Confederate flag license plate, which was turned down based upon public opposition by some who found the flag "offensive."

The impact of the *Walker* case is far from clear, and the later decision in *Matal v. Tam* (2017), which is the next case discussed below, states that *Walker* "likely marks the outer bounds of the government-speech doctrine." The appointments of Justices Kavanaugh and Barrett are also likely to limit the impact of *Walker*.

Justice Alito's dissent in *Walker* contends that it might apply to state- or state-university-sponsored billboards or other private, on-campus messages. What it will clearly apply to is other specialty license plates, particularly those with a controversial message. Indeed, Justice Alito pointed to the fact that Texas has permitted "Choose Life" license plates, while New York has rejected them because the message was "so incredibly divisive." Thus, *Walker* validates the state acting as public censor insofar as a private group wishes to proclaim its support of any controversial message that a majority of the Board of the Bureau of Motor Vehicles in a particular state may find incendiary.

By way of an historical footnote, the decision in *Walker* was issued on the same day a young white supremacist was arrested for murdering nine African Americans during a prayer meeting in an historic black church in Charleston, South Carolina. Ironically, photographs of the murderer, who was ultimately convicted and sentenced to death, soon surfaced showing him by an automobile that had a Confederate flag license plate prominently displayed on the front of the car.

DISPARAGING OR IMMORAL TRADEMARKS

As we noted at the beginning of this chapter, Justice Alito warned against growing incursions on the right of free speech in a 2017 commencement speech, observing that "The idea that speech can be banned if it expresses an idea that is offensive is spreading around the country." The expanding grasp of that idea is indeed manifested throughout the country, and particularly so on university and college campuses, and has even seeped into the lower schools. College students have, for example, been prohibited by their schools from wearing sombreros on Cinco de Mayo, and the display of American flags on that day was also criticized as being offensive to those of Mexican descent. Corporations, likewise, under fire from various groups speaking on behalf of particular constituencies, have also taken to punishing so-called offensive speech, taking it to the extent of terminating high officials accused by protest groups of such offenses.

In two cases, the Supreme Court countered this trend, upholding what it saw as free speech against the application of provisions of the trademark laws that prohibited registration of "disparaging" or "immoral or scandalous" marks.

The first of these cases to be decided involved the application of the trademark laws to ban registration of "disparaging" marks. Attacks against such marks have increased, with several groups leading the charge to ban them as offensive to their constituencies. Native Americans have been particularly vigorous in opposing use of their symbols or names by others, particularly by school sports teams, from the university level to the local grade school, as well as by professional sports teams. Many schools have responded by renaming those teams. Thus, since 1994, teams at St. John's University in New York are no longer known as the "Redmen," but instead as the "Red Storm," and the former Cleveland Indians are now the Cleveland Guardians. A university official explained that the St. John's nickname was changed "because of sensitivity to Native American Communities." The Native American protesters' most notable success came in convincing the Patent and Trademark Office to cancel the "Washington Redskins" football team's trademark, which they deemed offensive.

The Supreme Court stepped into the trademark aspect of this ongoing debate in *Matal v. Tam* (2017). That case involved the denial of trademark registration by the Patent and Trademark Office ("PTO") to the name "The Slants," used by an Asian rock group to "'reclaim' the term and drain its denigrating force."

Registration was denied to that mark under the Lanham Act trademark law, which prohibits registration of a trademark "which may disparage . . . persons, living or dead, institutions, beliefs, or national symbols, or bring them into contempt, or disrepute." The examining attorney at the PTO found that "there is . . . a substantial composite of persons who find the term in the applied-for mark offensive." He further observed that "several bloggers and commentators to articles on the band have indicated that they find the term and the applied-for mark offensive."

Not surprisingly, in view of his commencement comments, Justice Alito wrote the lead opinion, in part for the court, and in part for four justices, holding that the disparagement provision of the trademark law "violates the Free Speech Clause of the First Amendment. It offends a bedrock First Amendment principle: Speech may not be banned on the ground that it expresses ideas that offend."

All eight justices who participated in the decision agreed that the disparagement clause unconstitutionally discriminated on the basis of viewpoint. As Justice Alito explained, "Giving offense is a viewpoint." He rejected the concept that "The Government has an interest in preventing speech expressing ideas that offend." This was because "that idea strikes at the heart of the First Amendment. Speech that demeans on the basis of race, ethnicity, gender, religion, age, disability, or any other similar ground is hateful; but the proudest boast of our free speech jurisprudence is that we protect the freedom to express 'the thought that we hate'" (quoting a dissenting opinion of Justice Oliver Wendell Holmes).

The four concurring justices, in an opinion by Justice Kennedy, were even stronger in noting that the disparagement clause violated the First Amendment, and called for a heightened scrutiny standard of review. Justice Kennedy concluded his concurring opinion with the following remarks: "A law that can be directed against speech found offensive to some portion of the public can be turned against minority and dissenting views to the detriment of all. The First Amendment does not entrust that power to the government's benevolence. Instead, our reliance must be on the substantial safeguards of free and open discussion in a democratic society."

Those joining Justice Alito's opinion found it unnecessary to determine whether the heightened scrutiny standard applied, because the disparagement clause was not able to survive scrutiny under even a lesser standard. This was because "the disparagement clause is not narrowly drawn to drive out trademarks that support invidious discrimination . . . it is not an anti-discrimination clause; it is a happy-talk clause. In this way, it goes much further than is necessary to serve the interest asserted."

In finding a First Amendment violation, Justice Alito considered, and rejected, several arguments attempting to uphold the constitutionality of the disparagement clause. The most notable argument advanced by the defenders of the clause was that trademarks constitute government speech, which, as we saw in the *Walker* opinion discussed above, is not subject to the Free Speech Clause. Significantly, the opinion of the court in *Matal* observed that *Walker* "likely marks the outer bounds of the government-speech doctrine." In addition, it was significant that the PTO has long "made it clear that registration does not constitute approval of a mark."

The unanimous *Matal* decision sought to put a brake on the ever-growing campaign to limit "offensive" speech. Whether it will impact non-governmental entities, such as corporations and private schools, may be doubtful, but it should at least give them pause in determining how far they should choose to go in limiting or punishing speech.

In the view of some commentators, the *Matal* decision also brought into question the constitutionality of other provisions of the trademark laws. These include the provision denying trademark protection for any mark involving governmental symbols; provisions that specifically prohibit applicants from registering trademarks that provide certain types of truthful information, or that make subjective assertions, such as the characteristics of goods; and those marks that identify the geographic origin of goods.

In addition, the PTO had previously said that if the disparagement clause were to be ruled unconstitutional, then the separate provision denying registration to scandalous or immoral marks would also fall. That turned out to be accurate when the court in *Iancu v. Brunetti* (2019) reversed the PTO's decision to deny registration of the mark "FUCT" as "immoral or scandalous."

While Justice Kagan delivered the opinion of the court in *Iancu*, the case proved to be more controversial than *Matal*, generating four separate opinions, including three (by the Chief Justice, Justice Breyer, and Justice Sotomayor) dissenting in part.

Not surprisingly, Justice Kagan's opinion of the court relied heavily upon the *Matal* case. She pointed out that all of the justices in that case "agreed on two propositions," the first of which was "if a trademark registration bar is viewpoint-based, it is unconstitutional." In deciding whether to bar a trademark as "immoral or scandalous," she pointed out that the PTO determined whether a mark was one that "a substantial composition of the general public" would find "shocking to the sense of truth, decency, or propriety"; one that would give "offense to the conscience or moral feelings"; one that "called out for condemnation"; or one that was "disgraceful," "offensive," "disreputable," or "vulgar." The problem posed by defining "immoral" and "scandalous" was demonstrated both by the PTO criteria and standard definitions of the terms in dictionaries. The majority opinion concluded that "the statute, on its face, distinguishes between two opposed sets of ideas: those aligned with conventional moral standards and those hostile to them; those inducing social nods of approval and those provoking offense and condemnation. The statute favors the former, and disfavors the latter." Finally, Justice Kagan pointed out that trademarks in the areas of drug use, religious references, and references to terrorists were rejected when they were "offensive to many Americans," but approved when in conformity with majority views.

The majority found that the "immoral or scandalous" provision could not be saved by the limiting construction suggested in "the dissent's statutory surgery" because such a construction was inconsistent with the plain meaning of the statute.

In a concurring opinion, Justice Alito, who was the author of the *Matal* opinion, reinforced previous remarks he had made in his speeches and opinions, contrasting the American approach to that of "other countries with constitutions or legal traditions that claim to protect freedom of speech, [but where] serious viewpoint discrimination is now tolerated." Moreover, he repeated his view that "such discrimination has become increasingly prevalent in this country. At a time when free speech is under attack, it is especially important for this Court to remain firm on the principle that the First Amendment does not tolerate viewpoint discrimination." He went on to note, however, that Congress was free to adopt "a more carefully focused statute that precludes the registration of marks containing vulgar terms that play no real part in the expression of ideas."

The three dissenting opinions all relied on the opinion written by Justice Sotomayor, which was joined by Justice Breyer, and to which the chief justice referred to favorably. All of these three dissenting justices agreed that the "immoral" aspect of the statute could not be saved by a limiting construction. By contrast, they contended that the "scandalous" aspect, in the words of Justice Sotomayor, "can be read narrowly (to cover only offensive modes of expression)." She argued that interpreting "scandalous" "to regulate only obscenity, vulgarity, and profanity—would save it from unconstitutionality. Properly narrowed, 'scandalous' is a viewpoint-neutral form of content discrimination that is permissible in the kind of discretionary governmental program or limited forum typified by the trademark-registration system."

With the rulings in *Matal* and *Iancu*, trademarks that are deemed to be "disparaging," "immoral," or "scandalous" can be expected to seek trademark registration in large numbers. The only hope for some limitation is if Congress take steps to enact legislation limiting each of these terms to some concrete, objective standard that does not permit discrimination based upon the viewpoint conveyed by the proposed trademark. The most promising prospect for such legislation is to bar use of obscene, profanity-ridden, or vulgar terms that convey no actual expression of an idea. These are marks that, as Justice Alito indicated in his concurring opinion in *Iancu*, "generally signify nothing except emotion and a severely limited vocabulary."

STUDENT OFF CAMPUS VULGAR SOCIAL MEDIA POSTS

In *Tinker v. Des Moines Independent Community School District* (1969), the Supreme Court recognized that schools have a special interest in regulating on-campus student speech where it "materially disrupts class work or involves substantial disorder or invasion of the rights of others." Nevertheless, *Tinker* held that students do not "shed their constitutional rights to freedom of speech or expression at the schoolhouse gate." Thus, students were protected under the First Amendment in protesting the Vietnam War by wearing black armbands in school, even though the school had adopted a policy banning the wearing of such armbands on campus.

Tinker involved *on-campus* speech. In *Mahanoy Area School District v. B.L.* (2021), the court was called upon to decide whether a student could constitutionally be punished for vulgar off-campus posts on social media. In that case, after the student failed to make the school's varsity cheerleading squad, she posted two images on Snapchat, a social media app that permits the sharing of temporary images with selected friends. One of these images showed the student and her friend raising their middle fingers under a caption that used the vulgar *F* word three times. When the images were shared, several students became upset and approached the cheerleading coaches, who decided that the use of profanity violated team and school rules. They therefore suspended the student from the junior varsity cheerleading squad for one year.

In an opinion by Justice Breyer for eight members of the court, the student's off-campus social media posts were held to be constitutionally protected under the First Amendment. Although prior decisions recognized that, in certain circumstances, schools could regulate vulgar speech or speech that causes disorder when uttered on campus, here the off-campus location diminished the school's power to punish the student speaker. Moreover, while vulgar, the student's words and gestures were not legally obscene and did not amount to fighting words. Instead, they constituted remarks on public issues (as the majority saw it), which were transmitted to a group of friends. In addition, there was no substantial disruption at the school, but merely a few days' discussion in one class and a feeling of "upset" by some members of the cheerleading team.

Responding to any charge that the student's words were "unworthy of the robust First Amendment protections discussed herein," Justice Breyer concluded his opinion by stating that "sometimes it is necessary to protect the superfluous in order to preserve the necessary."

Significantly, the court rejected the appeals court's conclusion that schools had no power to regulate off-campus speech, noting that the parties to the appeal had identified bullying, harassment, threats, and failure to follow rules relating to school activities as areas that could be subject to regulation even if speech at issue occurred off campus. The court itself did not identify specific rules that would determine "precisely which of many school-related off-campus activities" fell within the school's power to regulate—"we do not now set forth a broad, highly general First Amendment rule stating just what constitutes as 'off campus' speech and whether or how ordinary First Amendment standards must give way off campus to a school's special need to prevent, *e.g.*, substantial disruption of learning-related activities for the protection of those who make up a school community."

As a general guide, the majority opinion went on to identify three features of off-campus speech that diminished a school's ability to regulate it. These included that the function of the school in place of the parents is minimal where activities occur outside the school. In addition, if schools were permitted to generally censor off-campus speech, this would mean the student was subject to school rules twenty-four hours a day. Finally, schools must protect "a student's unpopular expression, especially when the expression takes place off campus."

Justice Alito, joined by Justice Gorsuch, delivered a concurring opinion. Initially, he asked, "Why should enrollment in a public school result in the diminution of a student's free-speech rights?" Those attending private schools are not subject to such regulation.

While historically, the power of schools to regulate conduct was linked to the fact that the school was acting in the place of parents, it is necessary to determine how much authority parents delegate to public schools in which they enroll the children today. The concurring justices concluded that "parents are treated as having relinquished the measure of authority that the schools must be able to exercise in order to carry out their state-mandated educational mission, as well as the authority to perform any other functions to which the parents expressly or implicitly agree—for example, by giving permission for a child to participate in an extracurricular activity or to go on a school trip."

But "A public school's regulation of off-premises student speech is a different matter." Enrollment of a child in a public school "cannot be treated as a complete transfer of parental authority over a student's speech." Justice Alito went on to identify a number of situations in which "parents who enroll their children in a public school can reasonably be understood to have delegated to the school the authority to regulate the speech in question." These included extensions of the regular school program, as in online instruction or school trips. On the other hand, schools may not regulate "student speech that is not expressly or specifically directed at the school, school administrators, teachers, or fellow students and that addresses matters of public concern. Speech on such matters lies at the heart of the First Amendment's protection." Such speech cannot be regulated or punished "simply because it expresses ideas that are 'offensive or disagreeable.'"

In the case before the court, the school's justifications for suspending the student were weak. The messages and images were sent on her own time off premises and were circulated only to a group of friends for twenty-four hours. In addition, there was no significant disruption of classes. With respect to her language, the school did not claim authority "to regulate the vocabulary and gestures of all its students 24 hours a day 365 days a year."

Justice Alito concluded his opinion by stating that "If today's decision teaches any lesson, it must be that the regulation of many types of off-premises student speech raises serious First Amendment concerns, and school officials should proceed cautiously before venturing into this territory."

Only Justice Thomas dissented. His opinion documented the historic recognition that schools have broad discretion to discipline students under circumstances such as those in this case. He accused the majority of "depart[ing] from this historical rule," and "[choosing] intuition over history when it comes to student speech."

With respect to this student's vulgarity in speech and gesture, Justice Thomas pointed out that the majority gave little significance to the fact that her speech and gestures related to her decision to participate in an extracurricular activity, which constitutes an extension of the school day. In addition, the location of speech conveyed over social media is "a much trickier question than the majority acknowledges" since speech travels over social media and "where it is foreseeable and likely that speech will travel onto campus, a school has a stronger claim to treating the speech as on-campus speech."

PROHIBITING REGISTERED SEX OFFENDERS FROM ACCESS TO SOCIAL MEDIA

Sexual predators pose a significant and ever-increasing threat in our highly interlinked society, particularly to the young and to other vulnerable populations. In response to this threat, many laws have been enacted. For example, convicted sex offenders are required to register and to identify the place of their residence, as a cautionary method of notifying their neighbors of their presence among them. The State of North Carolina went further, barring access to most social media sites by registered sex offenders. This legislation is rooted in the recognition that social media sites are often utilized by sexual predators to identify and recruit children and other vulnerable members of society. Despite this laudatory purpose, the Supreme Court struck down the North Carolina law, finding that it was overbroad and thus in violation of the Free Speech Clause of the First Amendment (*Packingham v. North Carolina* [2017]).

The North Carolina law made it a felony for registered sex offenders "to access a commercial social networking Web site where the sex offender knows that the site permits minor children to become members or to create or maintain a personal Web pages." In North Carolina, this prohibition applied to approximately twenty thousand State residents, and more than one thousand people were prosecuted for violating the statute. The petitioner in the Supreme Court case was a registered sex offender who posted a message on his Facebook page praising God and Jesus separately for the dismissal of a parking ticket, thus relieving him of any fine or court costs. Although he made no attempt to contact any minor, Packingham was convicted and given a suspended prison sentence for violating the North Carolina statute.

While the three concurring justices expressed their concern on just how far free speech protections of internet sites might extend, all the justices agreed that the North Carolina statute was far too restrictive. North Carolina conceded that statute applied to sites such as Facebook, LinkedIn, and Twitter, and it was unclear how much further its prohibitions extended. Given this uncertainty, Justice Kennedy's majority opinion pointed out that the statute was so linguistically broad that it could, for example, bar a registered sex offender from ordering books from Amazon, from reading the *Washington Post* online, or from consulting WebMD on personal medical issues. (The concurring opinion used these exact same examples.) Justice Kennedy concluded that "Even convicted criminals—and in some instances especially convicted criminals—might receive legitimate benefits from these means for access to the world of ideas, in particular if they seek to reform and to pursue lawful and rewarding lives."

Much of Justice Kennedy's majority opinion is devoted to emphasizing the importance of the internet today as a means for permitting users "to gain access to information and communicate with one another about it on any subject that might come to mind." He points out, for example, that seven in ten adults use at least one social networking service, and that Facebook alone has 1.9 billion active users. In passages criticized by the concurring justices, Justice Kennedy goes on to describe social media and cyberspace as "the most important places (in a spatial sense) for the exchange of views," implicitly comparing them to streets and parks.

In an opinion concurring in the judgment on behalf of himself, Chief Justice Roberts, and Justice Thomas, Justice Alito criticized the majority opinion for its "undisciplined dicta" in its praise of the internet. He accused Justice Kennedy of "musings that seem to equate the entirety of the internet with public streets and parks," stating that he was "troubled by the implications of the Court's unnecessary rhetoric." In his view, "if the entirety of the internet or even just 'social media' sites are the 21st century equivalent of public streets and parks, then States may have little ability to restrict the sites that may be visited by even the most dangerous sex offenders." Justice Alito concluded that the court "should proceed circumspectly, taking one step at a time. It is regrettable that the Court has not heeded its own admonition of caution."

Given the concerns expressed in the concurring opinion, it will be left to later cases to decide both the standard of review with respect to restrictions on internet communications, as well as what restrictions may be lawful. With respect to sexual predators, however, both opinions make it clear, despite Justice Alito's concerns, that legislatures have the freedom to limit registered sexual offenders from internet access, so long as those limitations are narrowly tailored to further the government's legitimate interests in preventing use of the internet (in Justice Alito's words) "to facilitate the commission of sex crimes against a child."

VIOLENT VIDEO GAMES

Given the realistic depiction of increasingly gruesome violence in video games targeted at children, parents and other concerned citizens have sought to persuade legislatures to enact legislation banning such games. While they have been successful in some jurisdictions, the Supreme Court in *Brown v. Entertainment Merchants Association* (2011), ruled in a seven-to-two decision that the First Amendment protected violent video games. As such, the justices invalidated a California law banning the sale or rental of such games to children. Justice Alito, joined by Chief Justice Roberts, concurred in the judgment, but noted that this area might need to be reexamined in the light of future developments in the video game industry and its technology. As in the case of videos depicting animal cruelty, this is an area in which legislators seeking to limit the content of video games including violence will need to be very careful in drafting appropriate and narrowly crafted legislation.

APPAREL WITH POLITICAL MESSAGING AT POLLING PLACES

The State of Minnesota prohibited wearing any "political badge, political button, or other political insignia" inside a polling place on election days. The election judges were permitted discretion to decide whether any particular apparel violated this prohibition. By a seven-to-two vote, the Supreme Court struck down this prohibition as violative of the Free Speech Clause.

The petitioner in the case wore a button which read "Please I.D. Me," which referred to the need to show voter identification, which Minnesota did not require. He also wore a T-shirt with a Tea Party logo and the inscription "Don't Tread on Me." He was twice denied the right to vote, but ultimately was permitted to cast a ballot.

In an opinion by Chief Justice Roberts, the polling place was characterized as a nonpublic forum. Under this classification, the state was permitted to impose reasonable restrictions on apparel inside the polling place, including content-based restrictions on speech. Chief Justice Roberts explained that it was permissible generally to prohibit the wearing of political apparel inside a polling place in order to provide "an island of calm in which voters can peacefully contemplate their choices," recognizing that "It is a time for choosing, not campaigning." Thus, "The State may reasonably decide that the interior of polling places should respect that distinction."

Despite this general right to restrict wearing political apparel within the polling place, Minnesota's prohibitions violated the First Amendment because what is "political" was not defined by the statute and was left up to the election judge's discretion. Indeed, confusion as to what could properly be determined to be "political" was demonstrated by the oral argument in this case, where the state's counsel had difficulty explaining whether a shirt that read "All Lives Matter," or a shirt with a rainbow flag, violated the political apparel ban. Even more troubling, the counsel stated that a shirt with the text of the First Amendment would be allowed, while a shirt with the text of the Second Amendment would not.

The court's decision in the Minnesota case will have a limited application to apparel prohibitions in polling places. The majority opinion itself referred to laws in other states with more targeted restrictions as illustrative of a different and more "lucid" approach. It indicated that it was not passing on the constitutionality of those laws, but held that "if the State wishes to set its polling places apart as areas free of partisan discord, it must employ a more discernible approach than the one Minnesota has offered here." It must enact "objective, workable standards." Professor Jean Galbraith has remarked that this language suggests the need for "rules" (e.g., "don't exceed sixty miles per hour") rather than "standards" (e.g., "drive with caution").

NONUNION PUBLIC EMPLOYEES' PAYMENT OF UNION DUES

For many years, nonunion employees at unionized companies were required to pay "agency fees" to the unions. The Supreme Court originally upheld the legality of such fees in *Abood v. Detroit Bd. of Ed.* (1977). In a case that changed, rather than expanded, the reach of the Free Speech Clause, a divided Supreme Court overruled the *Abood* case, and held that public sector employee unions could not collect agency fees from employees who were not union members unless those employees affirmatively consented to paying those fees (*Janus v. American Federation of State, County & Municipal Employees* [2018]).

In the *Janus* case, the employee was required to pay an agency fee that was over 78 percent of the normal union membership dues. This percentage was alleged to be the portion of the fee representing activities by the unions which were "chargeable" under the rule of *Abood* as expenditures "germane" to the union's collective bargaining activities, as opposed to "nonchargeable" expenditures spent on such activities as political and ideological projects.

In an opinion for five members of the court, Justice Alito employed a standard of "exacting scrutiny" to hold that the "extract[ion]" of agency fees from nonunion members violated the First Amendment because it forced free and independent individuals to endorse ideas they found objectionable. Here, for example, the plaintiff disagreed with positions taken by the union not only on political and ideological matters, but also on efforts undertaken by the union as allegedly germane to its collective-bargaining efforts. The union efforts he objected to included activities directly related to public matters such as the Illinois State budget crisis and taxes, as well as to issues of collective bargaining related to education, child welfare, healthcare, and the rights of minorities.

The majority opinion noted that freedom of speech includes "the right to refrain from speaking at all," and that the First Amendment prohibits "forced associations." Moreover, where individuals are compelled to speak, they are "coerced into betraying their convictions."

Justice Alito spend a large part of the majority opinion in justifying the overruling of the *Abood* case. He summarized its perceived failings as including poor reasoning, the practical problems it had caused, the abuse attributable to its approach, and its inconsistency with later decisions of the Supreme Court. To begin with, *Abood*'s premise that permitting unions to charge nonmembers agency fees helped to preserve labor peace was seen to have been undermined by the fact that by 2018 there were no widespread or otherwise significant challenges to such peace either among the federal government's public sector employees or those in the twenty-eight states that prohibited unions from charging agency fees. In addition, the argument that nonmembers were getting a free ride unless they paid the fees was rejected on two principal grounds. First, the plaintiff argued that "he is not a free rider on the bus headed for a destination that he wishes to reach but is more like a person shanghaied for an unwanted voyage." Moreover, the "free rider" objection was typically not sufficient to overcome a First Amendment challenge, particularly where, as here, there was no compelling interest in charging such fees. Finally, in holding that it was permissible for unions to charge agency fees to nonmembers of the union, *Abood* employed a more deferential standard of review than was appropriate in deciding issues of free speech.

In dissent, Justice Kagan, joined by Justices Ginsburg, Breyer, and Sotomayor, clinically attacked the decision on two basic grounds. First, the majority purportedly overthrew the doctrine of *stare decisis* in a poorly reasoned and baseless opinion. Second, in a playful nod to Justice Scalia's dissenting opinion in the *Obergefell* case, Justice Kagan characterized the majority's approach as permitting "black-robed rulers [to] override . . . citizens' choices."

In the view of the dissenters, *Abood* provided a workable approach by distinguishing between activities which were germane to collective bargaining efforts and those which related to "non-workplace matters." While the dissenters admitted that there were "some gray areas," they argued that "everyone knows the difference between politicking and collective bargaining." Indeed, they emphasized that there have been few disputes over the years and relative "tranquility" in the lower courts regarding what activities were germane to collective bargaining, and what were not.

In further support of her opinion, Justice Kagan referred to the experience of twenty-two states, the District of Columbia, and Puerto Rico, all of which implemented the approach of *Abood.* This was particularly important under the reliance prong of the *stare decisis* doctrine because "thousands of ongoing contracts involving millions of employees" were negotiated in the context of this controlling approach. Indeed, some of those contracts do not have a severability clause, which may lead to entire contracts being abrogated under the majority's ruling. Moreover, in many decisions over nearly forty years, the Supreme Court itself had itself recognized *Abood* as a controlling First Amendment decision not limited to union issues. Indeed, one recent case had characterized the rule of *Abood* as "a general First Amendment principle."

The dissenters also argued that the court's decision supplies incentives for all union members to abandon the union. As more and more do so to avoid paying union dues, those who are left behind "begin to feel like suckers," and they also will eventually quit the union.

On a broader note, Justice Kagan's opinion accuses the majority of ignoring decades of First Amendment decisions, choosing instead to "weaponiz[e] the First Amendment, in a way that unleashes judges, now and in the future, to intervene in economic and regulatory policy." In doing so, "the majority has chosen the winners by turning the First Amendment into a sword, and using it against workaday economic and regulatory policy."

The *Janus* decision is likely to have a wide-ranging impact on both employees of public sector unions and upon the unions themselves. While it is important to note that the decision only applies to public sector employees (because the First Amendment only applies to governmental action), it is nevertheless estimated that the decision will apply to approximately five million government employees in twenty-two states. While those employees will save considerable money by being relieved of those fees, public employee unions will correspondingly suffer from a significant diminution of funds to support their collective bargaining efforts. A predictable result of this monetary shortfall will be that these unions, which regularly support the Democratic Party in any event, will use a greater portion of the funds that remain in their coffers to oppose Supreme Court candidates nominated by Republican presidents, as well as to reject Republican and other conservative candidates, both in general elections and in Democratic primaries.

The *Janus* decision could additionally put other involuntary assessments in legal danger. Commentators have pointed to assessments made by public universities as just one example.

LIMITING FEDERAL FUNDING

When Congress awards federal funding, it often places conditions on the spending of the money. In *Agency for International Development v. Alliance for Open Society International, Inc.* (2013), a divided court held by a six-to-two margin that the First Amendment precluded Congress from conditioning federal funding under the United States Leadership Against HIV/AIDS, Tuberculosis, and Malaria Act of 2003 on fund recipients adopting a policy explicitly opposing prostitution. In the opinion of the court written by Chief Justice Roberts, the majority ruled that a separate condition that prohibited the use of the funds themselves to promote or advocate prostitution sufficiently protected the congressional purpose. By going beyond this programmatic restriction, and requiring organizations additionally to "pledge allegiance to the Government's policy of eradicating prostitution," the government improperly sought to "leverage funding to regulate speech outside the contours of the program itself."

In a dissenting opinion, Justice Scalia, joined by Justice Thomas, saw the condition in question as a permissible "means of selecting suitable agents to implement the Government's chosen strategy to eradicate HIV/AIDS." They emphasized that "the First Amendment does not mandate a viewpoint-neutral government." In the dissenters' view, "So long as the unfunded organization remains free to engage in its activities 'without federal assistance,' . . . refusing to make use of its assistance for an enterprise to which it is opposed does not abridge its speech." In sum, "It is the reasonable price of admission to a limited government-spending program that each organization remains free to accept or reject."

Given controversies over whether and how government should fund certain activities, such as grants made to organizations that perform abortions, we can expect that this issue will continue to be litigated in multiple contexts in future years. Once again, careful legislative drafting may provide the remedy. As the court majority pointed out in its *Agency for International Development* opinion, the government may prohibit the use of its funds for particular purposes, but it may not go beyond such prohibitions to attempt to regulate the speech of the organization that it funded.

PROHIBITING NON-TERRORISTS FROM PROVIDING MATERIAL SUPPORT OR RESOURCES TO DESIGNATED TERRORIST GROUPS

Ever since the unprecedented terrorist attack on the United States on September 11, 2001, the American people have rightly been concerned regarding potential future attacks by terrorists within our country. Large-scale federal and state investigations have been undertaken in all fifty states, leading to numerous arrests and widespread surveillance of potential terrorists. A number of prosecutions of suspected terrorists who are alleged to have been assisting ISIS, al-Qaeda, and other Islamist terrorist organizations have been based upon a federal statute that prohibits any person from taking any action which provides "material support or resources" to any group that has been designated as a terrorist group.[5]

The Supreme Court had occasion to interpret the reach of this statute in *Holder v. Humanitarian Law Project* (2010). The pendency of the War on Terror led the court to interpret its language expansively, despite First Amendment concerns. In that case, human rights activists sought a ruling that they were free to provide humanitarian and nonviolent political activities training to two groups designated as foreign terrorist organizations. These groups, two of the thirty designated at that time as terrorist organizations by the Secretary of State, were from Kurdistan and Sri Lanka. (The case did not involve either ISIS or al-Qaeda.)

In a majority opinion written for six members of court, Chief Justice John Roberts rejected the position advanced by the human rights organizations and the individual petitioners. The court ruled instead that the material support statute barred petitioners from conducting activities such as training people from the terrorist groups in question how to petition for relief before the United Nations, how to present claims for disaster-related aid, and how to negotiate peace treaties. Chief Justice Roberts gave two principal reasons for so concluding. First, dollars are fungible, and money and skills could be transferred from their intended purposes to terrorist activities. Second, support from American human rights groups "helps lend legitimacy to foreign terrorist groups," thus making it easier for them "to persist, to recruit members, and to raise funds." As further support for the majority ruling, the opinion expressed its reliance partially on its deference to "the Government's conclusions" on these issues, noting the important foreign policy interests of the government at stake in combating terrorism.

Given its broad reading of the material support statute, this Supreme Court has empowered the federal government with broad authority to prosecute all types of activity that may be viewed as supporting terrorist organizations. As such, and as has been the case to date, multiple prosecutions are to be expected across the country, especially in the context of repeated attacks and multiple actions undertaken in this country to support and encourage designated terrorist organizations.

Despite the ruling in *Humanitarian Law Project*, the vast majority of the decisions discussed in this chapter demonstrate a strong commitment to expanding the right to free speech in a wide variety of contexts.

CAMPAIGN FINANCE LIMITS

Recent years have witnessed major controversy over the perception that "big money" is controlling the outcome of popular elections to governmental positions. Congress has reacted by enacting legislation placing limitations upon political contributions by both individuals and by corporate and other entities.

In addition to the First Amendment issues described above, the Supreme Court has delivered several controversial opinions that involved the application of the First Amendment's protection of free speech to issues of political campaign finance. In this area, the Supreme Court has overruled two of its prior decisions to strike down certain bans imposed under the Bipartisan Campaign Reform Act of 2002 on "electioneering communications" by corporations and unions, while at the same time upholding requirements that the identities of those funding the communications be disclosed.

The federal statute in question prohibited corporations and unions from using general treasury funds for advocating the election or defeat of a candidate. The case before the court involved a ninety-minute movie/documentary made by a nonprofit corporate entity that was critical of Senator Hillary Clinton, who was then running for the nomination of the Democratic Party for president.

In a five-to-four decision, with an opinion of the court written by Justice Kennedy, *Citizens United v. Federal Election Commission* (2010) found the bans on corporate speech to be an "unlawful" "outright ban" on speech by certain disfavored speakers. As such, the bans constituted "classic examples of [government] censorship" and unlawful "censorship to control thought." Corporations, the majority found, were actually "associations of citizens" and must be permitted to speak in an "open marketplace of ideas." Moreover, "political speech does not lose First Amendment protection simply because its source is a corporation."

In a dissenting opinion authored by Justice John Paul Stevens on behalf of four justices, the dissenters criticized the majority for overruling recent decisions, claiming that the current decision "threatens to undermine the integrity of elected institutions across the Nation." In addition, the majority allegedly ignored the governmental interest in preventing corruption, as prior decisions had recognized that "immense aggregations of [corporate] wealth" had "corrosive and distorting effects" on elections. As to corporations, Justice Stevens observed that corporate speech is "derivative speech, speech by proxy." Indeed, "The conceit that corporations must be treated identically to natural persons in the political sphere is not only inaccurate but also inadequate to justify the Court's disposition of this case."

Citizens United has provoked an ongoing storm of opposition, which still continues. Initially, President Obama dressed down the Supreme Court justices attending the State of the Union message, accusing the majority of permitting even foreign corporations to "bankroll" elections by their decision. (Justice Alito could be seen as mouthing, "Not true.") Liberal and progressive commentators have echoed the president and similarly assailed the decision. One such commentator called *Citizens United*, the worst Supreme Court decision since *Dred Scott*," while Professor Ronald Dworkin saw it as "regrettable" for allowing corporations "to buy unlimited time to defeat legislators who do not behave as they wish."[6] By contrast, the noted First Amendment litigator Floyd Abrams defended the decision. In his book, *The Soul of the First Amendment*, Abrams argued that media corporations, whose First Amendment rights have long been recognized and protected by the courts, should not have a "preferred" place in political discourse.[7] He quoted with approval Justice Alito's observation that "The question is whether speech that goes to the very heart of government should be limited to certain preferred corporations: namely, media corporations." Justice Alito suggested that a view "that the First Amendment protects only certain preferred voices should be disturbing to anybody who believes in free speech."[8]

Despite heated and continuous opposition, the Supreme Court refused to reexamine its ruling in *Citizens United* two years later, when it summarily reversed, in a five-to-four decision, *American Tradition Partnership, Inc. v. Bullock* (2012), a case in which the Supreme Court of Montana had upheld a similar ban on election communications by corporations. In addition, Justice Alito defended the decision in *Citizens United* in a November 2012 speech in which he pointed out that those who attack the outcome in that case did not question the outcome of cases such as *New York Times v. Sullivan* or the *Pentagon Papers* case, both of which upheld First Amendment rights of media corporations. As such, Justice Alito identified the issue as whether the First Amendment rights of free speech "should be limited to certain preferred corporations, namely those media organizations."

While the debate has been heated, the net effect of *Citizens United* on elections is still unclear. An analysis by *Bloomberg Businessweek* of contributions made to political action committees during the period from December 1, 2011, to May 31, 2012, for example, showed that corporate contributions to Super PACs constituted only 9 percent of the total in that period, while those made by unions, advocacy groups, family trusts, and other non-corporate entities accounted for nearly the same percentage. The vast bulk of the contributions during that period came from individuals, who had always been permitted to do so before *Citizens United*.[9]

The Supreme Court revisited the issue of campaign contributions, this time in the context of individual contributions, in *McCutcheon v. Federal Election Commission* (2014). In that case, the court ruled, once again by a five-to-four margin, that aggregate limits on individual contributions violated the First Amendment.

The Federal Election Campaign Act of 1971, as amended by the Bipartisan Campaign Reform Act of 2002, established two types of limitations on campaign contributions. Under the first limitation, base limits were established restricting the amount of money that could be contributed to any particular candidate or committee. Under the second limitation, aggregate limits restricted the amount of money one donor was permitted to contribute in total to all candidates or committees. The appellant McCutcheon had contributed to sixteen candidates, complying with the base limits for each. Under the law, however, the aggregate limits prohibited him from contributing to the additional twelve candidates he favored and to other political committees he wished to support.

Chief Justice Roberts delivered a plurality opinion for four justices stating that "There is no right more basic in our democracy than the right to participate in electing our political leaders." He went on to note that "If the First Amendment protects flag burning, funeral protests, and Nazi parades—despite the profound offense such spectacles cause—it surely protects political campaign speech despite popular opposition." While the court had previously decided in *Buckley v. Valeo* (1976) that an aggregate limit of $25,000 was constitutional, the plurality dismissed that ruling because the *Buckley* opinion itself noted that the issue had not been separately addressed by the parties and had devoted only three sentences in a 139-page opinion to the issue. In addition, the campaign finance laws had been changed and strengthened since *Buckley* was decided.

Chief Justice Roberts went on to conclude that the Supreme Court "has identified only one legitimate governmental interest for restricting campaign finances: preventing corruption or the appearance of corruption." However, "Congress may target only a specific type of corruption—'*quid pro pro*' corruption." The aggregate limits were not addressed to that problem because "Spending large sums of money in connection with elections, but not in connection with an effort to control the exercise of an officeholder's official duties, does not give rise to such *quid pro quo c*orruption." Even if the aggregate limits were viewed as aimed at preventing circumvention of the base limits, they still violated the First Amendment "because the statute is poorly tailored to the Government's interest in preventing circumvention of the base limits," and, as such, "impermissibly restricts participation in the political process."

The plurality opinion also noted the protections against corruption and abuse of the campaign finance system provided by the base limits themselves, and also by the disclosure requirements that provide the electorate with information regarding the sources of election-related spending. It also left open the possibility that Congress could adopt "a modified version of the aggregate limits, such as one that prohibits donors who have contributed the current maximum sums from further contributing to political committees that have indicated they will support candidates to whom the donor has already contributed." The existence of all those existing protections, as well as possible future legislative changes, demonstrated, in the view of the justices joining

Chief Justice Roberts's opinion, that the questioned restrictions on aggregate contributions unnecessarily abridged the donors' First Amendment rights.

The fifth vote to strike down the aggregate limitations came from Justice Thomas, who wrote an opinion concurring in the judgment. Justice Thomas stated that he would go further than the plurality justices by overruling *Buckley*, and by subjecting aggregate limits on campaign contributions to a strict scrutiny review "[under] which they would surely fail."

Justice Breyer wrote a dissenting opinion, in which Justices Ginsburg, Sotomayor, and Kagan joined. He began by stating that the same issue had been decided "[n]early 40 years ago" in the *Buckley* case which had "focused upon the same problem that concerns the Court today," and that it was "wrong" to overrule that case. As the dissenters saw it, the *McCutcheon* decision, together with *Citizens United*, "eviscerates our Nation's campaign finance laws, leaving a remnant incapable of dealing with the grave problems of democratic legitimacy that those laws were intended to resolve."

The dissenting opinion focused heavily upon attacking what it characterized as "a narrow definition of 'corruption' that excludes efforts to obtain 'influence over or access to' elected officials or political parties." Justice Breyer explained that the campaign finance laws implement a competing First Amendment interest to that identified by the plurality by seeking to "maintain . . . the integrity of our public governmental institutions." Indeed, a review of prior decisions reveals that they rested upon concerns regarding disproportional access to, or undue influence over, legislators and the appearance of corruption. Moreover, "Where enough money calls the tune, the general public will not be heard," and this "breaks the constitutionally necessary 'chain of communication' between the people and their representatives."

Justice Breyer then turned to the contention made in the plurality opinion that the existence of other laws was sufficient to address any lingering problems. He spent several pages of the dissenting opinion reviewing three detailed examples that gave rise in his view to the potential for circumvention of statutory limitations on contributions. He concluded, finally, that the court majority committed numerous errors, including "substitut[ing] judges' understanding of how the political process works for the understanding of Congress."

As with the *Citizens United* decision, *McCutcheon* was the object of heated commentary. The president of Democracy 21, for example, termed the decision a vote "to license the further corruption of our democracy," and accused the Supreme Court of re-creating "the system of legalized bribery today that existed during the Watergate days."[10] Whether or not all or most of the increase can be attributed to these two decisions, campaign contributions by outside groups have dramatically increased since 2010. The *New York Times* reported in July of 2014 that political advertising on television was "set to break $2 billion in congressional races, with overall spots up nearly 70 percent since the 2010 midterm election."[11] Three groups alone—one Republican, one Democrat, and the U.S. Chamber of Commerce—had already spent a total in excess of $80 million in congressional races by the end of July 2014.

In contrast to the campaign contribution cases discussed above, the Supreme Court upheld a provision of the State of Florida's Code of Judicial Conduct, which prohibited judicial candidates from personally soliciting campaign funds. In *Williams-Yulee v. Florida Bar* (2015), the court rejected a First Amendment attack on the restriction by a five-to-four margin. Chief Justice Roberts's majority opinion relied upon the interest of the State to preserve public confidence in the integrity of its judiciary. He reasoned that the public could lack confidence in a judge's ability to administer justice without fear or favor if he or she were elected by asking for favors.

COMPELLED DONOR DISCLOSURES

In *Americans For Prosperity Foundation v. Bonta* (2021), the Supreme Court struck down a California law requiring charitable organizations to disclose the identities of their major donors to the state attorney general. In a six-to-three decision, the court found that the disclosure requirement was facially invalid because it burdened donors' First Amendment rights and was not narrowly tailored to an important government interest.

Applying an "exacting scrutiny" standard, Chief Justice Roberts's majority opinion explained that the First Amendment protects freedom of association, and that prior cases noted "[i]t is hardly a novel perception that compelled disclosure of affiliation with groups engaged in advocacy may constitute as effective a restraint on freedom of association as [other] forms of governmental action."

Under the exacting scrutiny standard, there must be "a substantial relation between the disclosure requirements and a sufficiently important governmental interest." Moreover, "the disclosure requirement must be narrowly tailored to the interest it promotes." While "California has an important interest in preventing wrongdoing by charitable organizations," in this case "There is a dramatic mismatch . . . between the interest that the Attorney General seeks to promote and the disclosure regime that he has implemented in service of that end." Thus, the district court found that the collection of donors' names, addresses, and contributions did not lead to "a single concrete instance in which pre-investigation collection of [the data] did anything to advance the Attorney General's investigative, regulatory or enforcement efforts."

In addition, the attorney general had "multiple alternative mechanisms" by which he could obtain the same information after initiating an investigation.

Chief Justice Roberts also pointed out there were significant privacy concerns implicated in a compelled disclosure of the donors' contributions. Indeed, the petitioners "introduced evidence that they and their supporters have been subjected to bomb threats, protests, stalking, and physical violence." Moreover, "The gravity of the privacy concerns in this context is further underscored by the filings of hundreds of organizations as a*mici curiae* in support of the petitioners," including "organizations [which] span the ideological spectrum," such as the ACLU and Zionist and Muslim groups.

Concurring in the judgment, Justice Thomas indicated that, in his opinion, strict scrutiny was the appropriate standard to apply under the First Amendment in compelled disclosure cases. He also questioned the majority's application of the overbreadth doctrine, contending that "the court has no power to enjoin the lawful application of a statute just because that statute might be unlawful as-applied in other circumstances."

Justice Alito, joined by Justice Gorsuch, joined most of the majority opinion, but noted he did not agree that the exacting scrutiny standard was always appropriate. This was because he was "not prepared at this time to hold that a single standard applies to all disclosure requirements."

Justice Sotomayor dissented, joined by Justices Breyer and Kagan. She noted that the court's prior decisions required petitioners to show "concrete repercussions" in order to demonstrate an actual burden from a compelled disclosure. By contrast, the majority substituted, in her opinion, a "subjective preference for privacy" approach under which all compelled disclosure laws would be subject to close scrutiny. Justice Sotomayor argued in favor of a "flexible" or "nuanced" approach that would balance the governmental interest against the actual burden experienced by the petitioners.

She found several factors that suggested the burden in this case was not sufficient to overcome the governmental interest in gathering information to supervise charities. Thus, the disclosures made under the California law were not made public, and their confidentiality was protected by security measures imposed by the state.

Finally, the dissenters attacked the majority's conclusion that the law was facially invalid, reasoning that most donors choose to publicize their donations in order to manifest their support for the particular charity they are favoring by their contribution.

COMMERCIAL SPEECH

Day after day, in all sorts of media, including internet advertising, businesses market their products in loud and often exaggerated fashion to potential consumers. Can businesses hawking their wares be limited in what they say in their advertising? Expanding the reach of the First Amendment even further than the cases discussed above had done, the Supreme Court has also ruled that commercial speech is entitled to some First Amendment protection in ordinary commercial transactions. Two recent cases illustrate how the court has expansively applied the First Amendment to such transactions.

In *Sorrell v. IMS Health* (2011), the court held that a Vermont law violated the First Amendment by prohibiting, among other uses, the use for marketing by pharmaceutical manufacturers of pharmacy records that reveal the prescribing practices of individual doctors. Justice Kennedy's opinion of the court explicitly noted on its first page that "Speech in aid of pharmaceutical marketing . . . is a form of expression protected by the Free Speech Clause of the First Amendment." Despite legislative findings that pharmaceutical marketing programs conflict with governmental goals in multiple ways, including increasing the cost of healthcare and health insurance, and encouraging "hasty and excessive reliance on brand-name drugs," the court nonetheless struck the law down because it enacted "content- and speaker-based restrictions on the sale, disclosure, and use of prescriber-identifying information." As such, it "disfavors specific speakers, namely pharmaceutical manufacturers," and "burdens disfavored speech by disfavored speakers," while leaving others, including academic organizations, free to use the same information in their messaging.

Based on this reasoning, the court found that a heightened scrutiny standard of review was required because the law imposed "a regulation of speech because of disagreement with the message it conveys." Under this standard of review, the state was required to "show at least that the statute directly advances a substantial governmental interest and that the measure is drawn to achieve that interest." Since Vermont failed to do so, the statute violated the First Amendment.

Speaking for himself and for Justices Ginsburg and Kagan, Justice Breyer dissented. His opinion emphasized that prior decisions provided only limited First Amendment protections to commercial speech, imposing "tight restraints" only on governmental efforts to restrict such subjects as "'core' political speech,'" while "imposing looser constraints" on other types of speech, including commercial speech. By imposing a standard of heightened scrutiny to evaluate Vermont's law, the majority's approach "would transfer from legislatures to judges the primary power to weigh ends and to choose means, threatening to distort or undermine legitimate legislative objectives." Justice Breyer also noted the majority's approach would threaten all regulatory actions of both the federal and state governments, while ignoring the traditional deference extended to comprehensive regulatory regimes, which are reviewed only to make certain they are not arbitrary, capricious, or an abuse of discretion.

In a second decision, *Expressions Hair Design v. Schneiderman* (2017), the court held that a New York Business Law requirement that might be interpreted to bar merchants from informing their customers that a surcharge would be imposed for use of a credit card for payment, as opposed to a payment in cash, implicated First Amendment considerations.

Chief Justice Roberts, writing for a five-person majority, concluded that "the law does regulate . . . how sellers may communicate their prices," and by "regulating the communication of prices rather than the prices themselves, [the requirement at issue] regulates speech." The court did not make any ruling as to whether this regulation "survived First Amendment scrutiny," but instead remanded the case to the court of appeals to consider the First Amendment questions presented.

In a concurring opinion, Justice Breyer reprised his dissenting opinion in Sorrell, pointing out that "virtually all government regulation affects speech." As such, he concurred in the judgment, but suggested the proper inquiry was not whether the law in question regulated speech, but rather whether it "affects an interest that the First Amendment protects."

Although presented in a different context than the *Gilbert* case discussed above, the approach of the majority in both the *Sorrell* and *Expressions Hair Design* cases once again raises the question of how First Amendment protections may apply to regulatory laws, such as those covering communications by securities issuers regarding their companies.

NOTES

1. Richard Garnett, "Supreme Court Roundup," *First Things*, No. 227 (October 2012), 36.

2. Adam Liptak, "How Conservatives Weaponized the First Amendment," *New York Times*, June 30, 2018.

3. Michael McConnell, "A Free Speech Year at the Court," *First Things*, No. 216 (October 2011), 29.

4. Adam Liptak, "Court's Free-Speech Expansion Has Far-Reaching Consequences," *New York Times*, August 17, 2015.

5. For a discussion of the American laws aimed at terrorism, judicial decisions regarding their reach, and a listing of terrorist attacks in the United States, see Edward

F. Mannino, *The Roberts Court and Terrorism: A Citizen's Guide* (Amazon Kindle, 2016).

6. Darryl Pinckney, "Young Barry Wins," *New York Review of Books*, August 16, 2012, 42; Ronald Dworkin, "A Bigger Victory Than We Knew," *New York Review of Books*, August 16, 2012, 6.

7. Floyd Abrams, *The Soul of the First Amendment* (New Haven: Yale University Press, 2017).

8. Todd Ruger, "Alito Defends 'Citizens' in Speech to Federalist Society," The Blog of the LegalTimes, November 16, 2012.

9. Melissa Avstreih. "The Cash Behind the Super PACs," *Bloomberg Businessweek*, July 23–29, 2012, 28.

10. Andy Kroll, "The Supreme Court Just Gutted Another Campaign Finance Law. Here's What Happened," *Mother Jones*, April 2, 2014.

11. Ashley Parker, "Outside Money Drives a Deluge of Political Ads," *New York Times*, July 27, 2014.

Chapter 2

Free Exercise of Religion

Beyond the protections accorded to free speech, the First Amendment also prohibits Congress from making any law "prohibiting the free exercise" of religion. The Supreme Court has been inconsistent over the years in interpreting this provision, oscillating between enforcement of generally applicable laws over religious objections, on the one hand, and vigorous protection of religious believers, on the other hand.[1] Under the current court, the decisions have generally given the most generous protections to free exercise claims, including striking down pandemic-based restrictions on religious gatherings of all types, as exemplified by the cases noted below in the section discussing the confirmation of Justice Amy Barrett.

The free exercise decisions in the mid-twentieth century mostly favored minority religions, including Jehovah's Witnesses and Seventh-Day Adventists. By contrast, the more recent decisions of the court have favored mainstream Christian religions and Islam. The reasons for this shifting decision-making in the twenty-first century can be traced to several factors. First, the composition of the court has shifted from a principally liberal and moderate judiciary to one that is more conservative. Second, the emergence of law firms litigating pro bono on behalf of individuals claiming violations of their right to free exercise has led to several Supreme Court decisions vindicating those rights. Third, the base of the Republican Party has shifted to Christian conservatives championing the rights of their adherents. Fourth, Christian and Muslim groups have become more active in seeking legal protection for various beliefs and practices.

The leading early decision on the Free Exercise Clause was *Reynolds v. United States* (1879), which upheld a federal law prohibiting bigamy, including polygamy as then practiced in the Utah Territory by the Church of Jesus Christ of Latter-day Saints. In a test case, the Mormon hierarchy chose George Reynolds to challenge the government's power to prosecute those engaged in polygamy. Reynolds's argument was that he was free to practice polygamy because of his "religious belief or duty." In rejecting his argument, the Supreme Court concluded that Congress lacked power to legislate "over mere *opinion*, but was left free to reach *actions* which were in violation of social duties or subversive of good order."

A later group of cases involved the rights of the Jehovah's Witnesses to proselytize door-to-door and to hand out pamphlets attacking the Catholic religion, *Cantwell v. Connecticut* (1940), or in refusing to salute the American flag. In *Cantwell*, the Supreme Court ruled a complete prohibition against such activities violated the Free Exercise Clause.

The flag cases resulted in two opinions, the second of which overruled the first, despite the passage of only three years: *Minersville School District v. Gobitis* (1940), overruled by *West Virginia State Board of Education v. Barnette* (1943). In the first case, the Supreme Court followed the *Reynolds* case, ruling that "Conscientious scruples have not, in the course of the long struggle for religious toleration, relieved the individual from obedience to a general law not aimed at the promotion or restriction of religious beliefs. The mere possession of religious convictions which contradict the relevant concerns of a political society does not relieve the citizen from the discharge of political responsibilities."

In overruling *Gobitis*, the Supreme Court majority chose to view refusal to salute the flag as a question of free speech, not simply as an issue of free exercise of religion. The majority ruled that not saluting the flag is "a form of utterance," and, as such, that speech could only be suppressed where there was a clear and present danger of some action that the state had a right to prevent. In taking this approach, the court avoided questioning the rulings in *Reynolds* and *Gobitis* that permitted enforcing a rule of general applicability against religious believers who found the law to be violative of their religious beliefs.

In the 1960s and the 1970s, the Supreme Court took a proactive approach to defending the adherents of two minority religions to practice their faiths. In *Sherbert v. Verner* (1963), the court held that a Seventh-day Adventist could not be denied the benefits of unemployment compensation when she refused to work on Saturday, her Sabbath. Justice William Brennan wrote for seven members of the court that the denial of benefits "forces her to choose between following the precepts of her religion and forfeiting benefits, on the one hand, and abandoning one of the precepts of her religion in order to accept work, on the other hand." The treatment of this religious minority was particularly objectionable because state law permitted an exception for "the Sunday worshipper."

In *Wisconsin v. Yoder* (1972), Amish and Mennonite parents challenged a Wisconsin state law that required school attendance to the age of sixteen, because their faiths did not permit formal school education beyond the eighth grade. Chief Justice Warren Burger, writing for six members of the court, concluded that "a State's interest in universal education . . . is not totally free from a balancing process when it infringes on fundamental rights and interests, such as those specifically protected by the Free Exercise Clause of the First Amendment, and the traditional interest of parents with respect to the religious upbringing of their children so long as they . . . 'prepare [them] for additional obligations.'" In responding to the argument that the Wisconsin law applied uniformly to all citizens, the court ruled that "A regulation neutral on its face may, in its application, nonetheless offend the constitutional requirement for government neutrality if it unduly burdens the free exercise of religion."

While *Sherbert* and *Yoder* signaled a move away from the earlier decisions upholding the application of a general law against religious believers who viewed the law as infringing upon their beliefs, the pendulum swung back in *Employment Division v. Smith* (1990). In that case, two Native American workers were fired from their jobs at a private drug rehabilitation organization for taking peyote, an illegal drug, as part of a sacramental ritual in a Native American Church. Six members of the court joined an opinion by Justice Antonin Scalia, which held that a "valid and neutral law of general applicability" proscribing criminal conduct did not violate the Free Exercise Clause. *Sherbert* was distinguished because it did not involve conduct that was illegal. *Employment Division v. Smith* proved to be extremely controversial, and was eviscerated in its application to some restrictions on free exercise by the passage in 1993 of the Religious Freedom and Restoration Act, which is discussed at length below.

While the cases discussed above involved religious minorities, including Mormons, Jehovah's Witnesses, Seventh-day Adventists, and Amish and Mennonite believers, the more recent cases have involved claims principally by Christians and Muslims. There has been an exponential increase in cases claiming exemptions for these religious believers from laws of general applicability that are viewed by them as imposing mandates on their conduct that offend their religious beliefs. Religious believers, who have found themselves increasingly at odds with the now-dominant American culture, have relied on the Free Exercise Clause to protect them against governmental intrusion into the practice of their religions. This appeal to the First Amendment arises in multiple contexts. Here are some examples. First, several colleges and universities have mandated that any recognized student organization, including religious groups, must admit even those who do not share their beliefs as full, voting members. Second, religious schools have been sued for terminating the employment of teachers who did not adhere to core tenets of their religions. Third, churches and other religiously affiliated organizations have been denied benefits that are otherwise generally available to all applicants. Fourth, governmental authorities have mandated that both private employers and religious institutions provide contraception drugs to their employees, even when that violates the employers' beliefs. Pharmacists have also been required, in violation of their religious beliefs, to stock drugs they believe cause abortions. Fifth, prisoners have been required to abandon certain religious practices while incarcerated. Sixth, bakeries and photographers, among others, have been fined and otherwise penalized for declining to create custom-designed products to meet the specifications and demands of potential customers who wish to celebrate their same-sex marriages. Seventh, religious adoption and foster placement agencies are often required to place children with same-sex couples and gay adoptive parents, or lose their governmental certifications. Eighth, and finally, religious hospitals are pressured to perform abortions.

In commenting on such restrictions as these, Justice Alito, in his previously noted address to the Federalist Society, commented that "in certain quarters, religious liberty is fast becoming a disfavored right," with religious belief characterized as "an excuse for bigotry," which "can't be tolerated." Responding to these attacks on free exercise, the court has granted review in several of these cases, usually overturning mandates that conflicted with the religious beliefs of certain individuals, reaching results generally protective of these believers' rights to freely exercise their religions, most notably Christianity and Islam.

NON-BELIEVERS' MEMBERSHIP IN CAMPUS RELIGIOUS GROUPS

On many university campuses throughout the nation, student organizations that wish to receive the benefits of formal university recognition have been compelled to accept any applicant for membership, even if that applicant disagrees with the underlying goals of the student organization. In *Christian Legal Society v. Martinez* (2010), the Supreme Court confronted the issue of whether such organizations have any protection against such an invasion where their membership limitations are based upon adherence to the teachings of a particular religion. There, the court considered the constitutionality of a Hastings College of Law policy that required any organization that wished to be recognized as a registered student organization to accept all applicants for membership. The Christian Legal Society objected to this so-called all comers mandate because the group's tenets required members to sign a "Statement of Faith," which, among other things, affirmed the belief that no sexual activity should occur outside marriage between a man and a woman. "Unrepentant" homosexuals were thus excluded from membership in the group.

By a five-to-four majority, the Supreme Court upheld Hastings's policy as a reasonable condition on access to the forum of registered student organizations, pointing out that the policy was viewpoint-neutral. Justice Ruth Bader Ginsburg's opinion of the court noted that the Christian Legal Society was not compelled to accept any member if it was not a registered student organization, and that it still could obtain access to the law school's facilities for meetings and activities. As Justice Ginsburg saw it, "Hastings would do nothing to suppress CLS's endeavors, but neither would it lend RSO-level support for them."

The majority distinguished earlier decisions that struck down restrictions on access to school programs or recognition on the grounds that those cases compelled acceptance of members who did not share the group's ideas. Here, by contrast, Hastings was "dangling the carrot of subsidy, not wielding the stick of prohibition." In addition, the all-comers policy did not single out religious groups for their points of view, but applied to all student associations, whatever their beliefs.

In his dissenting opinion for four members of the court, Justice Alito focused on the fact that even the all-comers policy operated to force inclusion of members whose presence would "affect[t] in a significant way the group's ability to advocate public or private viewpoints." Moreover, in Justice Alito's view, the policy was not actually viewpoint-neutral because it was pretextual. This was because the policy was only adopted after the group's application was first denied under a separate nondiscrimination policy. Finally, the all-comers policy was seen by the dissenters to act in such a way that it "permits small unpopular groups to be taken over by students who wish to change the views that the group expresses." Indeed, "the consequence of an accept-all-comers policy is marginalization."

All-comers and nondiscrimination policies have been adopted by many colleges and professional schools. They have been most controversial, as in *Martinez*, when they are applied to religiously affiliated organizations. In the wake of the *Martinez* decision, several colleges and universities have opted to adopt similar nondiscrimination policies for recognized student organizations. Vanderbilt University in Tennessee, for example, adopted a nondiscrimination policy for such organizations that prohibited recognized campus groups from barring any applicant from either membership or from holding a leadership position. This aroused a storm of opposition. Indeed, Catholic Vanderbilt, the largest student group on campus, moved off campus to avoid the potential of a non-Catholic assuming a position of leadership, and some fifteen evangelical Christian groups severed their official ties with the university. In addition, an arm of student government at Tufts University in Massachusetts banned the Tufts Christian Fellowship for a violation of the university's nondiscrimination policy. This action was based on the fellowship's requirement that its leaders subscribe to the "basic biblical truths of Christianity." Other colleges and universities, including Harvard and the University of Iowa, also mandated nondiscrimination policies for registered student organizations. Iowa's efforts to eliminate approval of a Christian student group for refusing to permit a practicing homosexual to assume the office of vice president in the group was struck down by a federal district court because the university's "Human Rights Policy" was not "consistently and equally appl[ied]."[2]

In reaction to these university nondiscrimination policies, and in an effort to reverse them, several states have enacted legislation. The State of Kansas enacted legislation in February 2016 permitting faith-based organizations to restrict their membership to those who share their beliefs. Proponents hailed the Kansas law as protecting religious freedom, while opponents characterized it as legalizing discrimination. South Dakota followed in March 2019, when its legislature enacted HB No. 1087. That law provided, among other things, that "Access to, and use of, facilities at a public institution of higher education shall be equally available to all student organizations, regardless of the ideological, political, or religious beliefs of the organization. An institution may not prohibit an ideological, political, or religious student organization from requiring that its leaders or members of the organization affirm and adhere to the organization's sincerely held beliefs, comply with the organization's standards of conduct, or further the organization's mission or purpose, as defined by the organization."

The Supreme Court's five-to-four split in *Martinez*, and the controversies over subjecting campus religious groups to the mandates of the all-comers and nondiscrimination policies, reflect the real tensions in today's society between members of religious denominations that have become active in political debates and those individuals without any religious belief or affiliation. These tensions divide mainly between evangelical Protestants and conservative Catholics, on the one hand, and on the other side, the 25 percent of Americans who do not embrace any religion, and who wish to maintain a strict separation between church and state. Mirroring the split in the Supreme Court, the former see the policies at issue as marginalizing religion, while the latter see them as bringing outside influences into otherwise closed societies of like-minded individuals, thus fostering diversity and open discussion on university campuses. This debate shows no sign of abating, and there is no significant prospect for reaching a public consensus.

THE RIGHT OF RELIGIOUS GROUPS TO MAKE EMPLOYMENT DECISIONS

One of the recurring religious freedom issues that receives ongoing media attention relates to the rights of religious schools to terminate the employment of teachers and other staff. Religious schools won an important decision on this issue in *Hosanna-Tabor Evangelical Lutheran Church & School v. EEOC* (2012). In a unanimous opinion delivered by Chief Justice Roberts, the court held that a religious institution has considerable discretion to determine "who can act as its ministers," and that it can terminate such a minister without governmental second-guessing by the EEOC.

The *Hosanna-Tabor* case was brought by the EEOC to protect the rights of a schoolteacher at a Lutheran school who was terminated by the school, allegedly in retaliation for threatening to bring a disability-related lawsuit against the school. The teacher had been classified by the religious school as "called," rather than as a lay teacher, because she had received special training, including a course of theological study. The teacher had also been commissioned as a "Minister of Religion," taught a religion class as well as other classes, led prayers, and took her students to weekly chapel services.

The court held that its past decisions "confirm that it is impermissible for the government to contradict a church's determination of who can act as its ministers." Following the lead of some forty years of federal courts of appeals decisions, the court recognized for the first time in its history a "ministerial exception," which was required to "protect . . . a religious group's right to shape its own faith and mission through its appointments."

Without specifying any specific test for determining who qualifies as a minister, the court ruled that this teacher clearly functioned as such, given her title, training, teaching responsibilities, and use of her minister title to claim certain tax benefits. Given this finding, the EEOC's suit was barred by the First Amendment because "When a minister who has been fired sues her church alleging that her termination was discriminatory, the First Amendment has struck the balance for us. The church must be free to choose those who will guide it on its way."

It is important to note that the court emphasized that it was not ruling whether the ministerial exception bars other types of suits, such as those for "breach of contract or tortious conduct by their religious employers."

There were two concurring opinions. Justice Thomas indicated he would go further than the majority by deferring in all cases to a "religious organization's good-faith understanding of who qualifies as its minister." Justice Alito, joined by Justice Kagan, noted that they would not limit the ministerial exception to those formally ordained as ministers, but rather would apply it to any employee "who leads a religious organization, conducts worship services or important religious ceremonies or rituals, or serves as a messenger or teacher of its faith." Moreover, "The Constitution leaves it to the collective conscience of each religious group to determine for itself who is qualified to serve as a teacher or messenger of its faith."

Particularly in light of the result reached in *Christian Legal Society v. Martinez*, the unanimous decision in *Hosanna-Tabor* was an important reaffirmation of the First Amendment rights of all religious groups. The decision has been widely cited in cases involving issues of associational religious freedom to support the right of religious groups to conduct their affairs without governmental interference. Nevertheless, the decision does not confer an unlimited right to designate any employee as a "minister." Thus, Justice Alito's concurring opinion notes that "a purely secular teacher would not qualify for the 'ministerial' exception." On the other hand, he also observes that the fact that the teacher performs some secular duties in addition to religious ones does not void the exception.

Given the *Hosanna-Tabor* ruling, several religious institutions have attempted to include provisions in their employment contracts that designate all or most of their employees as "ministers," and/or have included contractual provisions requiring every employee to adhere to the tenets of that faith in their personal, as well as in their professional, lives. Thus, for example, the Catholic Diocese of Cleveland denominated its 2015–2016 contracts with its lay teachers as "Lay Teacher-Minister" agreements, and included a provision outlining in detail the teacher's "Role as Minister and Role Model of the Faith." This provision provides, in part, that "the Teacher-Minister further understands and acknowledges that it is the teaching of the Roman Catholic Church that teachers in a Catholic school are truly and in a very real sense engaged in a special ministry, or apostolate, of the Roman Catholic Church. . . . "[3] By contrast, after extensive negative publicity, the Catholic Archdiocese of San Francisco withdrew a proposed contractual provision that would have required teachers to "acknowledge that all faculty and staff are ministers engaged in this religious mission and thus serve their ministry of Catholic education, not only by the performance of their job duties, but also by their word and example, inside and outside the classroom, on and off campus."[4]

In addition to including, or attempting to include, contractual language designating teachers as ministers, both the Cleveland and San Francisco, as well as other Catholic dioceses, have sought to contractually require adherence to the religion's tenets in their employees' personal lives. The San Francisco Archdiocese 2015–2018 Collective Bargaining Agreement, for example, recites in its preamble that "the Union and its members recognize that all lay teachers covered by this Agreement shall perform all their duties as set forth in this Agreement in accordance with the doctrines and precepts of the Roman Catholic Church, and shall conduct themselves at all times during the performance of those duties in a manner in keeping with the standards of the Church," and that "teachers are expected to support the purpose of our Catholic schools in such a way that their personal conduct will not adversely impact their ability to teach in our Catholic High Schools." The Cleveland Diocese contract goes much further, specifying that a teacher-minister can be fired for "certain speech or actions that are considered to be contrary to the teachings of the Roman Catholic Church," including having or assisting an abortion and publicly supporting same-sex marriage.

Eight years later, the court revisited the ministerial exemption in *Our Lady of Guadalupe School v. Morrissey-Berru* (2020). Two combined cases again presented claims of employment discrimination, this time by two teachers at Catholic schools who claimed their employment was terminated, in one case to hire a younger teacher, and in the other, because the teacher had requested a leave of absence to obtain treatment for breast cancer. The court, in an opinion by Justice Alito for seven members of the court, applied the ministerial exemption to bar both claims.

The majority opinion explained that religious institutions do not have a general immunity from claims by employees, but are afforded "autonomy with respect to internal management decisions that are essential to the institution's central mission." As such, although the teacher in *Hosanna-Tabor* had a title of "minister," conferring such a title on a teacher is not sufficient, of itself, to apply the ministerial exemption, and the absence of such a title, as in these cases, is similarly not determinative. Nor is there any "rigid formula" that governs how to determine which employees are subject to the ministerial exception. "What matters, at bottom, is what an employee does."

In both cases before the court, the individual teachers "performed vital religious duties," and were "entrusted most directly with the responsibility of educating their students in the faith." In a key passage of the majority opinion, the court noted that "The religious education and formation of students is the very reason for the existence of most private religious schools, and therefore the selection and supervision of the teachers upon whom the schools rely to do this work lie at the core of their mission. Judicial review of the way in which religious schools discharge those responsibilities would undermine the independence of religious institutions in a way that the First Amendment does not tolerate."

The majority reviewed at length the facts that justified applying the exemption to these teachers. One petitioner was a grade-school teacher who taught religion, took religious education courses as required by the school, and was expected to attend faculty prayer services. She also entered into employment agreements that stated a school mission "to develop and promote a Catholic

School Faith Community." She was treated as a catechist, and, as such was "responsible for the faith formation of the students in [her] charge every day." She "provided religious instruction every day," "directed and produced an annual passion play," prayed with her students, and performed other religious duties.

The second petitioner was also a grade-school teacher. She signed an employment agreement similar to that of the other teacher. It "imposed commitments regarding religious instruction, worship, and personal modeling of the faith." This teacher "was required to teach religion for 200 minutes each week . . . and administered a test on religion every week." She also worshiped with her students, prepared them for Catholic mass, and prayed with her students every day, and at monthly masses.

Justice Thomas, joined by Justice Gorsuch, concurred in full with the majority opinion, but wrote separately to reiterate his belief, which was expressed in his concurring opinion in *Hosanna-Tabor*, that "the Religion Clauses require civil courts to defer to religious organizations' good-faith claims that a certain employee's position is 'ministerial.'" "[D]eference is necessary" because "What qualifies as 'ministerial' is an inherently theological question, and thus one that cannot be resolved by civil courts through legal analysis." Moreover, attempting to resolve the issue through litigation would raise the same entanglement questions that the court "usually goes to great lengths to avoid."

Justice Sotomayor dissented, joined by Justice Ginsburg. These justices pointed out that "the teachers taught primarily secular subjects, lacked substantial religious titles and training, and were not even required to be Catholic." They criticized the majority for "collap[sing] *Hosanna-Tabor*'s careful analysis into single consideration: whether a church thinks its employees play an important religious role. Because that simplistic approach has no basis in law and strips thousands of school teachers of their legal protections, I respectfully dissent."

The dissenters relied on a number of lower court decisions which interpreted the ministerial exception more narrowly, and pointed to the four "circumstances" the court considered in *Hosanna-Tabor* in determining whether to apply that exception. They concluded that "the ministerial exception applies to a circumscribed sub-category of faith leaders." Justice Sotomayor argued that the majority decision invites "potential for abuse," and constitutes "judicial abdication" by permitting religious institutions to engage in "any animus completely irrelevant to their religious beliefs or practices."

Cases decided by lower courts since *Hosanna-Tabor*, but before *Our Lady of Guadalupe School*, reached different results based upon careful reviews of the plaintiffs' job titles, religious duties, and other relevant factors. The ministerial exception was applied in these early cases to protect religious institutions from suit where the terminated employees held titles such as pastor, spiritual director, or music director, or where the employee led morning prayers and gave daily religious instruction. By contrast, the exception was held not to apply where the employee was a professor of exercise science, or a non-Catholic lay teacher who was not permitted to teach Catholic doctrine, or a lay teacher with no religious training, even though she attended and participated in prayer and religious services with students. See *Lee v. Sixth Mount Zion Baptist Church of Pittsburgh*, No. 17–3086 (3d Cir. Sept. 5, 2018) (collecting cases at 15–19).

Future cases decided by lower courts will need to determine that other employees are covered by the ministerial exemption, as well as the efficacy of employment contracts describing a school's mission or classifying employees as "ministers" to bar suits for unlawful termination or other alleged torts. Lines will be drawn in employment termination cases, with religion teachers, on the one hand, being ruled to be ministers. On the other hand, the after-hours janitor will fall outside the ministerial exception. Cases in the middle will prove more difficult, but the opinions in the *Hosanna-Tabor* and *Our Lady of Guadalupe School* cases suggest that close cases will be decided in favor of the religious institution that is sued. Finally, the nature of the claim will also be relevant, since only suits for employment discrimination were the subject of the *Hosanna-Tabor* and *Our Lady of Guadalupe School* decisions, and the court expressly noted that claims for breach of contract or for other tortious conduct might lead to a different result. For example, it is inconceivable that a claim for assault on an employee would be insulated from review by the ministerial exception.

DENIAL OF GENERALLY AVAILABLE BENEFITS TO RELIGIOUS INSTITUTIONS

The tension between the Establishment Clause and the Free Exercise Clause gives rise to difficult cases where benefits are granted by government to religious institutions or their members. In *Everson v. Board of Education* (1947), the first major Establishment Clause case, the Supreme Court ruled that it was constitutionally permissible to extend "general State law benefits to all . . . citizens without regard to their religious belief." The application of this principle to religious institutions (as opposed to their members) presents a different question than that resolved in *Everson*. This is a more difficult case, and it is particularly so under state constitutions that have adopted so-called Blaine Amendments that proscribe, in various versions, assistance being granted to religious institutions. The Supreme Court addressed this issue in

Trinity Lutheran Church v. Comer (2017), which was decided on the last day of the October Term, 2016.

Trinity Lutheran Church was a Missouri church that ran a preschool and daycare center. It applied for a grant under Missouri's Scrap Tire Program, which offered reimbursement grants to nonprofits that installed playground surfaces made from recycled tires to protect children who fall. The Missouri Department of Natural Resources made fourteen grants, and ranked the church's application fifth out of the forty-four applications it received, but it refused an award to the church under the Missouri Constitution. That constitution, in its 1875 Blaine Amendment, provided that "no money shall ever be taken from the public treasury, directly or indirectly, in aid of any church, sect or denomination of religion." The state Department of Natural Resources determined that this provision made the church "categorically ineligible to receive a grant."

In an opinion by Chief Justice Roberts, the Supreme Court held that denial of a grant to the church in these circumstances violated the Free Exercise Clause, which "'protect[s] religious observers against unequal treatment' and subjects to the strictest scrutiny laws that target the religious for 'special disabilities' based on their 'religious status.'" Chief Justice Roberts explained that the Supreme Court has repeatedly held that "denying a generally available benefit solely on account of religious identity imposes a penalty on the free exercise of religion that can be justified only by a state interest 'of the highest order.'" Nor did it matter that the state did not affect the religious practices of the church because "the Free Exercise Clause protects against 'indirect coercion or penalties on the free exercise of religion, not just outright prohibitions.'" Moreover, "Trinity Lutheran is not claiming any entitlement to a subsidy. It instead asserts a right to participate in a government benefit program without having to disavow its religious character. . . . Trinity Lutheran is a member of the community . . . , and the State's decision to exclude it for purposes of this public program must withstand the strictest scrutiny."

The court ruled that the state failed to defend its actions under the strict scrutiny standard, since it "offers nothing more than Missouri's policy preference for skating as far as possible from religious establishment concerns." As such, "the exclusion of Trinity Lutheran from a public benefit for which is otherwise qualified, solely because it is a church, is odious to our Constitution all the same, and cannot stand."

Chief Justice Roberts's opinion was joined, with one important exception, by five other justices, and Justice Breyer concurred in the judgment, making the count seven justices ruling against the state's practice of excluding religious institutions from generally available benefits. The significant exception was that Justices Thomas and Gorsuch refused to join in footnote 3, which provided that "This case involves express discrimination based on religious identity with respect to playground resurfacing. We do not address religious uses of funding or other forms of discrimination." In a concurring opinion for himself and Justice Thomas, Justice Gorsuch expressed the view that there is no useful distinction between laws that discriminate "on the basis of religious *status* and religious *use*." This was because the Free Exercise Clause "guarantees the free *exercise* of religion, not just the right to inward belief (or status)." The concurring justices also felt the footnote might suggest to some that the opinion applies only to a limited number of cases. He pointed out that "Such a reading would be unreasonable for our cases are 'governed by general principles, rather than ad hoc improvisations.' . . . And the general principles here do not permit discrimination against religious exercise—whether on the playground or anywhere else." Given the refusal of two justices to join in footnote 3, that footnote does not become binding precedent because only four justices joined in it. It should be noted, however, that Justice Breyer, who only concurred in the judgment, stated he "would leave the application of the Free Exercise Clause to other kinds of public benefits for another day."

Justice Sotomayor, on behalf of herself and Justice Ginsburg, wrote a dissenting opinion, parts of which she read from the bench, a tactic typically employed to underline the vigor with which a dissenting opinion is held. *Trinity Lutheran* was only the second time Justice Sotomayor had adopted this tactic in her eight years on the court, although she has continued to do so in more recent years in controversial cases such as that involving President Trump's so-called travel ban, a case that is discussed later in this book.

Justice Sotomayor saw the court's decision in *Trinity Lutheran* as having a dramatic negative impact on earlier precedent. She wrote that "This case is about nothing less than the relationship between religious institutions and the civil government—that is, between church and state. The Court today profoundly changes that relationship by holding, for the first time, that the Constitution requires the government to provide public funds directly to a church. Its decision slights both our precedents and our history, and its reasoning weakens this country's longstanding commitment to a separation of church and state beneficial to both." This was because "The Establishment Clause does not allow Missouri to grant the Church's funding request because the Church uses the Learning Center, including its playground, in conjunction with its religious mission." As such, this "impermissibly 'advanc[es] . . . religion.'"

Throughout her opinion, and not limited to the passage just quoted, Justice Sotomayor's rhetoric and approach recall the very early Establishment Clause decisions of the Supreme Court involving Catholic schools, where all aspects of that church's mission were seen as part of a pervasively sectarian approach to spreading its own religion. For example, Justice Sotomayor also observed that "The [Lutheran] Church seeks state funds to improve the Learning Center's facilities, which, by the Church's own avowed description, are used to assist the spiritual growth of the children of its members and to spread the church's faith to the children of nonmembers."

The dissenting justices also pointed out, in an extensive review of early efforts in our country to oppose subsidization of religion, that the decision not to fund religious activities "has deep roots in our Nation's history, [and] reflects a reasonable and constitutional judgment." Some thirty-eight states currently have provisions similar to that of the Missouri Constitution, and, in the view of the dissenters, those provisions were "all but invalidated today," and "the weighty interests they protect, and the history they draw on deserve more than this judicial brush aside." Justice Sotomayor ended her opinion by contending that "If this separation [of church and state] means anything, it means that the government cannot, or at the very least need not, tax its citizens and turn that money over to houses of worship. The Court today blinds itself to the outcome this history requires and leads us instead to a place where separation of church and state is a constitutional slogan, not a constitution commitment."

The dissenters also attempted to paint the provisions of the many state constitutions as not hostile to religion because "A State's decision not to fund houses of worship does not disfavor religion; rather, it represents a valid choice to remain secular in the face of serious establishment and free exercise concerns."

As with many of the Roberts Court's decisions, at the time it was decided, it was not clear how far its impact of *Trinity Lutheran* would reach. On the one hand, footnote 3, Justice Breyer's opinion concurring in the judgment, and the strong dissenting opinion of Justice Sotomayor suggested caution regarding reading the opinion too broadly. On the other hand, Justice Gorsuch's concurring opinion correctly noted that Supreme Court decisions are governed by "general principles."

In a five-to-four decision three years later, the court did extend the reach of *Trinity Lutheran* in *Espinoza v. Montana Department of Revenue* (2020). That case involved application of a Montana constitutional amendment which, along the lines of many state Blaine amendments, prohibited granting any aid to a school controlled by a "church, sect, or denomination." At issue was the disqualification of parents seeking scholarships for use in defraying tuition at schools operated by such religious entities from a scholarship program enacted to benefit parents who wished to send their children to private schools.

Writing for a majority of five, and relying heavily upon *Trinity Lutheran*, Chief Justice Roberts found this exclusion unconstitutional as applied to parents whose children attended a private Christian school which satisfied the statutory criteria for a qualified education provider. The majority ruled that the exclusion of religious entities from the scholarship program was an exclusion based upon religious *status*, an exclusion that ran contrary to *Trinity Lutheran*'s ruling that "disqualifying otherwise eligible recipients from a public benefit 'solely because of their religious character' imposes 'a penalty on the free exercise of religion that triggers the most exacting scrutiny.'"

The majority opinion took pains to note that the case "turns expressly on religious *status* and not religious *use*" (emphasis added). While the end goal may have been to prevent funds being used for religious or sectarian education, "Status-based discrimination remains status based even if one of its goals or effects is preventing religious organizations from putting aid to religious uses." As such, the majority distinguished the ruling in *Locke v. Davey* (2004), which had upheld a Washington state scholarship program that prohibited use of the scholarships to pursue theology degrees that prepared students to serve as religious clergy. Here, "By contrast, Montana's constitution does not zero in on any particular 'essentially religious' course of instruction at a religious school."

Writing for himself and Justice Gorsuch, Justice Thomas concurred but added comments on "how this Court's interpretation of the Establishment Clause continues to hamper free exercise rights." The two justices suggested that the Establishment Clause "likely has no application to the States or, if it is capable of incorporation, that the court employs a far broader test than the Clause's original meaning."

Justice Alito also filed a concurring opinion, recounting at length the history of the Blaine Amendments, versions of which still exist in thirty-eight states. He noted how Montana's constitutional provision was infected by the same anti-Catholic feeling that motivated Senator Blaine to propose his federal constitutional amendment, which is discussed below. As such, Montana's claim that its no-aid provision merely reflected an interest in preserving funding for public schools was improperly divorced from the historical context in which it was enacted.

Justice Gorsuch also filed a concurring opinion. He noted that he joined in full Chief Justice Roberts's majority opinion, but went on to question any distinction for purposes of the Free Exercise Clause between religious status and use, as he had done in his *Trinity Lutheran* concurring opinion. He argued that the Free Exercise Clause "protects not just the right to *be* a religious person, holding beliefs inwardly and secretly; it also protects the right to *act* on those beliefs outwardly and publicly."

JUSTICES GINSBURG, BREYER, AND SOTOMAYOR EACH DELIVERED DISSENTING OPINIONS

Joined by Justice Kagan, Justice Ginsburg pointed out that the Montana Supreme Court had struck down the entire scholarship program. This ruling, she argued, removed any discrimination between religious and secular schools, and thus placed no burden on the parents' religious exercise. She also contended that "A State may distinguish within a benefit program between secular and sectarian schools," and argued that this was what the Montana Supreme Court had done.

In his dissenting opinion, which was joined by Justice Kagan, Justice Breyer invoked language from *Locke v. Davey* stating there must be "play in the joints" between "what the Establishment Clause permits and the Free Exercise clause compels." He accused the majority of neglecting this doctrine, thereby "risk[ing] that kind of entanglement and conflict that the Religion Clauses are intended to prevent."

Justice Breyer wrote that the Montana law was "strikingly similar" to that considered in *Locke* because "Montana has chosen not to fund (at a distance) 'an essentially religious endeavor'—an education designed to 'induce religious faith.'" Moreover, since it is the parents who are the claimants in the current case, they are doing the same thing as was presented in *Locke*—seeking the funds to use to "obtain a religious education." After a lengthy review of history from the founding period regarding the dangers of using taxes to support "the teaching of religious truths," he noted that scholarship subsidies serve to underwrite, in part, salaries of teachers whom the opinion in the *Hosanna-Tabor* case identify as "'personif[ing] [the] beliefs' of the churches that employ them," legally becoming "ministers."

Justice Breyer favored what he termed "the flexible, context-specific approaches of our precedents," rather than the bright-line approach of the majority, which he characterized as "embracing mechanical formulas." In his view, there is "no test-related substitute for the exercise of legal judgment."

Justice Sotomayor wrote the final dissenting opinion, speaking only for herself. Initially, she agreed with Justices Ginsburg and Kagan that the striking down of the entire scholarship program by the Montana Supreme Court rendered the parents' claim moot. She went on to add that "Not only is the court wrong to decide this case at all, it decides it wrongly," and in doing so, "weakens this country's long-standing commitment to a separation of church and state beneficial to both."

In Justice Sotomayor's reading, the court's precedents require "not only differential treatment . . . but also a resulting burden on religious exercise."

Since the entire program was struck down, no one is receiving benefits and neither differential treatment nor any burden on religious exercise is present.

Finally, Justice Sotomayor reprised her dissent in *Trinity Lutheran*, contending once again that prior court rulings permitted religious entities to be singled out "for exclusion from otherwise generally applicable laws" because of "the unique status of religious entities." She found the *Locke* case to be controlling, and characterized the majority opinion's rulings as "perverse."

The Supreme Court considered the issue once again in *Carson v. Makin* (2022). In a decision for six members of the court, Chief Justice Roberts struck down a Maine law that disqualified parents from a program of tuition assistance if they chose to have their children attend a religious school because the program limited tuition assistance payments to children attending "nonsectarian" schools.

Not surprisingly, the majority noted that "The principles applied in *Trinity Lutheran* and *Espinoza* suffice to resolve this case." As such, the Maine program does not survive under strict scrutiny because the benefits are denied the parents who choose religious schools "solely because of [the schools'] religious character." Moreover, as previously decided in *Zelman v. Simmons-Harris* (2002), "a neutral benefit program in which public funds flow to religious organizations through the independent choices of private benefit recipients does not offend the Establishment Clause."

Justices Breyer, Sotomayor, and Kagan dissented, as they had done in the previous cases noted above. As he had written in *Espinoza*, Justice Breyer noted his concern that permitting religious schools to benefit indirectly from parents participating in a tuition assistance program could give rise to religious strife. He also relied upon the "play in the joints" approach taken in *Locke v. Davey* (2004).

Noting her "growing concern for where this court will lead us next," Justice Sotomayor accused the court of continuing "to dismantle the wall of separation between church and state that the Framers fought to build." She argued that the court should not have started down the path it did in *Trinity Lutheran* where it "revolutionized free exercise doctrine by equating a State's decision not to fund a religious organization with presumptively unconstitutional discrimination on the basis of religious status."

What the Supreme Court did not decide in these cases was the impact of the majority opinions on the constitutional viability of state Blaine Amendments, of which those of Missouri and Montana were types. The amendments in question derive their name from James G. Blaine, a Republican politician from Maine, who was his party's unsuccessful presidential standard bearer in the Election of 1884. In an earlier attempt to secure that nomination for the Election of 1880, Blaine had introduced a proposed constitutional amendment in 1875 that would have provided that "no money raised by taxation in any State for the support of public schools . . . shall ever be under the control of any religious sect." Blaine hoped by sponsoring this amendment to secure the support of the very vocal anti-Catholic populace of that time. The amendment passed the House of Representatives overwhelmingly, by a vote of 180 to 7, but it failed in the Senate by two votes to secure the two-thirds vote required for a constitutional amendment.

Blaine's proposal was recognized by all as aimed at Catholic schools, which at the time were the subject of vicious and repeated media attacks. Indeed, seventeen years before *Trinity Lutheran* was decided, four justices of the Supreme Court, in a plurality opinion written by Justice Thomas (cited by Chief Justice Roberts in *Espinoza*) noted that "Consideration of the [Blaine] amendment arose at a time of pervasive hostility to the Catholic Church and to Catholics in general, and it was an open secret that 'sectarian' was code for 'Catholic.'" Justice Thomas concluded that the "pervasive sectarian" doctrine was "born of bigotry, [and] should be buried now" (*Mitchell v. Helms* [2000]).

Despite what Justice Thomas characterized as their "pedigree," and despite Justice Sotomayor's comment that they were "all but invalidated" by *Trinity Lutheran*, the existing state Blaine Amendments are unlikely to be declared unconstitutional per se under the Free Exercise Clause, especially when applied to prohibit aid for particular religious uses. Instead, two other approaches are more likely. First, as in *Trinity Lutheran* and *Espinoza*, courts will not permit such amendments to justify excluding religious institutions or their members from receiving generally available benefits, at least where the exclusions are based on status. Second, courts may choose to restrictively interpret, and thus limit the scope of, Blaine Amendments, perhaps requiring demonstration of a historic basis for "zeroing in on" and prohibiting a particular religious use, such as was emphasized in *Locke v. Davey*.

Whether the court will ultimately abandon the status versus use dichotomy is unclear despite Justice Gorsuch's cogent arguments in his concurring opinions that the Free Exercise Clause protects both equally. Indeed, the majority opinion in *Carson* stated the previous decisions "never suggested that use-based discrimination is any less offensive to the Free Exercise Clause."

CORPORATIONS AND RELIGIOUS GROUPS DENIAL OF CONTRACEPTIVE COVERAGE TO THEIR EMPLOYEES

Federal and state laws, and particularly regulations promulgated under them, have increasingly been mandating that businesses provide their products or services to all who may wish to purchase them, even if providing such products or services will violate the consciences or religious beliefs of the business owner. Whether an individual has a constitutional right under the Free Exercise Clause to decline to obey a valid law has been the subject of much controversy in the Supreme Court, as the cases discussed above demonstrate.

Indeed, the decision in *Employment Division v. Smith* (1990) provoked an immediate hostile reaction. Congress initiated hearings on legislation to overturn the decision within a few months, and enacted the Religious Freedom Restoration Act (RFRA) virtually unanimously in 1993. That legislation stated a legislative purpose "to restore the compelling interest test" employed in *Sherbert v. Verner* (1963) and other earlier cases.

Under RFRA, the plaintiff must first show that the legislation at issue substantially burdens his or her exercise of religion. To the extent that showing is made, the burden then shifts to the government to prove it has a compelling interest in enforcing the law, and that no less restrictive means is available to secure that interest.

In *City of Boerne v. Flores* (1997), RFRA was held only to apply to actions of the federal government, a holding that led many states to enact parallel visions of the law to restrict governmental infringement of religion within their state borders. Thus, in states where no state RFRA has been enacted, the religion-restrictive test of the *Employment Division* case still applies, while the RFRA statutory standards are applied to test federal free exercise claims.

The Supreme Court under Chief Justice Roberts has issued four opinions interpreting the reach of RFRA and a similar statute, upholding the free exercise claims in the first three cases on statutory, as opposed to constitutional, grounds. In the fourth case, resolved only after the death of Justice Scalia, the court declined to decide the issues presented, instead remanding the case to the appellate courts to explore the possibility of a negotiated settlement.

In the first of these cases, *Gonzales v. O Centro Espirita Beneficente Uniao Do Vegetal* (2006), the court essentially reached the opposite result as *Employment Division*, holding that the American branch of a Brazilian church was free to distribute communion in the form of a tea brewed from plants which contained a controlled substance regulated by federal law. Chief Justice Roberts, writing his first Supreme Court opinion, ruled for a unanimous court that the United States had failed to demonstrate a compelling interest to ban the use of the sacramental tea by the church. It placed partial reliance on the fact that the federal drug laws permitted exceptions, and that the use of peyote by Native American churches had been exempted for thirty-five years.

While the court's *O Centro* decision provoked little controversy, the court's second RFRA opinion created firestorms in liberal circles. On June 30, 2014, the last day of its 2013 term, the Supreme Court announced its highly controversial decision in *Burwell v. Hobby Lobby Stores, Inc.* By a five-to-four margin, the court ruled that three closely held corporations did not have to comply with a mandate promulgated by the Department of Health and Human Services under the Affordable Care Act. That HHS Mandate required them to provide certain contraceptive services to their employees as part of their health insurance coverage. In a majority opinion by Justice Alito, the court held that this mandate violated the rights of these corporations under RFRA.

Since commentary on the Burwell opinion has consistently been ideologically skewed by both the right and the left both at the time of the decision and thereafter, it is important to set forth exactly what the case actually held. In short, the majority found that "a federal regulation's restriction on the activities of a for-profit closely-held corporation must comply with RFRA" and that "The contraceptive mandate, as applied to closely-held corporations, violates RFRA."

Four principal issues were decided by the majority. First, the court held that corporations fall within the protections provided by RFRA. The opinion was at its broadest on this issue, following the federal Dictionary Act's definition of *person* as including corporations and other entities. Justice Alito reasoned that "protecting the free-exercise rights of corporations like Hobby Lobby, Conestoga, and Mardel protects the religious liberty of the humans who own and control those corporations."

Second, the majority ruled that at least some corporations can "exercise . . . religion" within the meaning of RFRA. The court left open the question of whether a publicly owned corporation could exercise religion. Justice Alito pointed out that "HHS has not pointed to any example of a publicly traded corporation asserting RFRA rights, and numerous practical restraints would likely prevent that from happening." Given that state of affairs, "we have no occasion in these cases to consider RFRA's applicability to such companies. The companies in the cases before us are closely-held corporations, each owned and controlled by members of a single family, and no one has disputed the sincerity of their religious beliefs."

Third, the court held that the HHS Mandate did "substantially burden" the closely held corporations' exercise of religion, stating that "We have little trouble concluding that it does." Justice Alito supported this view by summarizing the financial penalties which would be imposed for noncompliance with the mandate, which in Hobby Lobby's case would be $475 million a year. The court further ruled that courts should not second-guess whether sincerely held religious beliefs of the owners of closely held corporations are reasonable because "the federal courts have no business addressing . . . whether the religious belief asserted in a RFRA case is reasonable."

Fourth, the majority assumed without deciding, as a threshold matter, that the HHS Mandate did further a compelling governmental interest, and then turned to the second requirement, that the mandate must further that interest by use of the least restrictive means available. Noting that the least restrictive means test "is exceptionally demanding," Justice Alito suggested that the government had other, less restrictive options available to it. Thus, the government could itself provide contraceptive coverage at its own cost, or, alternatively, it could provide to closely-held for-profit corporations the same accommodation it provided for nonprofit corporations with religious objections. Those corporations were entitled under the mandate to "self-certify that [they] oppose providing coverage for particular contraceptive services."

In the final pages of the majority opinion, Justice Alito pointed out that no woman would lose coverage for any mandated contraceptive services because the nonprofit accommodation provided by the mandate assured that the contraceptive services will be provided to them without any cost-sharing. Moreover, he summarized several additional considerations that would work to limit the scope of the court's holding. For example, the majority opinion notes that different considerations apply to immunizations aimed at combating the spread of infectious diseases, as well as to practices of racial discrimination allegedly based on religious objections. In the latter case, the government has a compelling interest in "providing an equal opportunity to participate in the workplace without regard for race."

On behalf of herself, and Justices Breyer, Sotomayor, and Kagan, Justice Ginsburg filed a vigorous dissenting opinion. She characterized the majority opinion as a "decision of startling breadth," permitting commercial enterprises "to opt out of any law (saving only tax laws) they judge incompatible with their sincerely held religious beliefs." Justice Ginsburg pointed out that no precedent existed under which a for-profit corporation had been exempted on religious grounds from complying with a generally applicable law. She further argued that while the majority opinion indicated that its holding was limited to closely held corporations, nevertheless "its logic extends to corporations of any size, public or private." Moreover, in her view, the majority "invites for-profit entities to seek religion-based exemptions from regulations they deem offensive to their faith."

Justice Ginsburg also contended that the ruling would have an impact on "thousands of women . . . or [their] dependents." As such, she argued that the majority was ignoring that recognizing closely held corporations as capable of exercising rights under RFRA "significantly impinge[s] on the interests of [these] third-parties." In Justice Ginsburg's view, the majority opinion "would deny legions of women who do not hold their employers' beliefs access to contraceptive coverage that the [Affordable Care Act] would otherwise secure."

The dissenters also pointed out that the ruling was not based upon the Free Exercise Clause, and that constitutional decisions under that part of the First Amendment had not recognized rights of the type secured by the majority opinion. As such, the majority erred in the view of the dissenters because the legislative history of RFRA indicated that its intent was simply to restore Free Exercise precedent as it existed prior to the decision in *Employment Division v. Smith* (1990).

Finally, Justice Ginsburg contended that there was no substantial burden placed upon the closely held corporations since the connection between their religious objections and the contraceptive coverage requirement was "too attenuated to rank as substantial." She also contended that the "let the government pay" for the contraceptive coverage argument paved a slippery slope that could be abused in many circumstances.

With respect to corporations and other for-profit organizations, the holding in *Hobby Lobby* is unlikely to be extended significantly. To begin with, the decision was highly controversial, and the five-justice majority included the now-deceased Justice Antonin Scalia, although his replacement, Justice Neil Gorsuch, did reach the same conclusion in his dissenting opinion in the *Hobby Lobby* case when he served on the Tenth Circuit. Moreover, it appears, despite Justice Ginsburg's concerns, that the majority opinion will have limited applicability. To fall under the majority opinion's holding, such a corporation will have to be closely held and its controlling persons will need to show an actual history of religious beliefs followed by the corporation. While the rights, if any, of publicly held corporations under RFRA were not decided, it is unlikely that any such corporation will ever invoke RFRA, for practical as well as for public relations purposes, and even less likely that they would prevail if they did. With respect to the least restrictive means issue, the government is unlikely to prevail on this point so long as it grants exemptions to multiple corporations which received grandfathering relief, or as long as it provides accommodations to non-profit corporations. In addition, Justice Ginsburg's contention that "legions of women" would lose contraceptive coverage as a result of the majority opinion ignored Justice Alito's point that the nonprofit corporation accommodation which the majority found to be an acceptable least restrictive means for closely held for-profit corporations would assure that no woman would lose any contraceptive coverage mandated by the regulations.

Following the decision in *Hobby Lobby*, a flurry of litigation in the lower courts was instituted by religious groups, including religious orders and religious colleges and universities, contending that the nonprofit corporation accommodation applied to for profit, closely held corporations in *Hobby Lobby* was not sufficient to protect their religious beliefs in opposition to the HHS Mandate. Their reasoning, which was rejected by most of the lower courts on grounds of proximate causation, was that certifying to HHS their opposition to providing contraceptives sets in motion a process ending in the provision of those contraceptives to their employees, in contravention of the religious entity's religious beliefs. While the court did not decide the substance of any of these cases, it did initially issue orders enjoining enforcement of the HHS Mandate pending filing and disposition of a petition for certiorari in several of them. See, for example, *Zubik v. Burwell*, No. 14A1065 (June 29, 2015). Each of these orders specifically noted that it did not affect the ability of the employees of the affected organizations "to obtain, without costs, the full range of FDA approved contraceptives," and that the Order "should not be construed as an expression of the Court's views on the merits" (*Ibid.*). Then, after accepting the issue for review, the court in *Zubik v. Burwell* (2016), laboring under the tension of a divided eight-member court, dodged that issue, remanding the cases to the lower courts to seek a compromise resolution. In a unanimous per curiam opinion in this, its fourth RFRA-related case, the justices jointly justified this approach by reference to the results of a supplemental briefing, where the parties agreed that it might be possible to provide contraceptive coverage through petitioners' insurance companies without mandating the form of notice objected to by the religious institutions. The court specifically noted that "The Court expresses no view on the merits of the cases. In particular, the Court does not decide whether petitioners' religious exercise has been substantially burdened, whether the Government has a compelling interest, or whether the current regulations are the least restrictive means of serving that interest." In order to preserve the status quo, the court additionally ruled that "the Government may not impose taxes or penalties on petitioners for failure to file the relevant notice" while the efforts to reach an accommodation were ongoing.

Following the court's decision, the regulatory authorities at Health and Human Services under the Obama Administration called for public comments on the issue of a possible resolution, but the *Zubik* petitioners reported that the Obama regulators were not receptive to their conscience-based objections. As such, the possibility for a negotiated settlement between the Obama government officials and the religiously affiliated nonprofit organizations seemed dim, and it appeared that the court might have to grapple with the questions presented in those cases sometime in the future. That possibility was initially minimized with the election of Donald Trump to the presidency in 2016, after which the Department of Health and Human Services and the Treasury Department promulgated two regulations in 2017 that relieved religious entities and certain employers that had moral objections to providing contraceptives to their employees from compliance with laws and regulations burdening their exercise of religion. Those regulations, however, were challenged in court, with initial decisions finding that the regulations were not required under RFRA and were improperly promulgated. On appeal to the Supreme Court, the lower courts were reversed, and the regulations were upheld (*Little Sisters of the Poor Saints Peter and Paul Home v. Pennsylvania* [2020]).

In a seven-to-two opinion authored by Justice Thomas, the court ruled that the regulations were properly promulgated because the departments were granted broad discretion under the Affordable Care Act to issue "comprehensive guidelines" to implement the mandate to provide "additional preventive care and screening," and no limits were placed on that discretion by the statute. In sum, "the plain language of the statute clearly allows the Departments to create the preventive care standards as well as the religious and moral exemptions."

While the majority went on to reject the argument that the departments were not authorized to consider whether RFRA compelled promulgation of these exemptions, it did not rule on whether RFRA required such, but did observe that "the contraceptive mandate is capable of violating RFRA." As such, "it is unsurprising that RFRA would feature prominently in the Departments' discussion of exemptions that would not pose similar legal problems."

Finally, the majority concluded that the objections to the promulgation of the rules lacked merit.

In a concluding paragraph, the majority noted the Little Sisters of the Poor and many other religious objectors for seven years "have had to fight for the ability to continue in their noble work without violating their sincerely held religious beliefs."

In a concurring opinion, Justice Alito, joined by Justice Gorsuch, stated they would decide the RFRA issue, and rule under a detailed analysis set forth in their opinion that that law "compels an exemption for the Little Sisters and any other employer with a similar objection to what has been called the accommodation to the contraceptive mandate." Justice Alito indicated that they would decide this issue now because under Justice Kagan's concurring opinion (which is discussed below), the regulations might still be attacked on the grounds that they were arbitrary and capricious under the Administrative Procedure Act. Justice Alito would instead "bring the Little Sisters' legal odyssey to an end."

Justice Kagan, writing for herself and Justice Breyer, concurred in the judgment, noting that the regulations at issue fell within the "statutory authority to exempt certain employers from the contraceptive-coverage mandate, but for different reasons that the court gives." They stated that deference to the departments "long-standing and reasonable interpretation" regarding the grant of discretion to the departments over who shall be covered was called for." But, they noted, "that does not mean the Departments should prevail when these cases return to the lower courts." That was because the concurrence questioned whether "the exemptions can survive administrative law's demand for reasoned decisionmaking. That issue remains open for the lower courts to address." Justice Kagan pointed to the fact that the regulations "exempted all employers with objections to the mandate, even if the accommodation met their religious needs," and was thus overbroad. Instead, they "should have exempted only employers who had religious objections to the accommodation—not those who viewed it as a religiously acceptable device for complying with the mandate."

These concurring justices also expressed doubts regarding whether there was adequate support for the extension of the exemptions to publicly traded corporations and to employers "who have moral, rather than religious, objections to the contraceptive mandate."

Justice Kagan concluded her opinion by stating that "None of this is to say that the Departments could not issue a valid rule expanding exemptions from the contraceptive mandate."

In the final opinion, Justice Ginsburg dissented, joined by Justice Sotomayor. They accused the majority of "cast[ing] totally aside countervailing rights and interests in its zeal to secure religious rights to the *n*th degree." These justices cited government estimates that "between 70,500 and 126,400 women would immediately lose access to no-cost contraceptive services." This "imbalanced result" "condone[s] harm to third parties occasioned by entire disregard of their needs."

Justice Ginsburg also reviewed at length the legislative history and statutory text of the ACA, as well as the court's prior rulings. She concluded that none of them supported the conclusion reached by the majority and by Justices Kagan and Breyer. The focus of the dissenters was principally upon the the need for contraception, the harm to women who are excluded from free contraceptive services, and the need for "equal access to preventive services, thereby advancing public health and welfare and women's well-being."

Given the opening left by Justice Kagan's concurring opinion, that "odyssey" of the Little Sisters is not over, but has continued, coming to resemble the storied fictional case of *Jarndyce v. Jarndyce* created by Charles Dickens in his novel *Bleak House.*

PRISONERS' RIGHTS TO EXERCISE THEIR RELIGION

In *Holt v. Hobbs* (2015), the Supreme Court decided another statutory free exercise case, construing what it referred to as a "sister statute" to RFRA. *Holt* unanimously held that a state prison inmate had the right to grow a one-half-inch beard in accordance with his Muslim religion even though the state correctional policy prohibited inmates from growing beards unless they had a skin condition. Because the Religious Land Use and Institutionalized Persons Act (RLUIPA) conferred the same statutory protections for prisoners to freely exercise their religion as RFRA did more generally, Justice Alito's opinion in *Holt* repeatedly cited the *Hobby Lobby* opinion and applied its analytical framework for determining whether the prisoner's religious exercise had improperly been restricted. The *Holt* opinion concluded the correctional policy "substantially burdens petitioner's religious exercise," that the prohibition of short beards did not further a compelling interest of the prison officials regarding the hiding of contraband, or the disguising of identities, and that the officials failed in any event to show that their policies were the least restrictive means for furthering any compelling interest.

Justice Alito pointed out that RLUIPA specifically mandated that it be "construed in favor of a broad protection of religious exercise, to the maximum extent permitted by the terms of this chapter and the Constitution." Given this broad mandate, the opinion first held that the prisoner satisfied his burden of proving that the grooming policy substantially burdened his exercise of religion because forcing him to shave his beard would require him to "engage in conduct that seriously violates [his] religious beliefs."

In a significant ruling, Justice Alito further noted that although not all Muslims believe that men must grow beards, the protections of the statute were "not limited to beliefs which are shared by all of the members of a religious sect," and there was no contention that the prisoner did not sincerely believe that his religion required him to grow a beard. Moreover, in another part of the opinion, Justice Alito stressed, quoting the *Hobby Lobby* opinion, that the compelling interest test focuses on the specific litigant before the court—"the particular claimant whose sincere exercise of religion is being substantially burdened."

Given these findings, the burden then shifted to the prison officials to show, under the express terms of RLUIPA, that the refusal to permit the prisoner to grow a one-half-inch beard furthered a compelling governmental interest, and was also the least restrictive means of furthering that interest. Here the court first rejected the defense that the prohibition of all beards was necessary to prevent the concealing of contraband. This was a defense the court explicitly found "hard to take seriously." Next, Justice Alito reasoned that even if the concern regarding contraband were accepted, the no-beards policy still was unsupportable under the independent least restrictive means inquiry. Thus, any legitimate security concerns could be satisfied "by simply searching petitioner's beard." Finally, the court went on to reject a second defense advanced by the prison officials—that the no-beards policy was necessary to prevent inmates from disguising their identities, which could facilitate their escape or make their recapture more difficult. The court held that this concern could be addressed by requiring photographs to be taken of the prisoner at intake, when he could be required to shave his beard, with additional photographs being taken thereafter. Moreover, the court pointed to the fact that the existing correctional policy did permit the growth of a one-quarter-inch beard for medical reasons even though this permission arguably would also pose a risk of deception.

The court also relied on the fact that "the vast majority of States and the Federal Government permit inmates to grow 1/2-inch beards, either for any reason or for religious reasons." While it is noted that this was not dispositive, it suggested that less restrictive means were available to meet the concerns of the correctional officials.

Finally, the court noted that prison officials could question the authenticity of a prisoner's religious claims if they "suspect . . . that an inmate is using religious activity to cloak illicit conduct." In addition, "an institution might be entitled to withdraw an accommodation if the claimant abuses the exemption in a manner that undermines the prison's compelling interests." These comments appear to have been addressed to Justice Sotomayor's concurring opinion, which emphasized the need for granting discretion to prison officials "[i]n the dangerous prison environment," which necessitates regulations to "maintain good order, security and discipline."

Three notable points emerge from the *Holt* decision. First, the decision was widely anticipated because it was simply inconceivable that the majority justices who joined in the *Hobby Lobby* decision would expose themselves to the criticism that they protected the free exercise rights of Christian-led corporations, but not those of Muslim prisoners. Second, the court reaffirmed the important point that the free exercise claims of individuals cannot be determined based upon the views of their fellow religionists. Thus, the fact that some Muslims believe that men do not have to grow a beard as a requirement of Islam was not dispositive of the prisoner's individual case, since it was conceded that he sincerely believed that his religion did require him to grow a beard. Indeed, RLUIPA specifically provides that "religious exercise" be understood to include "any exercise of religion, whether or not compelled by, or central to, a system of religious belief." One may therefore wonder whether a Catholic prisoner who sincerely felt that he was required to honor the historic Catholic practice of abstaining from meat on all Fridays would have to be accommodated by prison officials even though the practice was no longer a mandatory religious requirement of the Catholic Church outside of the Lenten season, or whether a Jewish prisoner might be entitled to be provided with kosher food for all his meals. Third, the considerable length to which the seven justices who joined Justice Alito's opinion went to knock down the justifications offered by the prison officials shows just how vigorously the court will cross-examine claims of a compelling governmental interest, and also what a stringent burden the least restrictive means requirement places upon all government officials, whether under RFRA or RLUIPA.

DAMAGE REMEDIES UNDER RFRA

Once it has been determined that a violation of RFRA has occurred, the question arises as to what remedies may be appropriate. In *Tanzin v. Tanvir* (2020), the Supreme Court determined that litigants may, when appropriate, obtain money damages against federal officials in their individual capacities for violating their rights under RFRA. The case involved three practicing Muslims who claimed that agents of the FBI placed them on a "No Fly List" in retaliation because they refused to act as informants against their religious communities. The Supreme Court did not determine whether the actions of the agents violated RFRA, but only addressed the issue of whether damages are available for a violation of RFRA.

In a short, unanimous opinion for eight members of the court, with Justice Barrett not participating, Justice Thomas carefully reviewed the text of RFRA in reaching this conclusion. The statute expressly provides that a person whose religious exercise has been unlawfully burdened has the right to "obtain appropriate relief against a government." In turn, "government" is defined to include, among others, an "official (or other person acting under color of law) of the United States." This resolved the issue regarding whether an individual government agent could be sued.

What constitutes "appropriate relief" raised a more difficult question since there is no statutory definition of the term. Justice Thomas pointed out that "damages have long been awarded as appropriate relief" in suits against government officials. Indeed, in the words of the majority opinion "A damages remedy is not just 'appropriate' relief. . . . It is also the *only* form of relief can remedy some RFRA violations. For certain injuries, such as respondents' wasted plane tickets, effective relief consists of damages, not an injunction."

That money damages are generally available as a RFRA remedy did not end the case, however, as Justice Thomas was careful to note, in a footnote at the end of the opinion, that the government officials who were sued in the case "are entitled to assert a qualified immunity defense when sued in their individual capacities for money damages under RFRA."

PHARMACISTS' RIGHTS TO REFUSE TO STOCK EMERGENCY CONTRACEPTIVES

Governmental mandates that businesses provide to customers certain products even if such provision would violate the business owners' consciences or religious beliefs go far beyond the HHS Mandate on contraceptives. Thus, to take just one example, a pharmacy in Washington State declined to stock emergency contraceptives, based on a religious belief held by its pharmacists that providing emergency contraceptives "is tantamount to abortion." The pharmacy's action violated regulations issued by the Washington State Board of Pharmacy. Those regulations required all pharmacists to provide emergency contraceptives, specifically mandating that no pharmacist could refuse to do so based on religious grounds. The Ninth Circuit, on appeal from a district court ruling which enjoined enforcement of the regulations, rejected the pharmacy's First Amendment challenge to those regulations. No RFRA claim could be made since the federal RFRA statute only applies to federal laws, and the State of Washington does not have state RFRA legislation.

The pharmacy's attempt to obtain Supreme Court review (which requires a vote of four justices to hear an appeal) fell one vote short. Three justices dissented from the refusal to hear the case, joining an opinion written by Justice Alito for himself, Chief Justice Roberts, and Justice Thomas (*Stormans,* Inc. v. Weisman [2016]).

Justice Alito cautioned that the denial of review provided "an ominous sign," reasoning that "if this is a sign of how religious liberty claims will be treated in the years ahead, those who value religious freedom have cause for great concern."

There were several key factors identified by Justice Alito that made the case a good candidate for Supreme Court review. First, the importance of the case was made clear by the fact that some thirty-eight national and state pharmacy associations urged the court to hear the case, contending that the regulations in question constituted "a radical departure from past regulation of the pharmacy industry," and might cause small, independent pharmacies to close, reducing patient access to medication. Second, the case placed "important First Amendment interest at stake." Third, there was strong evidence of a discriminatory legislative intent aimed at religious believers. Thus, for example, the State Human Rights Commission made threats of personal liability against the pharmacy board members if they passed a regulation permitting referral to another pharmacy for religious or moral reasons. In addition, the governor indicated she could remove the board members after they initially voted to permit a conscience exemption. This, plus additional evidence, had persuaded the trial court, following a twelve-day hearing, to issue an injunction barring enforcement of the regulations, an injunction which the Ninth Circuit dissolved.

Justice Alito's dissenting opinion provided additional reasons for the Supreme Court to review the case. He pointed to several factors indicating that women seeking emergency contraceptives could obtain them with ease, given the presence of more than thirty other pharmacies located within five miles of the petitioning pharmacy. In addition, the widely utilized and accepted practice of "facilitated referral" permitted all pharmacies to refer patients to other pharmacies to obtain drugs they did not stock. The record in the trial court indicated that other pharmacies not involved in litigation utilized the facilitated referral option "at least several times a day" for drugs of all types.

Finally, even though the authorities vigorously and successfully lobbied against providing a religious exemption, the regulations nevertheless provided certain other, secular exemptions, one of which permitted pharmacists to decline to provide drugs to Medicaid patients because of low reimbursement rates.

While the dissenting justices provided strong reasons for the Supreme Court to hear the case, it is questionable whether the pharmacy would have prevailed had the court done so in 2016. To begin with, it is likely that the four most liberal judges would have voted against the pharmacy, unless they were persuaded that religious believers were in fact targeted by the Washington State regulators. Second, it is noteworthy that Justice Kennedy did not vote to hear the case, putting in question how he would have voted if the issue had been presented for decision. Third, even if Justice Kennedy would have voted for the pharmacy, that would only have resulted in a four-to-four split, with the decisive vote to be cast by a then unknown new justice to be appointed by the new president.

Since Justice Gorsuch was confirmed thereafter, in April of 2017, this problem was ameliorated, and the court agreed, after considering whether to take the case at fourteen different conferences, to hear *Masterpiece Bakeshop v. Colorado Civil Rights Commission,* in which certiorari was granted on June 26, 2017, the last day of the October 2016 term.

BAKERS' RIGHTS TO REFUSE TO CREATE A CAKE FOR A SAME-SEX WEDDING

In *Masterpiece Cakeshop,* the court agreed to hear the following question: "Whether applying Colorado's public accommodations law to compel the petitioner to create expression that violates his sincerely held religious beliefs about marriage violates the free speech or free exercise clauses of the First

Amendment." Although that was the question accepted, it was not the one the court decided. Instead, the court ruled that the Colorado Civil Rights Commission violated the Free Exercise Clause of the First Amendment by demonstrating a "clear and impermissible hostility toward the sincere religious beliefs motivating [the baker's] objection" (*Masterpiece Cakeshop, Ltd. v. Colorado Civil Rights Commission* [2018]).

The baker told the petitioners, and a total of six same-sex couples, that he would not create a wedding cake for a same-sex wedding reception because of his religious objections to same-sex marriage. The petitioners then contended this refusal constituted illegal discrimination based on sexual orientation under Colorado's public accommodations law.

In his majority opinion, Justice Kennedy stated it was possible that the creation of a wedding cake could constitute an exercise of protected speech, observing that while the gay couples' rights must be protected, "the religious and philosophical objections to gay marriage are protected views and in some instances protected forms of expression." Nevertheless, "Whatever the confluence of speech and free exercise principles might be in some cases, the Colorado Civil Rights Commission's consideration of this case was inconsistent with the State's obligation of religious neutrality." As such, the Colorado Commission violated the Free Exercise Clause of the First Amendment.

Justice Kennedy noted that a state must apply any public accommodations law in a manner that is neutral toward religion, holding that a government cannot pass judgment on religious beliefs, or enact laws that are hostile to such beliefs. Flaunting this requirement, Colorado, in the majority's view, demonstrated an extreme hostility toward the baker's religious beliefs. For example, one commissioner disparaged the baker's beliefs as despicable, noting that religion was used to defend slavery in some instances. The same commissioner went on to compare the baker's objections to the Holocaust. The majority opinion went on to note a second example of hostility, stemming from the different treatment of bakers who refused to create cakes disparaging same-sex marriage without being held to have violated the public accommodations law.

While the baker won his case, with the penalties against him vacated, the court's opinion was a narrow and limited one, and the question accepted for review was left undecided. Indeed, although seven justices agreed the baker had been improperly discriminated against, four justices noted in their concurring or dissenting opinions that absent the hostility demonstrated by the Colorado Commission to religion, it would have been permissible for an agency to sanction a baker for refusing to create a cake for a same-sex couple. These four justices pointed to several excerpts from Justice Kennedy's majority opinion, including his observation that the general rule was that it is illegal to deny any protected class equal access to goods and services.

Thus, in a concurring opinion for herself and Justice Breyer, Justice Kagan wrote that "Colorado can treat a baker who discriminates based on sexual orientation differently from a baker who does not discriminate on that or any other prohibited ground." Justice Ginsburg, in a dissenting opinion for herself and Justice Sotomayor, indicated the same views, again quoting at length from the majority opinion's statements in favor of the rights of gay people not to be discriminated against. Justice Ginsburg went on to attempt to distinguish the cases of the bakers who refused to create cakes opposing same-sex marriage from the case before the court.

While these four justices indicated views that would be hostile to religious objections to creating specialty goods or services for same-sex couples, three other justices noted (or suggested) they would find such religious objections constitutionally protected. The clearest exposition of this view came in Justice Thomas's concurring opinion, which was joined by Justice Gorsuch. Justice Thomas indicated that the creation and design of a cake is expressive and constitutes protected speech. As such, no public accommodations law can be utilized to penalize a vendor unless it passes strict scrutiny. Without deciding whether the Colorado law passed this test, Justice Thomas went onto counter the same-sex couple's argument that the law protects them from the degradation of their dignity. Citing multiple Supreme Court decisions, Justice Thomas indicated that a state "cannot punish protected speech because some group finds it offensive, hurtful, stigmatic, unreasonable, or undignified." Justice Gorsuch joined Justice Thomas's opinion, but it is notable that neither Chief Justice Roberts nor Justice Alito did so, leaving unclear their views on the original question accepted for review.

In a second concurring opinion, written by Justice Gorsuch and joined by Justice Alito, there was a recognition that wedding cakes convey a message, but no express statement that they constitute protected speech. Instead, this opinion faulted Colorado for failing to apply "a consistent legal rule," finding that the baker should have been given the same rights to decline to create a cake favoring same-sex marriage, as were given to those refusing to create cakes opposing same-sex marriage. Justice Gorsuch concluded that "Mr. Phillips has conclusively proven a First Amendment violation and, after almost six years facing unlawful civil charges, he is entitled to judgment."

Where, then, does this leave the question the court originally agreed to decide? There are three important points to note here. First, the court wisely agreed not to decide an important and sensitive constitutional issue on which there is significant disagreement among members of the public. In taking this course, the court avoided the criticism it experienced by making early determinations declaring a constitutional right to abortion, *Roe v. Wade* (1973), *overruled* in *Dobbs v. Jackson Women's Health Organization* (2022), and a constitutional right to same-sex marriage (*Obergefell v. Hodges* [2015]). This course also permitted the lower courts an opportunity to develop a body of law based on the specific facts and circumstances of particular cases, which will create factual records that will form the basis for appropriate adjudications in these individual cases. The Supreme Court was sensitive to this issue, noting that in the case before it, the baker's objections to creating a cake celebrating same-sex marriage had a greater force because Colorado had not recognized a right to such marriage at the time the same-sex couple asked him to design their wedding cake. Second, the majority opinion has all the hallmarks of a minimalist, compromise decision that was required to gain a majority, and particularly to obtain the vote of Justice Kennedy. Justice Kennedy, it must be remembered, was at the time perhaps the court's strongest advocate of gay rights, and included several statements in his opinion for the majority recognizing the necessity "to protect the rights and dignity of gay persons who are, or wish to become married, but who face discrimination when they seek goods and services." Third, by strongly declaring that religious objections must be treated fairly by government decision-makers without any bias demonstrated toward religious practice, the court sent a message that the current, increasing hostility to religion is not acceptable in government decision-making. Thus, Justice Kennedy emphasized that "the religious and philosophical objections to gay marriage are protected views and in some instances protected forms of expression." In an interesting development abroad, the Supreme Court of the United Kingdom echoed this passage and held that a Christian baker had the right to decline to make a cake with the message, "Support Gay Marriage." The unanimous British court reasoned that "The objection was to the message on the cake, not on any personal characteristics of the messenger" (*Lee v. Ashers Baking Company*, 2018 UKSC 49 [Oct. 10, 2018]).

It is significant to note that the Supreme Court's decision did not immediately end the baker's problems with the Colorado Civil Rights Commission. Indeed—in what was clearly not a coincidental development—on the same day the Supreme Court originally decided to hear the *Masterpiece Cakeshop* case, a lawyer visited the baker, requesting him to make a custom cake celebrating a "gender transition." The baker again refused to do so, based again on his religious beliefs. The Colorado Commission found probable cause that his actions violated the Colorado anti-discrimination statute. In response, the baker filed a federal lawsuit against the commissioners. Ultimately, however, the Colorado Commission and Phillips settled, with the commission voluntarily dismissing its administrative action unanimously after it came to light in Phillip's federal case that one commissioner had called him a "hater" on Twitter, and two other commissioners had announced that they supported the negative comments made by the commissioner whose comments were cited in the Supreme Court's opinion. One of these other commissioners had stated that "I was actually proud of what she said, and I agree with her." Phillips also voluntarily dismissed his federal lawsuit, and each side agreed to bear their own legal fees and costs.

In all, Phillips was under attack by the Colorado Commission for almost seven years. In an OpEd for the *Denver Post*, he stated that "I lost the right to live out my freedom for nearly seven years. I don't want that to happen to anyone else. . . . Here's hoping that we as a nation learn to tolerate and respect our differing beliefs and that governments stop harassing people whose faith they dislike."[5]

Despite Mr. Phillips's hopes, the basic issue of the rights of a business to decline to serve potential customers based on religious belief is not about to go away, and it is to be expected that the Supreme Court will eventually have to decide this issue. Mark Movsesian has aptly summed up three reasons why litigation is likely to continue on these issues of religious freedom in declining to provide goods or services to individuals whose views offend the religious beliefs of the vendor. He notes that "*Masterpiece Cakeshop* reflects very broad cultural and political trends that drive those conflicts and shape their resolution: a deepening religious polarization between Nones and the Traditionally Religious, an expansive understanding of equality as sameness, and an activist state dedicated to enforcing that understanding in large areas of our common life."[6]

Indeed, even Phillips has not been left alone. He was sued again in June 2019, this time by the same transgender plaintiff who had complained to the Colorado Commission in its second proceeding against the bakery. This latest complaint was filed in Denver district court, alleging discrimination and deceptive and unfair trade practices. Phillips lost at the trial level, and was fined $500, the maximum penalty under the Colorado Anti-Discrimination Act. The decision of the trial court was upheld at the first the appellate level, and an appeal is being pursued.

Significantly, the cake in question differed from that involved in the Supreme Court case, as it did not involve any creativity but only had a "simple design of blue and pink," which "Defendants admit that they were willing to make the requested cake until Ms. Scardina identified that she chose the colors to reflect and celebrate her identity as a transgender female." The district court expressly noted that "Perhaps the analysis would be different if the cake design had been more intricate, artistically involved, or overtly stated a message attributable to Defendants."

RELIGIOUS INSTITUTIONS AND SAME-SEX FOSTER PLACEMENTS

Fulton v. City of Philadelphia (2021) presented the court with an opportunity to overrule or limit *Employment Division v. Smith* (1990), which, as discussed above, declined to permit an exception based on religious belief to justify noncompliance with a law that was neutral and generally applicable. While three members of the court would have overruled *Smith*, the majority chose not to do so.

Fulton presented a First Amendment free exercise challenge to the decision of the City of Philadelphia not to refer children for foster placement to Catholic Social Services ("CSS") any longer because that organization would not certify same-sex couples for foster child placement. The city took this punitive action despite the facts that there had been no attempts by LGBT couples to seek certification from CSS, and that CSS had an exemplary record in making foster child placements over many years. Indeed, the city on appeal acknowledged that "CSS has 'long been a point of light in the city's foster-care system.'"

In an opinion for six members of the court, Chief Justice Roberts noted that "CSS seeks only an accommodation that will allow it to continue serving the children of Philadelphia in a manner consistent with its religious beliefs; it does not seek to impose those beliefs on anyone else." On the merits, the majority opinion concluded that *Smith* did not justify the city's action in refusing to contract with CSS because "This case falls outside *Smith* because the City has burdened the religious exercise of CSS through policies that do not meet the requirement of being neutral and generally applicable." The majority opinion explained that *Smith* itself recognized that a law that provided for individual exceptions was not a law that was neutral and generally applicable because "where the state has in place a system of individual exemptions, it may not refuse to extend that system to cases of 'religious hardship' without compelling reason." Here, Philadelphia's standard foster care contract granted "sole discretion" to the commissioner or his or her designee to grant exceptions to providers from the requirement that no rejection of a foster care applicant should be made based on the applicant's sexual orientation.

Concurring in the judgment, Justice Alito, joined by Justices Thomas and Gorsuch, performed a tour de force attacking the decision in *Smith*, and contending in a closely argued originalist approach focused on the text and original understanding of the Free Exercise Clause that *Smith* should be overruled.

Justice Alito began his opinion by documenting in detail the historic leadership of religious groups in protecting orphans and abandoned children which, at least until the early twentieth century, exceeded the efforts of government to do so. He then criticized the majority opinion as leaving a large loophole by which the city could evade the decision by simply dropping the exemption provision in its form contract. Should it do so, the parties will be in exactly the same position they were when *Fulton* was argued, and the court will be forced to determine whether *Smith* should be overruled or limited.

Turning into the *Smith* decision, Justice Alito pointed out there were four dissents, and that *Smith* essentially sidestepped earlier decisions such as *Sherbet v. Verner* (1963), which required a compelling state interest to justify burdening religious practice. *Sherbert* provided this standard as the controlling law for some thirty-seven years. In addition to the four dissents, *Smith* provoked a strong negative response and energized Congress to pass the Religious Freedom and Restoration Act by overwhelming majorities in both houses, restoring the compelling interest test to cases to which it applied.

The concurring opinion also pointed out that *Smith* ignored the text and original understanding analysis commonly followed by originalists, choosing instead to simply ask whether the majority's reading of the Free Exercise Clause was "permissible." Justice Alito then performed an elaborate analysis, reminiscent of the approach Justice Scalia followed in the *Heller* right to bear arms opinion. Alito began with the text of the First Amendment, pointing out that the key phrases were "prohibiting" and "free exercise of religion." This text, in his view, did not lend any support to the *Smith* rule that religious practice could be burdened by a neutral and generally applicable law. The concurring opinion then reviewed at length the historical record which was claimed to support a plain reading of the broad text of the Free Exercise Clause. Looking first at the twelve of the thirteen original states' constitutions which included a protection for religious practice, the concurring justices noted that the prevalent approach taken in these early constitutions was to protect religious practice broadly, providing exceptions only for practices which endangered the public peace or safety. The actual practices in both the colonies and the states similarly showed a willingness "to grant exemptions—even when the generally applicable laws served critical state interests." One telling example was the religious exemptions given to religious groups, including the Quakers and Mennonites, which objected to military service in the militia for religious reasons.

Justice Alito concluded that *Smith* should be overruled and its rule replaced with the rule followed prior to its decision—"A law that imposes a substantial burden on religious exercise can be sustained only if it is narrowly tailored to serve a compelling government interest."

Justice Gorsuch also wrote a concurring opinion that was joined by Justices Thomas and Alito. He pointed out that the court has granted certiorari "to decide whether to overrule" *Smith*, but the majority "seek to sidestep the question." Agreeing with Justice Alito, Justice Gorsuch concluded that *Smith* should be overruled because it "failed to respect this Court's precedents, was mistaken as a matter of the Constitution's original public meaning, and has proven unworkable in practice."

Justice Gorsuch also contended that the court's failure to overrule *Smith* would inevitably lead to additional years of litigation between the city and CSS. On that point, he cited the experience of the baker, Jack Phillips, who is still being sued because the court in the Masterpiece Cakeshop case failed to resolve the underlying question of whether his religious beliefs justified his refusal to design a cake for a same-sex wedding.

Justice Alito's seventy-seven-page opinion concurring in the judgment was so comprehensive that several legal scholars have concluded that it was originally drafted as a majority opinion but fell two votes short of achieving that status. Particularly damaging were the votes of Justices Barrett and Kavanaugh, both of whom joined in Chief Justice Roberts's opinion. In a separate concurring opinion, Justice Barrett, joined by Justice Kavanaugh, explained that many of those involved in the appeal, including "Justices of this Court have made serious arguments that *Smith* ought to be overruled." Moreover, "In my view, the textual and structural arguments against *Smith* are more compelling. As a matter of text and structure, it is difficult to see why the Free Exercise Clause—lone among First Amendment freedoms–offers nothing more than protection from discrimination." Why, then, did these two justices not join in the call to overrule *Smith*? Justice Barrett explained that her concern was "what should replace *Smith*?" She pointed out that she was "skeptical about swapping *Smith*'s categorical anti-discrimination approach for an equally categorical strict scrutiny regime, particularly when this Court's resolution of conflicts between generally applicable laws and other First Amendment rights—like speech and assembly—has been much more nuanced."

Thus, *Smith* survived, if only by a slim thread, and it can be expected that future cases will more closely analyze what more "nuanced" standard of review might replace *Smith*'s "categorical anti-discrimination approach."

NOTES

1. For a detailed discussion of the early decisions interpreting the Free Exercise Clause, see Edward F Mannino, *Shaping America: The Supreme Court and American Society* (Columbia: University of South Carolina Press, 2009), 187–94.

2. The Iowa case is *Business Leaders in Christ v. The University of Iowa*, C.A. No.17-cv-00080-SMR-SBJ (S.D. Iowa January 23, 2018).

3. Patrick O'Donnell, "Cleveland Diocese adds detailed 'morality clause' to high school teachers, too," *The Plain Dealer*, April 8, 2015.

4. Joan Frawley Desmond, "San Francisco High-School Teachers Approve Contract, Amid Ongoing Tensions," *National Catholic Reporter*, August 23, 2015, 1.

5. For further information on the *Masterpiece Cakeshop* matter, see Joy Pullman, "After More Evidence of Its Anti-Christian Animus, Colorado Commission Suspends Harassment of Cake Baker," *The Federalist.com*, March 6, 2019; Kristen Waggoner, "Jack Phillips Wins Again," *National Review Bench Memos*, March 11, 2019; Jack Phillips, "Jack Phillips: Can I just be a cake artist again?" Op-Ed, *Denver Post*, March 8, 2019.

6. Mark Movsesian, "*Masterpiece Cakeshop* and the Future of Religious Freedom," 42, *Harvard Journal of Law & Public Policy* (Summer 2019), 711, 750.

Chapter 3

Establishment of Religion

While the First Amendment forbids Congress from "prohibiting the free exercise" of religion, it also prohibits it from enacting any law "respecting an establishment of religion." The proper interpretation of the Establishment Clause has been one of the most contentious topics in the court's jurisprudence, and has caused acrimonious public debate, particularly regarding the decisions that banned school prayer and Bible reading in the public schools.[1]

As the Supreme Court has recently expanded its interpretation of the Free Exercise Clause, it has constricted the prohibitions of the Establishment Clause. The principal reason for both of these changes has been the appointment of three conservative justices by President Donald Trump, resulting in a conservative majority of six justices on the current court. Persistent criticism by both liberal and conservative commentators of the twentieth-century court's confusing explication of what the Establishment Clause does and does not prohibit provides an additional explanation of the court's new approach. Finally, the prior decisions were mostly unpopular, supplying a favorable public opinion for the changes that have been made.

The Supreme Court's historic approach to the Establishment Clause was muddled, at best, in its decisions and opinions. The earliest opinions often reflected a religious bias of the largely Protestant judiciary to Catholic schools, a bias from which the court largely retreated after Chief Justice Rehnquist and Justices Scalia and Thomas took their seats on the court. Nevertheless, Justice Scalia criticized the court thereafter for what he perceived to be "the Court's hostility to religion," as well as for failing to utilize any "consistently applied principle" in its Establishment Clause decisions. The debate regarding the Establishment Clause is an ongoing one in both the court and in the public arena, as the strong dissenting opinions of Justice Sotomayor in *Trinity Lutheran* and *Kennedy v. Bremerton School District* (discussed below) and of Justice Ginsburg in *American Humanist Ass'n* (also discussed below) demonstrate.

The most recent decisions of the Supreme Court have limited the reach of the Establishment Clause, calling into question the continuing viability of many earlier decisions.

The seminal case interpreting the Establishment Clause is *Everson v. Board of Education* (1947). In *Everson*, a sharply divided Supreme Court upheld a New Jersey school district policy which permitted reimbursing the parents of Catholic school students for the costs of their bus transportation to school. While the parents won that case, it proved to be a Pyrrhic victory because the court adopted a strict Jeffersonian "wall of separation" template for adjudicating future Establishment Clause cases. Indeed, Justice Black's opinion for the majority expressly stated that the wall of separation between Church and State "must be kept high and impregnable."

One year after Everson, the court struck down a "released time" program under which clergy of various denominations were permitted to come into Illinois public schools during regular hours once a week to teach religious classes. *McCollum v. Board of Education* (1948). Writing for eight members of the court, Justice Black ruled that "this is beyond all question the utilization of the tax-established and tax-supported public school system to aid religious groups to spread their faith. And it falls squarely under the ban of the First Amendment . . . as we interpreted it in Everson v. Board of Education." By contrast, in *Zorach v. Clauson* (1952), by a vote of six to three, the Supreme Court upheld a version of released time implemented in New York under which students left the public school to attend religious services during the public school day at other locations. Significantly, the ACLU and the American Jewish Congress opposed even this approach for reconciling free exercise claims with Establishment Clause concerns.

While the released time decisions were themselves controversial, the most vocal opposition to the Supreme Court's approach to the Establishment Clause came later with the school prayer and Bible-reading prohibitions it imposed in the 1960s. In *Engel v. Vitale* (1962), the court struck down a nondenominational prayer which was said aloud at the beginning of class at the start of the school day in New York State. Recitation of the prayer was not compulsory, and any student who wished not to say it was excused. Justice Black wrote a majority opinion for six members of the court, ruling that the prayer was unconstitutional because "the constitutional prohibition against laws respecting an establishment of religion must at least mean that in this country it is no part of the business of government to compose official prayers for any group of the American people to recite as part of a religious program carried on by government." Only Justice Potter Stewart dissented, with two members of the court not participating in the decision.

One year after *Engel*, the Supreme Court reignited the controversy by striking down Bible reading in the public schools by a vote of eight to one.

Abington School District v. Schempp (1963). While "the place of religion in our society is an exalted one," Justice Tom Clark's majority opinion observed that the Bible was "an instrument of religion," and concluded that "it is not within the power of government to invade th[e] citadel [of the individual heart and mind], whether its purpose or effect be to aid or oppose, to advance or retard. In the relationship between man and religion, the State is firmly committed to a position of neutrality." As such, to withstand an attack under the Establishment Clause, "there must be a secular legislative purpose and a primary effect that neither advances nor inhibits religion."

The court's rulings against school prayer continued in several cases, with even a fairly bland nondenominational graduation prayer struck down by the court in *Lee v. Weisman* (1992) by a vote of five to four. Justice Kennedy's majority opinion found that the "dominant facts" were that "state officials direct the performance of a formal religious exercise at promotional and graduation ceremonies for secular schools." This was found to be "pervasive" governmental involvement with religion, and the majority specifically declined the request of the United States to reconsider the *Lemon* decision (discussed below) and its three criteria. The court also invalidated student-led prayers at high school football games in *Santa Fe Independent School District v. Doe* (2000), finding a close "entanglement" between the school and the prayers.

Turning to the teaching of evolution in the public schools, the court also struck down an Arkansas law that prohibited the teaching of that subject in those schools. Justice Abe Fortas described that law as "a product of the upsurge of 'fundamentalist' religious fervor of the twenties," ruling that "the law's effort is confined to an attempt to blot out a particular theory because of its supposed conflict with the Biblical account, literally read." Other attempts to confine the teaching of evolution also failed the Establishment Clause test. Thus, in *Edwards v. Aguillard* (1987), seven members of the court found a Louisiana statute unconstitutional because it prohibited the teaching of evolution unless "creation science" was taught at the same time. Justice William Brennan explained that the law failed because it had a religious, rather than a secular, purpose. He wrote that the sponsor of the law made it clear that the legislative intent was "to restructure the science curriculum to conform with a particular religious viewpoint." Foreshadowing future developments in the Establishment Clause jurisprudence, Chief Justice Rehnquist and Justices Thomas, Scalia, and Kennedy dissented. Justice Scalia delivered an influential dissenting opinion joined by those justices, questioning the view that the Establishment Clause "forbids legislators . . . to act upon their religious convictions." He contended that the legislative purpose was appropriate to prevent indoctrination of students, choosing to let them "be free to decide for themselves, about the origin of life."

Many other cases decided during this time struck down a wide variety of laws that attempted to provide books, services, and salary reimbursements to religious schools and their teachers. A prime example of these rulings was featured in the highly controversial decision in *Lemon v. Kurtzman* (1971), which as seen in the more recent cases discussed in this chapter is essentially a dead letter now. That case reviewed the constitutionality under the Establishment Clause of several aspects of aid to private schools in Pennsylvania and Rhode Island. The most significant discussion was devoted to the laws' salary subsidization feature for teachers of secular subjects in religious schools. Payments were made either to the teachers or to their schools on the condition that the subsidized teachers could not teach religion and could only use teaching materials that were used in the public schools or were approved by the state secretary of education. The states monitored compliance in various ways, including post-audit programs and written pledges by teachers that they would not teach religion. Despite these attempts to satisfy the Establishment Clause concerns, Chief Justice Warren Burger's majority opinion struck the laws down by adding a third test to the secular legislative purpose and principal or primary effects tests used in prior cases. The court added a further requirement that "the statute must not foster 'an excessive government entanglement with religion.'" By monitoring teacher compliance, the majority concluded that these "prophylactic contacts" would involve "excessive and enduring entanglement between state and church," which, in turn, would give rise to "divisive political potential," with different groups warring with each other over state aid.

Professor Noah Feldman has accurately characterized *Lemon v. Kurtzman* as "the high point of legal secularism." Following that decision, while the court continued to strike down some laws which provided aid to religious schools, and continued to ban the recitation of prayers in public school activities, the court generally took a more accommodating view toward religious interests in its future Establishment Clause decisions, affected in part by the confirmation of more conservative justices on the court. Two cases well illustrate this change.

Mitchell v. Helms (2000) upheld a federal program under which "secular, neutral, and non-ideological" educational materials and equipment were lent to public and private schools. Private schools received about 30 percent of the dollars distributed, with the majority of those dollars going to Catholic schools. Writing for four justices in a plurality opinion, Justice Clarence Thomas found this federal program permissible under the Establishment Clause, based upon "the principles of neutrality and private choice." Three justices dissented, invoking the "pervasively sectarian" doctrine, which typically was invoked against Catholic schools that were charged with "religious indoctrination." In a striking passage attacking that doctrine, Justice Thomas charged that "hostility to aid to pervasively sectarian schools has a shameful pedigree we do not hesitate to disavow. . . . Opposition to aid to 'sectarian' schools acquired prominence in the 1870's with Congress's consideration (and near passage) of the Blaine Amendment, which would have amended the Constitution to bar any aid to sectarian institutions. Consideration of the amendment arose at a time of pervasive hostility to the Catholic Church and to Catholics in general, and it was an open secret that 'sectarian' was code for 'Catholic.'" Justice Thomas concluded that "*This doctrine, born of bigotry, should be buried now*."

The aid program was upheld, but the votes of Justices Sandra Day O'Connor and Stephen Breyer were necessary to achieve a majority, and they did not joining Justice Thomas's comments, finding instead that the program was constitutional because it consisted of a lending of materials, with no money distributed directly to the schools.

The second and more controversial decision came in *Zelman v. Simmons-Harris* (2002). That case upheld as constitutional under the Establishment Clause a state program under which vouchers were awarded to public school parents for their use in paying for private school tuitions for their children. Some 96 percent of the participating families chose to use their vouchers for their children to attend religious schools, principally those affiliated with the Roman Catholic religion, even though two out of three of the participating families were not Catholic.

The majority opinion in *Zelman* was written by Chief Justice William Rehnquist. It marked his triumph in beginning to remake the Supreme Court's jurisprudence under the Establishment Clause. His opinion noted that the voucher program was one of the government neutrality, with the allocation of monies resulting from "true private choice," a phrase that appears repeatedly in the majority opinion. Moreover, the aid that reached religious schools did so "only by way of the deliberate choices of numerous individual recipients." As such, those choices could not be attributed to the government, and the voucher program was "entirely neutral with respect to religion."

Three justices dissented. Justice John Paul Stevens saw the program as advancing "religious indoctrination at state expense," and as increasing the risk of "religious strife." Justice David Souter indicated his view that the Establishment Clause imposed a flat ban on any aid for "religious teaching," and predicted that the decision would lead to a "scramble for money" among "competing sectarians." Finally, Justice Breyer expressed a concern that the voucher program would lead to "religiously based social conflict." He saw the voucher program as particularly dangerous because it involved "direct financing of the core function of the church: the teaching of religious truths to young children."

Against the background of this very muddled precedent, the Supreme Court has most recently decided several cases involving Establishment Clause issues. In *Trinity Lutheran*, as discussed above, the majority chose to frame the case as implicating the Free Exercise Clause, while the dissenters saw it as presenting serious issues under the Establishment Clause. The other recent cases, discussed immediately below, involved whether prayer was constitutionally permissible at public meetings or on a public-school football field, and whether state maintenance of a war memorial featuring a cross violated the Establishment Clause.

PRAYER AT PUBLIC MEETINGS

State and local governmental entities, historically and today, often begin their meetings with the recitation of a prayer, usually proclaimed by a citizen voter. The governmental entities which have engaged in such practices have often been dragged into court by the ACLU or by other civil liberty organizations which charge violations of the Establishment Clause. The Supreme Court most recently decided one such challenge in *Town of Greece v. Galloway* (2014). There, the court had occasion to revisit its earlier precedent regarding whether the Establishment Clause barred legislative bodies from opening their sessions with a prayer. It ruled, by a five-to-four margin, that opening a town board meeting with a prayer was constitutionally permissible under the Establishment Clause. Two citizens who had attended these town board meetings had filed suit claiming that the board's practices violated the Establishment Clause by preferring the Christian religion over other faiths.

The record demonstrated that while the clergy offering the prayer had nearly always been Christian, the opportunity to give the prayer was theoretically open to all denominations. The town, however, was mainly Christian, and only in recent times had other denominations been permitted to participate, and then only after protests had been made as to the overtly Christian nature of the prayers that had been offered. Rather than generic prayers directed to an unidentified supreme being, some of the past prayers had invoked "Lord Jesus," the "Holy Spirit," Pentecost, and the Resurrection. Significantly, the prayers were offered before the legislative activity began, and the town board had given no guidance as to the content of permissible prayer and did not prescreen the prayers to be offered.

The majority opinion by Justice Kennedy placed great reliance upon the decision in in *Marsh v. Chambers* (1983), which had upheld a legislative prayer. Justice Kennedy noted that there had been a long history of permitting legislative prayer in both Congress and state legislatures. As such, the court was called upon to decide if the town's practice "fits within the tradition long followed in Congress and state legislatures." Despite the sectarian Christian nature of many of the prayers which had been offered in the town meetings, the court quickly rejected the claim that only non-sectarian prayers were permissible. In the view of the majority justices, "An insistence on nonsectarian or ecumenical prayer as a single, fixed standard is not consistent with the tradition of legislative prayer outlined in the Court's cases." Justice Kennedy went on to reject the endorsement test set forth in *County of Allegheny v. ACLU* (1989) as dictum, and concluded that there was no constitutional rule that "invocations must be nonsectarian."

The majority also concluded in a critical passage that "The First Amendment is not a majority rule, and government may not seek to define permissible categories of religious speech. Once it invites prayer into the public sphere, government must permit a prayer giver to address his or her own God or gods as conscience dictates, unfettered by what an administrator or judge considers to be nonsectarian." Moreover, "Absent a pattern of prayers that over time denigrate, proselytize, or betray an impermissible government purpose, a challenge based solely on the content of a prayer will not likely establish a constitutional violation."

In a section of his opinion joined only by Chief Justice Roberts and Justice Alito, Justice Kennedy rejected the claim that the town's legislative prayer practice was coercive as to non-adherents of the Christian religion. Observing that "Offense . . . does not equate to coercion," Justice Kennedy considered the prayers at issue not to be coercive. Nevertheless, he cautioned that the constitutional viability of a legislative prayer involves a test which is a "fact-sensitive," one which "considers both the setting in which the prayer arises and the audience to whom it is directed." Since the prayers at issue were directed to the legislators, and the public was not required to participate, there was no Establishment Clause violation, and the prayers had a "permissible ceremonial purpose." On this point, Justice Thomas, who was joined by Justice Scalia, expressed a far more limited view of what might constitute impermissible coercion. In view of these two justices, only "actual legal coercion," rather than "subtle coercive pressures," would be sufficient to make out a constitutional violation of the Establishment Clause.

The principal dissenting opinion was delivered by Justice Kagan, and joined by Justices Ginsburg, Breyer, and Sotomayor. Justice Kagan conceded at the beginning of her dissenting opinion that a town hall meeting "need not become a religion-free zone," but found a problem with the Town of Greece's practices since the prayers at issue were "predominantly sectarian in content." To document this conclusion, she devoted a lengthy paragraph to quoting from some of the prayers offered at the town board meetings. These included prayers which referred to "the saving sacrifice of Jesus Christ on the cross," and the "life and death, resurrection and ascension of the Savior Jesus Christ." In the view of the dissenting justices, these invocations of Christian beliefs violated controlling "principles of religious neutrality" that, in the words of the *County of Allegheny* case rejected by Justice Kennedy, prohibited demonstrating "a preference for one particular sect or creed (including a preference for Christianity over other religions)." Justice Kagan went on to offer three hypotheticals involving sectarian prayers in other venues (a court, a polling place, and a naturalization ceremony) to dramatize the negative emotional impact of prayers based upon the tenets of one religion on non-adherents of that religion.

Justice Kagan's dissenting opinion discussed at length the *Marsh* case so heavily relied upon by the majority. While agreeing with the observation made in *Marsh,* as well as in other cases, that Americans "are a religious people," she nevertheless concluded that "the circumstances here demand . . . the recognition that we are a pluralistic people too." Focusing upon other religions, she cautioned that "In this country, when citizens go before the government, they go not as Christians or Muslims or Jews (or what have you), but just as Americans." Kagan further characterized *Marsh* as involving only prayer directed to legislators, contrasting that with the case at issue, which she saw as involving interaction between residents and public officials, constituting citizen participation in governmental affairs.

In their final analysis, the dissenters would have struck down the practices followed in the Town of Greece as a violation of the Establishment Clause because citizens "even in a partly legislative body . . . should not confront government-sponsored worship that divides them along religious lines."

In assessing the future reach of the *Town of Greece* decision, there are two points of particular note. First, each of the opinions in the case emphasized the limited nature of the court's ruling, and/or the need for fact-specific inquiries in each case of legislative prayer. Justice Alito's concurring opinion, for example, states that "All that the Court does today is to allow a town to follow a practice that we have previously held is permissible for Congress and state legislatures." Even though the majority opinion validates legislative sectarian prayers in language which equally could be applied in other venues, including public school functions and activities and public displays, it is most unlikely that the three justices who joined in all of Justice Kennedy's opinion would vote to extend the ruling to these other venues, particularly where schoolchildren (rather than what Justice Kennedy referred to as "adult citizens") would be those affected. Second, and conversely, the majority opinion makes it quite clear that it will be extremely difficult to successfully challenge a legislative prayer in the absence of an impermissible governmental purpose or an overt denigration or proselytization of non-adherents made by the person who offers the prayer. Given the majority opinion's strong language upholding the town board's meeting prayer, and the additional language requiring fact-specific inquiries into future prayers, it seems apparent that the court is unlikely to take another legislative prayer case in the foreseeable future, leaving it to lower courts to sift through the facts of any future case. The *Town of Greece* decision is thus likely to lead to an increased incidence of the invocation of prayers at the beginning of legislative sessions.

PRAYER ON A PUBLIC-SCHOOL FOOTBALL FIELD

Joseph Kennedy was a public high school football coach who offered a thirty-second personal prayer at the end of each game, kneeling at the fifty-yard line. Over time, a majority of his players joined him, and the coach began to give "short motivational speeches," which initially contained religious content but which the coach later dropped in response to the school district's concerns. Based on these activities, he lost his job because of the school district's fear that allowing such prayer on public school grounds would violate the Establishment Clause.

In a six-to-three decision, with the majority opinion written by Justice Gorsuch, the Supreme Court ruled that Kennedy's private prayer was protected by the Free Speech and Free Exercise clauses.

The majority opinion relied heavily upon the fact that during the same period of time when Kennedy was offering his prayer, other school district employees were permitted to attend to different personal matters such as making restaurant reservations and checking their email. Thus, terminating Kennedy's employment was not done pursuant to a policy that was neutral or generally applicable. As such, the court expressly held that the Establishment Clause does not require any governmental entity "to single out private religious speech for special disfavor."

On Kennedy's free exercise claim, the majority held that plaintiff had met his burden to show that the school district's policy was not neutral or generally applicable because of the exceptions granted to other school district employees for personal matters other than prayer.

As to his free speech claim, the applicable test when a party is engaged in commenting on matters of public concern is to balance the competing interests of the private citizen and school district's interests in regulating government speech. Here, Kennedy was not speaking within his duties as a coach and his prayers therefore were nongovernment speech and the school district's interests to avoid an Establishment Clause violation did not satisfy strict scrutiny. In reaching this conclusion, Justice Gorsuch indicated that those defending the policy relied heavily upon the discredited test of *Lemon v. Kurtzman* (1971), an opinion that "this court long ago abandoned . . . and its endorsement test offshoot." The applicable test, shown by the discussion of the recent cases discussed in this chapter, is to refer to "historical practices and understandings."

Pointing out that the prior cases which relied on the Establishment Clause to ban certain out-of-classroom activities all involved findings that students were coerced to participate in religious activities, the court ruled that there was no evidence of such coercion. In sum, "Rather than respect the First Amendment's double protection for religious expression, [the school district defenders] would have us preference secular activity."

There were two concurrent opinions, by Justice Thomas and Justice Alito. Both pointed out that the majority opinion left open other issues, including what standard to apply in cases involving government employees' rights as well as what burden to place on an employer to justify restricting religious expression.

Justice Sotomayor wrote a dissenting opinion, joined by Justices Breyer and Kagan. She initially noted that "this Court consistently has recognized that school officials leading prayer is constitutionally impermissible. Official-led prayer strikes at the core of our constitutional protections for the religious liberty of students and their parents, as embodied in both the Establishment Clause and the Free Exercise Clause of the First Amendment."

The dissenters also accused the majority of having "misconstrue[d] the facts." While Kennedy did drop "overtly religious references" from his post-game speeches, he still permitted students to participate in his activities on school property. In addition, he consistently refused all suggested accommodations, insisting on a right to engage in "demonstrative prayer." Moreover, these prayer activities were highly publicized, leading to both media and some government officials attending.

Justice Sotomayor also accused the majority of overruling *Lemon v. Kurtzman* and many subsequent cases that implemented its threefold test. She pointed out that most of the criticisms of *Lemon* appeared in separate concurring or dissenting opinions.

In the dissenters' view, while the majority acknowledged that the "Establishment Clause prohibits government from coercing participation in religious exercise," they nevertheless "appl[y] a nearly toothless version of the coercion analysis." But the coercion standard is important to protect children who are "uniquely susceptible to 'subtle coercive pressure.'" In addition, Kennedy's speech on school property violated the Establishment Clause's "concerns about endorsement" and about coercion because of the "immense social pressure" on students to participate, including their desire to obtain college letters of recommendation from their coach.

The majority was also criticized for failing to recognize the "conflicting pressures" between the Establishment Clause and the Free Exercise Clause, characterizing them as "work[ing] in tandem," changing prior precedent to prioritize free exercise and by substituting a "history and tradition" standard which will be hard for school administrators to apply.

Justice Sotomayor concluded the dissenting opinion by characterizing the majority opinion as one which "elevates one individual's interest in personal religious exercise . . . over society's interest in protecting the separation between church and state, eroding the protections for religious liberty for all."

The recent cases discussed in this chapter show, once again, how the court has changed prior law, as the dissenting opinions document. In addition to replacing prior precedent with a history and tradition standard, these decisions also employ a standard which compares the activities which are permitted for others under the same circumstances to those prohibited for individuals seeking to exercise their religious beliefs. This approach, used in the *Kennedy* case, was also employed in other recent cases involving free exercise, including *Fulton v. City of Philadelphia* (discussed in the prior chapter), and the shadow docket decisions striking down restrictions on religious services because of health concerns related to the ongoing pandemic. By permitting other similarly situated actors to engage in their chosen activities while denying such rights to religious adherents demonstrates that the laws in question are not neutral or generally applicable, and thus will not survive strict scrutiny.

WAR MEMORIALS AND MUNICIPAL FLAGS

The constitutionality of state-sponsored religious monuments and displays has also been a source of great confusion and contention in Supreme Court cases. See Mannino, *Shaping America: The Supreme Court and American Society* (2009) at 182–87. Attempts to apply the teachings of the court's nearly fifty-year-old decision in *Lemon v. Kurtzman* (1971) have also been largely unsuccessful in several Establishment Clause contexts, and that precedent itself has come under significant attack or questioning by both legal commentators and by several of the justices themselves, including in the *Kennedy* case just discussed. *Lemon* established a three-part test, mandating that state action must have a secular legislative purpose; its principal or primary effect must be one that neither advances nor inhibits religion; and the state action must not foster an excessive government entanglement with religion.

In *American Legion v. American Humanist Association* (2019), the court confronted the Establishment Clause conundrum once again, as it was called upon to review the constitutionality of a ninety-four-year-old, forty-foot-tall stone-and-concrete cross erected in the Washington suburbs at a busy intersection, and known as the "Peace Cross." The cross honored local soldiers killed in World War I, and the American Legion symbol appeared at its center, identifying the monument's sponsor. No religious language appeared on any part of the monument.

While a majority of the justices on the case criticized the *Lemon* test, or at the least, declined to apply it to this religious monument, it was not overruled. Instead, the majority opinion emphasized that the cross had become a central symbol of World War I, giving it a secular meaning in the context of the Peace Cross monument. It pointed out the great impact on the public imagination of the poem "Flanders Field," which commemorated the deaths of the World War I soldiers buried there, where "the poppies blow/ Between the crosses, row on row." The majority reasoned that the cross took on historical (and secular) importance by memorializing the many sacrifices of life by the Maryland county's soldiers. Justice Alito therefore concluded for the majority that "The cross is undoubtedly a Christian symbol, but that fact should not blind us to everything else that the Bladensburg Cross has come to represent."

The majority opinion also pointed out how many Christian symbols have become secularized. Note was made of the inclusion of the cross on the trademarks of Blue Cross/Blue Shield, Johnson & Johnson, and the Bayer Group, as well as the remarks of the president of the secular government of France, who praised the historical significance for the country of the Notre Dame Cathedral, which had just sustained major fire damage. The majority opinion also noted the many American cities which had religious names, such as Corpus Christi (Latin for "The Body of Christ"), Texas, and the mottos of several states, including that of Florida, "In God We Trust."

Perhaps most significantly, the majority opinion also relied heavily upon the age of the monument, contending that older monuments should be accorded a presumption that they are constitutional when the issue presented is whether to tear them down. As Justice Alito put it for the majority, "destroying or defacing the Cross that has stood undisturbed for nearly a century would not be neutral and would not further the ideals of respect and tolerance embodied in the First Amendment." Indeed, ordering the removal of the cross would evince "a hostility toward religion that has no place in our Establishment Clause traditions."

The majority also placed emphasis on determining whether long-standing monuments reflect "respect and tolerance for differing views, an honest endeavor to achieve inclusivity and nondiscrimination, and a recognition of the important role that religion plays in the lives of many Americans." It concluded that the Peace Cross satisfied each of these elements.

Two parts of Justice Alito's opinion which were joined by three other justices (Chief Justice Roberts and Justices Breyer and Kavanaugh) severely criticized the *Lemon* opinion, pointing out that the test it prescribed could not resolve many Establishment Clause issues. In a heavily footnoted discussion of the "shortcomings" of that test, these four justices concluded that the *Lemon* test should not be utilized in cases of "long-standing monuments, symbols, and practices." Notably, although she did not join in the criticism of the *Lemon* test in the majority opinion, Justice Kagan found "much to admire in this section of the opinion."

Other justices were even more critical of *Lemon*. In a concurring opinion, Justice Thomas indicated that he "would take the next logical step and overrule the *Lemon* test in all contexts." In addition, Justice Gorsuch said that he would dismiss the objections to the Peace Cross because in his view, "offended observer[s]" lacked standing. Notably, he observed that permitting standing to such complainants was a result of the *Lemon* test, and that *Lemon* should be abandoned as a "misadventure," which "left us only a mess." In its place, he contended that the approach adopted in the *Town of Greece* opinion discussed above should be utilized. Moreover, Justice Kavanaugh, who joined the entirety of Justice Alito's opinion, also wrote a concurring opinion, in which he contended that "the *Lemon* test is not good law and does not apply to Establishment Clause cases in any of the five categories" he outlined in his concurring opinion.

In sum, some six justices criticized the use of the *Lemon* test in all or in at least some of the varying categories of Establishment Clause cases, and three called for it to be abandoned entirely.

By contrast, while agreeing that the Peace Cross did not offend the Establishment Clause, both Justice Breyer and Justice Kagan wrote separately that they preferred a case-by-case approach and would not discard the *Lemon* approach in all contexts.

In addition to the majority opinion, there were six other opinions. In total, seven of the justices either joined the majority opinion or concurred in its disposition of the case. Only Justice Ginsburg, joined by Justice Sotomayor, filed a dissenting opinion, portions of which she read in open court.

Justice Ginsburg began her opinion by referring to the Peace Cross as "an immense Latin cross," a description she supported by including a picture of the cross in an appendix. Justice Ginsburg relied heavily on prior cases which "reaffirmed the Constitution's commitment to neutrality" among all religious faiths and between religion and nonreligion. Since the Latin cross "is the foremost symbol of the Christian faith," and its "defining symbol," maintaining the Peace Cross on a public highway, she reasoned, "elevates Christianity over other faiths, and religion over nonreligion." The Establishment Clause prohibits such action because, in her view, that clause was meant to incorporate Jefferson's view that "a wall of separation" should be erected between church and state. In the case of the Peace Cross, that wall of separation is breached because its display on public property raises a presumption that the government "endorse[s] its religious content."

The future impact of *American Legion v. American Humanist Ass'n* and *Kennedy v. Bremerton School District* is likely to be felt in several areas. First, the test enunciated in *Lemon v. Kurtzman* is, at best, on life support, and is unlikely ever to be relied upon again in any Establishment Clause decision, even more so in light of the decision in the *Shurtleff* case discussed below. Second, as demonstrated in Justice Kavanaugh's concurring opinion in *American Legion*, and in prior opinions by Justice Thomas, at least some of the justices favor a test in Establishment Clause cases that turns on whether the government action is actually "coercive."

The court dealt with another Establishment Clause issue in *Shurtleff v. City of Boston* (2022). In an unanimous decision, the court held that the City of Boston erred in refusing to permit a Christian group to raise what was described as a "Christian flag" on one of three flagpoles on City Hall Plaza, alongside the American flag and the flag of the Commonwealth of Massachusetts, because of Establishment Clause concerns.

Writing for a majority of six, Justice Breyer's majority opinion concluded that flying the Christian flag did not qualify as government speech, and the city's ability to decide what flags could be flown was not unlimited. Instead, the city's decision in refusing to allow the flag to be flown violated the Free Speech Clause of the First Amendment. That was because when the government is not speaking for itself, it may not exclude private speech based on a religious viewpoint since such governmental action would constitute impermissible viewpoint discrimination.

There were two lengthy concurring opinions, by Justices Alito and Gorsuch, with Justice Thomas joining both. Justice Alito devoted his opinion to an analysis of what properly could be construed as government speech. Justice Gorsuch, by contrast, blamed the problem in the case on the continuing reliance by lower courts on the discredited, but never overruled, fifty-one-year-old *Lemon* precedent, as he also did in the subsequent majority opinion he wrote in the *Kennedy* case. Since the *Lemon* precedent established such a "malleable" test, it placed "risk-adverse local officials . . . in an ironic bind" between the Establishment Clause and the Free Speech and Free Exercise Clauses. As in the *City of Boston* case, "local governments have sometimes violated the First Amendment in the name of protecting it." Characterizing *Lemon* as having "interrupted [a] long line of precedents," Justice Gorsuch pointed out that the court in its more recent decisions had refused to apply its test. Moreover, that test made it easier for governments to discriminate against religion. Concluding that *Lemon* was seriously flawed in its interpretation of the Establishment Clause, Justice Gorsuch wrote that "it is past time for local officials and lower courts to let it lie."

NOTE

1. The early opinions of the Supreme Court on the Establishment Clause are reviewed in detail in *Shaping America, supra*, 157–87, and in Edward F. Mannino, "The Sinking Wall of Separation: The Supreme Court and the Establishment Clause, 1947–2005," in *The American Experiment Religious Freedom* (Portland: University of Portland Press, 2008). The latter article explores the issue of anti-Catholic bias in the early Establishment Clause decisions. For a detailed review of the historical background of the debate over separation of church and state dating back to the late eighteenth century, see Philip Hamburger, *Separation of Church and State* (Cambridge: Harvard University Press, 2002).

Chapter 4

Unlawful Searches and Seizures

The Fourth Amendment provides that "The right of the people to be secure in their persons, houses, papers, and effects, against unreasonable searches and seizures, shall not be violated, and no Warrants shall issue, but upon probable cause, supported by Oath or affirmation, and particularly describing the place to be searched, and the persons or things to be seized." Advances in technology have forced the Supreme Court over the last ninety years to confront how the introduction of various new technologies affects these requirements. The most recent decisions reflect an increasing societal concern to protect privacy against what is perceived as governments "spying." The justices, both liberal and conservative, have typically disagreed on how to resolve the issues presented by those advances, and have repudiated the approach of the early cases, effectively overruling an earlier precedent.

In an early and seminal case, the Supreme Court considered whether wiretapping constituted a "search" within the meaning of the Fourth Amendment. Writing for the five-member majority in *Olmstead v. United States* (1928), Chief Justice William Howard Taft concluded that it did not, noting that the meaning of search and seizure under the Fourth Amendment was to be construed in light of what was considered to be a search and seizure "when it was adopted." Since wiretapping is performed "without trespass upon any property of the defendants," Taft concluded that "the amendment did not forbid what was done here. There was no searching. There was no seizure." In dissent, Justice Louis Brandeis took a broader view, contending that the Fourth Amendment banned "every unjustifiable intrusion by the government upon the privacy of the individual, whatever the means employed." Another dissenting justice, Pierce Butler, took a more nuanced approach, concluding that "Under the principles established and applied by this court, the Fourth Amendment safeguards against all evils that are like and equivalent to those embraced within the ordinary meaning of its words."

Olmstead remained the law for almost forty years. It was not until *Katz v. United States* (1967) that the Supreme Court finally concluded, after confronting the issue in several cases, that *Olmstead*'s "underpinnings . . . have been so eroded by our subsequent decisions that the 'trespass' can no longer be regarded as controlling." Seven members of the court, in an opinion by Justice Potter Stewart, ruled that "the Fourth Amendment protects people—and not simply 'areas'—against unreasonable searches and seizures." Despite this ruling, the Supreme Court did not adopt Justice Brandeis' view, finding instead that "The Fourth Amendment cannot be translated into a general constitutional 'right to privacy.'" Justice Hugo Black filed the only dissenting opinion in *Katz*. Channeling Chief Justice Taft, he wrote that he did not believe that "the words of the Amendment will bear the meaning given them by today's decision," and that "the language of the Amendment is the crucial place to look in construing a written document such as our Constitution." Looking at that language, "A conversation overheard by eavesdropping, whether by plain snooping or wiretapping, is not tangible and, under the normally accepted meanings of the words, can neither be searched nor seized." In conclusion, Black warned against "the ingenuity of language-stretching judges."

The introduction of new technologies continues to pose interpretive problems for the Supreme Court under the Fourth Amendment, even applying the broadened interpretation established in *Katz*. The Supreme Court has decided several recent cases interpreting the requirements of the Fourth Amendment. The cases discussed below dealt in part with the need to interpret the Fourth Amendment in the contexts of the use of tracking technologies and smart phones.

TRACKING TECHNOLOGY

When they wish to track individuals suspected of engaging in criminal activity, law enforcement officials have a number of ways available to them to do so. They include placing trackers on suspect's vehicles and using a wide variety of electronic surveillance methods, including accessing factory-installed GPS trackers or stolen vehicle detection systems. A critical question with respect to use of most of these tracking methodologies is whether a warrant is required under the Fourth Amendment before tracking can be implemented. In *United States v. Jones* (2012), the Supreme Court ruled that a warrant was required before a tracker could physically be attached to a vehicle being used by a drug trafficking suspect. The various opinions in the case clarify that the necessity for a warrant can be triggered in two separate ways. Initially, any "physical intrusion" or trespass on property of the suspect, such as by placing a tracker on a vehicle, triggers the requirement that a warrant be secured before installing the tracker. This follows the *Olmstead* approach. Second, a warrant is also required when the suspect has a reasonable expectation of privacy under the circumstances in question. This reflects the *Katz* approach.

The privacy inquiry is much more problematic than the physical intrusion inquiry for law enforcement to resolve. Thus, in *Jones*, four justices concurred in the decision, but divided on the issue of privacy. Justice Sotomayor suggested that even short-term monitoring would require a warrant, while Justice Alito, joined by three other justices, suggested that short-term monitoring would not be a violation of privacy, but noted that four weeks of monitoring would be too long to be permitted without a warrant.

In other, earlier decisions, the Supreme Court had held that the use of beepers would not require a warrant (*United States v. Knotts* [1983]; *United States v. Karo* [1984]). Nevertheless, the *Jones* opinions left open the question of what type of electronic surveillance methods might require the prior issuance of a warrant, and under what circumstances they would do so.

In any event, the court suggested that the existence of exigent circumstances will obviate any necessity first to obtain a warrant. Where there are time constraints, or where there are other reasons that seeking a warrant may not be feasible, law enforcement officials should prevail in any challenge to such surveillance. Thus, for example, in the case of suspected terrorists, warrantless searches should be permissible, based upon both the inherent secrecy of terror plots, as well as a suspected terrorist's lack of any reasonable expectation of privacy in his or her activities. Indeed, Justice Alito's concurring opinion in *Jones* explicitly notes (without deciding the question) that even "prolonged GPS monitoring" might be permissible in "the context of investigations involving extraordinary offenses."

SEARCHES OF CELL PHONES

In a second decision deciding when a warrant must be obtained prior to conducting a search, a unanimous Supreme Court held that the exception to the Fourth Amendment that permits police to make a warrantless search incident to a lawful arrest does not automatically authorize them to search digital information on an individual's cell phone. Chief Justice Roberts's opinion of the court in *Riley v. California* (2014) thus held that "officers must generally secure a warrant before conducting such a search."

The lead defendant in *Riley* was stopped by the police because he was driving with expired registration tags. The car was then impounded and searched, and the defendant was arrested for possession of loaded firearms concealed under the car's hood. When his smartphone was searched incident to arrest, it revealed his association with a street gang, and the data on his phone ultimately led to his indictment in connection with a gang shooting. The police sought to justify the search as one conducted incident to arrest, and thus permissible under prior Fourth Amendment decisions. The exception to the Fourth Amendment warrant requirement upon a search incident to arrest is rooted in both the interest of preserving officer safety, and also in the prevention of the destruction of evidence.

Finding no "precise guidance from the founding era," the court used a Fourth Amendment balancing test that weighs the intrusion upon an individual's privacy against any legitimate governmental interests that may be served by conducting a warrantless search. In making this analysis, the court concluded that there was a great intrusion upon personal privacy implicated in a cell phone search, but insufficient governmental interest generally to justify conducting such a search without a warrant.

With respect to personal privacy, Chief Justice Roberts cited data that indicated that cell phones were materially different from items normally seized by the police incident to an arrest. Thus, cell phones have an "immense storage capacity" and store information that often includes "a digital record of nearly every aspect of [individual] lives," including pictures and videos, as well as streams of personal email correspondence. As such, the search of a cell phone without a warrant implicates significant privacy interests because such a search will reveal "[t]he sum of an individual's private life."

By contrast, the two principal threats traditionally used to justify warrantless searches incident to an arrest were not found by the court to be present in the two cases before it. First, there was no threat to the safety of a police officer from the cell phones, nor was there the possibility of using the cell phone to escape custody. Second, there was little potential for the destruction of evidence by such methods as remote wiping or data encryption. Moreover, the police could independently address any such threat by disabling the cell phone's locking mechanism or by placing it in an enclosure isolating it from radio waves, such as in a Faraday bag, which is an inexpensive sandwich bag–like container with aluminum foil that is already in use by a number of law enforcement agencies.

The court did leave an avenue open to the police to conduct a warrantless search of a cell phone incident to an arrest if there were "exigent circumstances," such as the arrest of a kidnapper whose cell phone might disclose the location of an abducted child.

In a concurring opinion, Justice Alito urged the court to leave open the possibility for legislatures to enact legislation that would draw "reasonable distinctions based on categories of information or perhaps other variables" detailing the circumstances under which the police might conduct a warrantless search of a cell phone.

Much like the Second Amendment decision in the *District of Columbia v. Heller* (2008), the court's decision in *Riley* reflects current public opinion. Here, the need to protect individual privacy has become a libertarian bellwether, particularly among younger individuals. In addition, this concern for maintaining personal privacy has become paramount throughout the country and among all age groups, particularly after disclosures of widespread and secretive incursions on privacy by the National Security Agency and by freelance or foreign-government backed hackers, as well as by social media platforms and by spying devices incorporated in new technology. Significantly, the court was able to respond to this public concern without unduly hampering the police by recognizing the possibility of a need to conduct a warrantless search of a cell phone where exigent circumstances were present. In the end, courts will have to decide on a case-by-case basis whether such circumstances were present when a warrantless search was undertaken.

CELL PHONE LOCATION RECORDS

In *Carpenter v. United States* (2018), the Supreme Court continued its focus on the need to protect individual privacy where new technology has the ability to reveal sensitive personal data. There, the court divided five to four on whether police could obtain a defendant's cell phone location records from a third-party wireless carrier without a warrant. In an opinion by Chief Justice Roberts, the majority held that a warrant was required where the prosecutors had obtained defendant's cell phone location records after one of his accomplices had identified him and others as involved in the robberies. The records obtained from the carriers revealed the defendant's location over 129 days, four of which placed him in close proximity to the scene of four of the robberies. The prosecutors lawfully obtained these records under the Stored Communications Act, which permits records to be obtained where they are "relevant and material to an ongoing investigation," but they did not apply for a warrant.

In the context of this particular factual background, the court held that the search was illegal in the absence of a warrant because defendant had a legitimate and reasonable expectation of privacy in his cell phone location records. As it had done in *Riley*, the court focused on "the seismic shifts in digital technology" that permitted "detailed, encyclopedic, and effortlessly compiled" information to be collected that contained "deeply revealing" information about the cell phone user.

While previous decisions had held that a defendant does not have a reasonable expectation of privacy in records which are turned over to, and held by, a third party, the majority distinguished these cases based on the much greater volume of sensitive information that is stored in the cell phone location records. Quoting previous decisions of the court, the majority noted that the Fourth Amendment "protects people, not places," and that the Framers of the Constitution aimed "to place obstacles in the way of a too permeating police surveillance."

The court also held, despite the opinions voiced by several of the dissenting justices, that the protections of the Fourth Amendment are not limited to property-based interests. Moreover, the authorization obtained under the Stored Communications Act did not excuse the necessity to obtain a warrant, since the Fourth Amendment requires a showing of probable cause, which represents a much higher burden than reliance and materiality.

Finally, Chief Justice Roberts emphasized at considerable length that the holding in *Carpenter* was very limited, and applied only to cell phone location records. The focus of the holding was to prevent "unlimited access to a wireless carrier's database" for cell phone location records. The Chief Justice also noted that no warrant would be required where exigent circumstances existed, including "bomb threats, active shootings, and child abductions." In addition, it might not be necessary to seek a warrant where shorter periods of time were involved, or where access was sought under different circumstances. In addition, the majority opinion indicated that the court did not question the use of traditional surveillance methods, such as security cameras.

There were four dissenting opinions.

In opinion for himself and for Justices Thomas and Alito, Justice Kennedy contended that the approach taken by the majority was too restrictive and placed criminal investigations at serious risk. He wrote that "Cell-site records . . . can serve an important investigative function, as the facts of this case demonstrate." These dissenters went on to criticize the majority for failing to give "clear guidance to law enforcement."

Justice Kennedy also argued that the court's prior cases relied on "property-based concepts." As such, "The the only question necessary to decide is whether the Government searched anything of Carpenter's when it used compulsory process to obtain cell-site records from Carpenter's cell phone service providers." This is because "Fourth Amendment rights . . . are personal." The dissenters concluded that the records in question were simply third-party business records in which cell phone users had no Fourth Amendment protection based on prior caselaw.

Finally, Justice Kennedy pointed out that the prosecution subpoenaed the records properly under federal law, and that a subpoena satisfies the Fourth Amendment so long as the materials sought are relevant, reasonable, and appropriately limited.

In a lengthy opinion written for himself alone, Justice Thomas indicated that the only question presented in the case was "*whose* property was searched," and that the records in question belonged to the wireless providers, not to Carpenter. He went on to argue that majority's reliance on Justice Harlan's concurring opinion in *Katz v. United States* (1967) was misplaced because its "reasonable expectation of privacy" standard "has no basis in the text or history of the Fourth Amendment." After a extensive discussing of *Katz* and other prior precedent relying on it, Justice Thomas concluded that "the *Katz* test is a failed experiment," and that "this Court is duty bound to reconsider it."

A third dissenting opinion was written by Justice Alito, who was joined by Justice Thomas. They contended that the approach taken by the majority "guarantees a blizzard of litigation while threatening many legitimate and valuable investigative practices upon which law enforcement has rightfully come to rely." Moreover, it was "revolutionary" to allow a defendant to object to "the search of a third party's property." Indeed, there was no "search" in this case because the records were obtained through a lawful subpoena duces tecum. Justice Alito set forth a lengthy review of English and American precedents which had approved of using such subpoenas to obtain documents. He concluded that the Fourth Amendment therefore "did not apply to the compulsory production of documents at all." Finally, Justice Alito noted that "The desire to make a statement about privacy in the digital age does not justify the consequences that today's decision is likely to produce." Instead, Congress is better equipped to pass specific legislation to deal with these problems created by new technologies.

The final dissenting opinion was written by Judge Gorsuch. He reviewed three possible approaches to the Fourth Amendment issues raised by new technologies. First, he criticized the third-party approach, agreeing with legal scholars that it was "quite dubious" to argue that such an approach accurately reflects "subjective expectations of privacy." He also found it "pretty unlikely" that the courts would permit the use of third-party doctrine to justify seizing all a person's emails or the results of DNA tests. A second approach would be to discard the third-party doctrine, and to use instead the *Katz* "reasonable expectation of privacy" standard when adjudicating whether materials held in the hands of third parties can only be obtained under a warrant. Judge Gorsuch concluded that this approach would not work because it would leave the court with the same problems outlined by Justice Thomas in his dissenting opinion. Third, he evaluated use of what he referred to as "the traditional approach," which "asked if a house, paper or effect was *yours* under law." He pointed out that something can be "yours" even if it is in the possession of a third party, giving examples including neighbors who care for your dog while you travel. Based on these examples, Judge Gorsuch argued that emails should be treated like traditional mail "as a bailment in which the owner retains a vital and protected legal interest." Judge Gorsuch concluded that it was possible that Carpenter's cell phone records could qualify as "*his* papers or effects under existing law," but since Carpenter had never raised this issue, he had forfeited the argument.

The five opinions in *Carpenter* reveal a deeply divided court, with even the dissenters disagreeing on a proper approach to the application of the Fourth Amendment in the context of new technologies. The dissenting justices call for a more restrictive, property-based approach, while the majority follow a looser, privacy-based approach. The extent to which a privacy-based approach applies in these situations was left undefined, and Justices Kennedy and Alito were correct in stating that such a nebulous approach may hamper legitimate law-enforcement efforts and create confusion given the court's lack of "clear guidance" to law enforcement. The majority opinion responds to this criticism by attempting to limit its holding, emphasizing that what it is seeking to protect is large amounts of private information.

The approach suggested by some of the dissenters, which relies upon finding that there is no Fourth Amendment protection where materials are held by a third party, suffers from equally objectionable shortcomings, as several of the opinions reflect. Considering all the issues raised by the various opinions, Judge Gorsuch suggests an approach that may be the best under all the circumstances, by focusing on whether particular materials, even if they are in the possession of a third party, are properly considered as materials in which the defendant has a significant interest and are therefore deserving of protection.

SEARCH OF A VEHICLE PARKED IN A DRIVEWAY

In *Collins v. Virginia* (2018), a police officer walked up the driveway outside the defendant's house to search a motorcycle that was partially hidden under a tarp. He had probable cause to do so based on his investigation of two traffic incidents involving a distinctive orange-and-black motorcycle identical to the one he saw in the driveway, but he did not seek a warrant before conducting the search.

By an eight-to-one margin, the Supreme Court held that the warrantless search was illegal under the Fourth Amendment. The majority rested its decision on the view that the curtilage—the area immediately by a house—is considered part of the home under the Fourth Amendment. Justice Sotomayor's opinion of the court noted that "When a law enforcement officer physically intrudes on the curtilage to gather evidence, a search within the meaning of the Fourth Amendment has occurred."

The majority rejected the argument that the so-called automobile exception justified the search in question because that exception to the requirement to obtain a warrant is based upon the quickness with which a vehicle can be moved. As such, any search made under the automobile exception is limited in its scope to the boundaries of the vehicle itself.

The court ordered the case remanded to the lower court to decide whether other possible exceptions to the Fourth Amendment warrant requirement, such as that recognizing exigent circumstances, might justify the search.

In his dissenting opinion, Judge Alito contended that the search was reasonable, and fell within the automobile exception, because that exception permitted the police to search a vehicle on public streets if there was probable cause to do so. He characterized the majority opinion as a "strikingly unreasonable decision" that was "based on a misunderstanding of Fourth Amendment basics." Indeed, he observed that "An ordinary person of common sense" would react to the court's decision the way a character in Dickens's *Oliver Twist* did, by concluding that if that were the law, "the law is an ass—a idiot." The search was reasonable in Justice Alito's view because the motorcycle was just as mobile as any vehicle would be; that the "short walk up the driveway did petitioner or his girlfriend [no] harm"; and that the officer did not damage any property or observe anything that he could not have seen from the street.

While the *Collins* decision was a limited one, it goes back to a property-based approach. The court often uses this approach in cases not involving new technologies because it provides a straightforward resolution of the Fourth Amendment issue.

RENTAL CAR RECORDS OF A DRIVER NOT LISTED ON THE RENTAL AGREEMENT

The driver of a rental car was stopped by the state police for a traffic violation. The police discovered that the car was rented, that the driver was not listed as an authorized driver, and that the driver had prior drug and weapons convictions. The police proceeded to search the car without a warrant authorizing the search. The search revealed body armor and forty-nine bricks of heroin stored in the trunk.

In a unanimous decision in *Byrd v. United States* (2018), the Supreme Court held that a driver in lawful possession or control of a rental car does not automatically lose Fourth Amendment protections for an otherwise reasonable expectation of privacy just because he or she is not listed on the car rental agreement. Utilizing property law concepts, Justice Kennedy's majority opinion pointed out that "one who owns or lawfully possesses or controls property will in all likelihood have a legitimate expectation of privacy by virtue of the right to exclude." The opinion pointed out that the possession of the car had to be lawful, and that a car thief, for example, would not have a reasonable expectation of privacy even where he or she had sole possession and control of the car. The car thief analogy was relevant because the evidence showed the driver had persuaded a woman to rent a car in her name, and that she then turned over the keys to the car to the driver immediately after she left the rental car office.

The court left for the court of appeals to decide on remand whether one who intentionally enlists a third party to rent a car to facilitate a crime should be treated as a car thief or, alternatively, whether there was probable cause in any event such as to permit the state police to conduct the search without a warrant. On remand, the Third Circuit Court of Appeals concluded that the police had probable cause, and that the search was legal.

While the Supreme Court's decision may seem strange in potentially protecting a fraudster, it makes sense in a broader context, as Judge Michael Fisher of the Third Circuit pointed out at a legal conference. Judge Fisher noted that it is common for married or partnered couples to share the driving of a rental car. If the driver at the time the car was stopped by police was not listed on the rental agreement as an authorized driver, a contrary decision by the Supreme Court would lead to an curious result wherein one partner had Fourth Amendment protections, but the other did not.

It is also noteworthy that the majority opinion points out that the recent decisions of the court clarify that the *Katz* expectation of privacy standard "supplements, rather than displaces, 'the traditional property-based understanding of the Fourth Amendment.'" In the future, therefore, cases will continue to be decided on property concepts where they are applicable, and reasonable expectation of privacy concepts where they are not.

DRAWING BLOOD FROM AN UNCONSCIOUS DRIVER

When blood may be drawn without actual consent, and without a warrant, from a driver suspected of drunk driving has not been clear from prior decisions of the Supreme Court. In *Mitchell v. Wisconsin* (2019), a divided court set forth "a rule for an entire category of cases," generally permitting a warrantless blood test when the suspect is unconscious. In a plurality opinion joined by the chief justice and by Justices Breyer and Kavanaugh, Justice Alito found that a state of unconsciousness presented an exception under the exigent circumstances doctrine to the requirement to obtain a warrant to conduct a blood test.

Three factors led the plurality to its conclusion. First, the court has repeatedly recognized that highway safety is a paramount interest. Second, blood alcohol limits advance that interest, and have been proven to work. Third, the unconsciousness of a driver presents a medical emergency requiring the police to seek urgent care. Since blood-alcohol concentrations dissipate quickly, to require police to obtain a warrant under these circumstances would create the risk of the drunk driver going free because the passage of time required to obtain medical care could reduce his blood alcohol level to an acceptable point.

Justice Thomas concurred only in the result, stating that he would adopt a per se rule that "the natural metabolization of alcohol in the blood stream 'creates an exigency once police have probable cause to believe the driver is drunk,' regardless of whether the driver is conscious."

Justice Sotomayor, joined by Justices Ginsburg and Kagan, dissented. The dissenters contended that the rule under the Fourth Amendment "is clear: If there is time, get a warrant." Here, the State of Wisconsin, in the view of the dissenters, conceded that it had time to get a warrant to compel the blood draw, "and that should be the end of the matter." Moreover, prior case law established that "there is no categorical exigency exception [to obtaining a warrant] for blood draws," and that any exigent circumstances must be decided on a case-by-case basis.

Justice Gorsuch dissented in a separate, one-paragraph opinion, stating that the case should have been dismissed because Wisconsin did not raise the issue of exigent circumstances in appealing to the Supreme Court.

COMMUNITY CARETAKING EXCEPTION

In 1973, the Supreme Court recognized an exception to the Fourth Amendment requirement to seek a warrant before undertaking a search in cases in which officers who patrol public highways discharge noncriminal "community caretaking functions" (*Cady v. Dombrowski* [1973]). That case upheld the legality of a warrantless search of an impounded vehicle for an unsecured firearm. Forty-eight years later, the court limited the exception recognized in *Cady.*

In *Caniglia v. Strom* (2021), the Supreme Court dealt with the legality of a search of their home after the petitioner's wife had called the police to request a welfare check after he had threatened suicide and asked her to shoot him with a gun he had placed on their dining room table. When the police arrived, they called an ambulance to take the husband to the hospital for a psychiatric evaluation. Although the husband requested the police not to take his firearms as a condition to his agreement to go to the hospital, they nevertheless seized his guns once he had left for the hospital.

In a unanimous decision, the court held that the community caretaking exception did not justify either the search of the home or the seizure of the husband's weapons. In a short opinion joined by four other members of the court, Justice Thomas delivered the majority opinion. He noted that *Cady* involved the search of an impounded vehicle, not a home, and that opinion itself recognized "a constitutional difference" between the two. The majority concluded that the community caretaking exception was "not an open-ended license to perform [community services] anywhere."

Although the decision was unanimous, there were three concurring opinions. Chief Justice Roberts, joined by Justice Breyer, wrote a one-paragraph opinion stating that he joined the majority opinion because nothing in it was contrary to prior rulings holding that a warrant to enter a home was not required where there was a "need to assist persons who are seriously injured or threatened with such injury."

Justice Alito also concurred, highlighting "some important questions that the Court does not decide." On that understanding he joined the majority opinion in full. Those undecided questions included what, if any, Fourth Amendment restrictions apply to "a short-term seizure conducted for the purpose of ascertaining whether a person presents an imminent risk of suicide," and the legality under the Fourth Amendment of so-called red flag laws under which police may seize guns under a court order "to prevent their use for suicide or the infliction of harm on innocent persons." In addition, the majority opinion left open whether a warrant was required to search a home "for the purpose of ascertaining whether a resident is in urgent need of medical attention and cannot summon help." Justice Alito also reiterated that "there is no special Fourth Amendment rule for a broad category of cases involving 'community caretaking.'"

The third and final concurring opinion came from Justice Kavanaugh. While joining the court's opinion in full, he sought to "underscore and elaborate" on the point made in the Chief Justice's concurring opinion "that the Court's decision does not prevent police officers from taking reasonable steps to assist those who are inside a home and in need of aid." He cited a previous concurring opinion by Chief Justice Roberts which would have permitted warrantless searches under exigent circumstances, including where there was "an objectively reasonable basis for believing" that help was needed to assist persons inside the home who were seriously injured or threatened with such injury. Justice Kavanaugh concluded that the court's exigency precedents "permit warrantless entries when police officers have an objectively reasonable basis to believe that there is a current, ongoing crisis for which it is reasonable to act now."

While the decision in *Caniglia* suggests that the future application of the community caretaking exception will be limited to searches of cars, the three concurring opinions make it clear that many situations such as that presented in *Caniglia* can be addressed under other accepted theories, most typically the exigent circumstances theory.

HOT PURSUIT AND WARRANTLESS ENTRY

When an individual suspected of committing a felony evades the police and engages in flight from them, the Supreme Court had previously upheld a warrantless entry into the suspect's home made during a "hot pursuit" of the suspect. In *Lange v. California* (2021), the court considered whether the same result was constitutional in the pursuit of a subject suspected of committing a misdemeanor.

Lange drove by a California Highway Patrol officer honking his horn and playing loud music. The officer signaled him to stop, but Lange did not do so, instead entering his driveway and driving into his garage. The officer followed him into the garage, observed signs of intoxication, and tested his blood alcohol level, which was found to be three times the legal limit. Lange was charged with the misdemeanor violation of driving under the influence.

On appeal, the Supreme Court unanimously held that there was no categorical right to perform a warrantless entry into a home (here an attached garage) when in pursuit of a fleeing misdemeanor suspect. Instead, a case-by-case assessment of exigencies was required.

The majority opinion written by Justice Kagan was joined by six other justices in whole or in part. Four justices wrote or joined in concurring opinions.

While recognizing that "A great many misdemeanor pursuits involve exigencies allowing warrantless entry," Justice Kagan went on to state that "whether a given one does so turns on the particular facts of the case."

The key in deciding the legality of warrantless searches is whether they involve exigent circumstances—that is, when "'the exigencies of the situation make the needs of law enforcement so compelling that [a] warrantless search is objectively reasonable.'" Prior decisions identified a number of such situations including providing emergency assistance to an injured occupant, protecting an occupant from imminent injury or to ensure his own safety, preventing the imminent instruction of evidence, or preventing a suspect's escape.

In rejecting a categorical rule permitting warrantless searches in any case of flight from a police officer where commission of a misdemeanor is suspected, the court noted that such exceptions are "'jealously and carefully drawn,'" because the "'home is entitled to special protection.'" Moreover, a misdemeanor offense is typically a "minor" infraction, and the added factor of flight does not necessarily pose dangers which rise to the level of exigent circumstances.

Finally, a review of the common law in place at the time of the Constitution demonstrated that it "did not recognize a categorical rule enabling . . . an entry in every case of misdemeanor pursuit."

The principal concurring opinion, which concurred only in the judgment, was written by Chief Justice Roberts and joined by Justice Alito. The opinion was nineteen pages long, three more than Justice Kagan's majority opinion.

Throughout this book, we have documented how the Supreme Court has overruled or changed prior rulings on constitutional law. In *Lange*, we have the chief justice himself accusing his colleagues of doing just that. Chief Justice Roberts's main point was that hot pursuit "is itself an exigent circumstance," "not merely a setting in which other exigent circumstances justifying warrantless entry might emerge." Looking at prior rulings, he contended that "We have repeatedly and consistently reaffirmed that hot pursuit is itself an exigent circumstance."

Chief Justice Roberts emphasized the importance of such general rules because "they provide 'guidance on how police should handle [such] cases.'" Moreover, "In determining what is reasonable under the Fourth Amendment, we have given great weight to the essential interests in readily administrative rules." "As such, "I would not override decades of guidance to law enforcement in favor of a new rule that provides no guidance at all."

Against this background, the majority's rule is "famously difficult to apply," especially since the difference between felonies and misdemeanors often "is esoteric, to say the least." Indeed, different states have classified certain offenses differently, some choosing to label them as felonies, while others consider them to be only misdemeanors.

Justice Kavanaugh wrote a brief concurring opinion contending that "there is almost no daylight in practice between the Court's opinion and the chief justice's opinion concurring in the judgment." While the chief justice's opinion "concludes that pursuit of a fleeing misdemeanant should *itself* constitute an exigent circumstance," most such cases will also involve some recognized exigent circumstance.

In his concurring opinion, joined in part by Justice Kavanaugh, Justice Thomas's main point was that the case-by-case rule adopted by the majority "is subject to historical, categorical exceptions." These include when a person is arrested and escapes; when the police are in "hot pursuit of a person who committed an affray"; when "pre-felonies" are involved; or where the defendant breached the peace.

Given that the ruling requires a case-by-case analysis, the issue of warrantless searches of a suspect thought to have committed a misdemeanor and who flees from the police is unlikely to return to the Supreme Court, but will be committed to the sound discretion of the trial court.

SEIZURES

The Fourth Amendment prohibits unreasonable *seizures* as well as unreasonable *searches*. Over the dissent of three justices, the Supreme Court under Chief Justice Roberts once again extended earlier precedent by giving an expansive reading to the key term "seizure" in *Torres v. Madrid* (2021).

Torres presented an extreme factual situation. When police attempted to arrest the defendant under the terms of an arrest warrant, she claimed she believed the officers were carjackers and therefore accelerated to escape them. The two officers fired thirteen shots at her, striking her twice in the back, but she nevertheless escaped capture at the time. She later brought a civil suit for damages, claiming that the officers applied excessive force, making the shooting an unreasonable seizure. As such, the case presented the question as to whether the bullets that struck her constituted a "seizure."

In the opinion by Chief Justice Roberts for five members of the Court (Justice Barrett not participating), the court ruled that "Under our cases, an officer seizes a person when he uses force to apprehend her." The court relied heavily upon its earlier decision in *California v. Hodari D.* (1991), as illuminated by many English common law rulings. It concluded that there was a necessity for an objective test for seizure and ruled that "The application of physical force to the body of a person with intent to restrain is a seizure even if the person does not submit and is not subdued."

Justice Gorsuch wrote a dissenting opinion, joined by Justices Thomas and Alito. He pointed out that previous cases required "taking possession of someone or something" to constitute a seizure, and that "Countless contemporary dictionaries define a 'seizure' or the act of 'seizing' in terms of possession." He distinguished the earlier opinion in *Hodari D.* by pointing out that the passage relied upon by the defendant was only dicta and therefore not controlling. Justice Gorsuch concluded that "To rule as it does, the majority must endow the term 'seizure' with two different meetings at the same time. It must disregard the dominant rule of the common law. It must disparage this Court's existing caselaw for erasing distinctions that never existed."

As the majority opinion itself acknowledged, it does not answer the question whether Ms. Torres was entitled to a remedy of civil damages against the officers. This was because no determination was made as to whether the seizure was unreasonable, nor was any opinion given regarding whether the officers were entitled to qualified immunity. Given these unresolved issues, the *Torres* case is unlikely to assist criminal defendants who are subjected to an application of force by arresting officers under similar circumstances, the occurrence of which is unlikely in any event.

Chapter 5

Race

From the horror of slavery to more subtle forms of discrimination, racial prejudice has been a recurrent stain on the fabric of American democracy. The Supreme Court has struggled with racial discrimination issues for over 175 years. It has rendered decisions that have been overturned by constitutional amendment (*Dred Scott v. Sandford*) or by the court itself (*Plessy v. Ferguson*), but it has also vindicated civil rights in several twentieth-century decisions, including by overturning the separate but equal doctrine of *Plessy* (*Brown v. Board of Education*) and by upholding the Civil Rights Act of 1964 (*Heart of Atlanta Motel, Inc. v. United States; Katzenbach v. McClung*), and the Voting Rights Act of 1965 (*South Carolina v. Katzenbach*). Despite these rulings, racial strife continues in the twenty-first century and is fanned on both sides by organized groups.[1]

Against this background, the Supreme Court has recently followed a more conservative approach to these and other emerging issues. Two of the significant issues coming before the court currently involve challenges to restrictions on voting, and the use of diversity to give preferential treatment to minority students in college admissions. Both these issues have sharply divided the populace. The Republican Party and many of its members, led by former President Trump, have claimed widespread fraud in voting, and they lobby to impose strict limits on who may vote and to place further restrictions on voting procedures, such as mail-in ballots and ballot harvesting. The use of diversity in college admission procedures has similarly divided the nation, but a majority of the population opposes such usage. The divisive nature of both these issues is discussed more fully below in the analysis of the decisions of Supreme Court in these areas.

The Supreme Court has grappled with issues of racial discrimination from the middle of the nineteenth century, beginning with *Dred Scott v. Sandford* (1857). There, a divided Supreme Court held that African Americans whose ancestors had been slaves were not "citizens" within the meaning of the Constitution and thus were not able to sue as such in the federal courts. It also questioned whether Congress had any power over slavery in the territories and whether the Missouri Compromise was thus invalid. It took a bloody Civil War with over seven hundred thousand deaths and the subsequent ratification of the Thirteenth Amendment to overturn the *Dred Scott* decision.

Even after the ratification of the Thirteenth, Fourteenth, and Fifteenth Amendments, the Supreme Court in the latter half of the nineteenth century issued a number of rulings that, with one exception, severely limited the protections of those amendments. In the *Slaughterhouse Cases* (1873), over three dissents, the court held that the Privileges and Immunities Clause of the Fourteenth Amendment only guaranteed the rights held by citizens of the United States, as opposed to rights held by citizens of particular states. Citizens of the United States had only limited protections, such as the right of peaceable assembly and habeas corpus. Other rights were the province of the states to confer on their citizens. The court did not "see in those [Civil War] amendments any purpose to destroy the main features of the general system." Otherwise, in the majority's opinion, the Supreme Court would become "a perpetual censor upon all legislation of the States, on the civil rights of their own citizens, with authority to nullify such as it did not approve as consistent with those rights, as they existed at the time of the adoption of this amendment." Such a result would "radically change . . . the whole theory of the relations of the State and Federal governments to each other and of both those governments to the people."

The subsequent decision in the *Civil Rights Cases* (1883) continued a restrictive interpretation of the Civil War Amendments, invalidating congressional legislation that prohibited discrimination in "inns, public conveyances on land or water, theaters, and other places of public amusement." Over only one dissent, the court struck down the Civil Rights Act of 1875, ruling that the Fourteenth Amendment did not give Congress the "power to legislate upon subjects which are in the domain of state legislation," nor did it enact a "code of municipal law regulative of all *private rights between man and man in society*." In the court's view, the Fourteenth Amendment only empowered Congress to enact "corrective legislation" to combat illegal state action. Justice Bradley's majority opinion went on to characterize the freed slaves as taking "the rank of *mere citizen*," ceasing to be "*the special favorite of the laws.*" As such, the rights of the freed slaves "are to be protected in the ordinary modes by which the other men's rights are protected."

Following a distinction made by the *Civil Rights Cases* between political and social rights, the Supreme Court next upheld a Louisiana law requiring railroads to provide "equal but separate accommodations for the white, and colored, races." The eight-justice majority ruled that the Fourteenth Amendment "could not have been intended to abolish distinctions based upon color, or to enforce *social, as distinguished from political, equality*, or a co-mingling of the two races upon terms unsatisfactory to either." The court went on to observe that "If one race be inferior to the other socially, the constitution of the United States cannot put them upon the same plane." As such, "social prejudices may [not] be overcome by legislation." In a powerful dissent that would be relied upon in several twentieth-century decisions protecting the rights of all citizens, Justice John Marshall Harlan argued that the Civil War Amendments "removed the race line from our governmental systems," and noted that "our constitution is color-blind, and neither knows nor tolerates classes among citizens. In respect of civil rights, all citizens are equal before the law."

A final nineteenth-century decision, *Yick Wo v. Hopkins* (1885), showed the future promise of the Fourteenth Amendment to serve as a guarantor of the civil rights of all persons living in the United States. In that case, the court found unconstitutional the application to Chinese aliens of a local San Francisco ordinance that required any person seeking to operate a laundry in a wooden building to obtain the consent of the local board of supervisors. Yick Wo had operated such a laundry for twenty-two years in the city but was nevertheless imprisoned for ten days when he declined to obtain the mandated consent and failed to pay a required fine. A unanimous Supreme Court held that the application of the local ordinances to Yick Wo violated the Equal Protection Clause of the Fourteenth Amendment because the ordinances, while appearing fair on the surface, were applied in a discriminatory fashion against the two hundred Chinese aliens operating laundries in wooden buildings, all of whom had been denied consent to operate their laundries. By contrast, all eighty non-Chinese petitioners' applications had been approved.

Significantly, the opinion first noted that "the Fourteenth Amendment to the Constitution is not confined to the protection of citizens," but its provisions "are universal in their application to all persons within the territorial jurisdiction, and without regard to any differences of race, color, or of nationality, and the equal protection of the laws is a pledge of the protection of equal laws."

In a series of decisions on the protections afforded by the Fifteenth Amendment, the Supreme Court in its nineteenth-century decisions followed the same restrictive interpretation of that amendment as it had with the Fourteenth Amendment. In *United States v. Reese* (1876) and a companion case, *United States v. Cruikshank* (1876), the court held that, since the Fifteenth Amendment "interferes with" state electoral laws and effects "a radical change," it requires Congress to spell out explicitly any intended interference with the rights of states to regulate the qualifications of their citizens to vote. The opinion reiterates at length the discussion in the *Slaughterhouse Cases* of the differences between the rights of citizens of the United States and those of the states, and the importance of states' rights and federalism in the American system of government. Once again, as with the *Civil Rights Cases*, the Civil War Amendments were not seen as designed to alter this fundamental structure and the corresponding limitations upon federal power in areas viewed as involving states' rights.

In the twentieth century, the Supreme Court slowly changed course to begin protecting racial minorities against discrimination. By the middle of the century, it gradually expanded those protections, by utilizing a more expansive view of the Fourteenth Amendment and by upholding federal legislation opening public accommodations to all and protecting the voting rights of those minorities. In the early case of *Shelley v. Kramer* (1948), the court ruled that the judicial enforcement of restrictive covenants in real estate transactions that limited the use or occupancy of real estate to members of the white race constituted impermissible state action under the Equal Protection Clause, even though they regulated only private conduct. Two other cases outlawed differential treatment of African Americans in higher education without overruling *Plessy*. Those unanimous decisions ruled that African American students had been discriminated against in admission to, or treatment in, previously all-white schools. In *Sweatt v. Painter* (1950), the Supreme Court, for the first time in its history, ordered the admission of an African American student to the University of Texas Law School at a time when there had been no law school for black students in Texas when the student applied to that law school. Chief Justice Fred Vinson's opinion compared the University of Texas Law School to a law school that had just opened to serve black students. The comparison demonstrated startling differences between the schools regarding their faculties, their libraries, and the numbers of students such that they could not be considered "equal." As such, and further considering the reputations of the two schools, the court found that there was a denial of "substantially equality in educational opportunities offered white and Negro law students by the State."

In a second case, decided the same day, the Supreme Court dealt with the separate question of what protections were available to an African American student who *had* been admitted to a previously all-white school. *McLaurin v. Oklahoma State Regents* (1950) portrayed the incredibly discriminatory treatment accorded to a student who had been admitted to the University of Oklahoma to pursue a doctorate in education. Initially, he "was required to sit apart at a designated desk in an anteroom adjoining the classroom; to sit at a designated desk on the mezzanine floor of the library, but not to use the desks in the regular reading room; and to sit at a designated table and to eat at a different time from the other students in the school cafeteria." While those conditions subsequently improved somewhat, the court nevertheless unanimously ruled that "The Fourteenth Amendment precludes differences in treatment by the state based upon race," and found that the state had set the student apart from other students, handicapping him in his pursuit of effective graduate instruction. As such, the University of Oklahoma was ordered to extend to McLaurin "the same treatment" as was extended to "students of other races."

In a final case, decided the same day as the higher education cases, the court ruled that segregated facilities in dining cars on interstate railroad routes violated a probation of the Interstate Commerce Act, but did not reach any constitutional issue (*Henderson v. United States* [1950]).

While each of these decisions was narrowly drawn to avoid deciding broader issues, including the continued viability of *Plessy v. Ferguson*, the decisions nevertheless established the foundation from which the Supreme Court would deliver its broader rulings barring segregation in public education throughout the United States. In *Brown v. Board of Education* (1950), a decision that both liberals and conservatives today deem to be a "super precedent," the Supreme Court finally overruled *Plessy* and concluded that "In the field of public education the doctrine of 'separate but equal' has no place. Separate educational facilities are inherently unequal." In reaching this conclusion, the court relied upon its previous decisions in *Sweatt* and *McLaurin*, as well as on "intangible considerations." In rejecting Plessy, the unanimous opinion written by the new chief justice, Earl Warren, concluded that "whatever may have been the extent of psychological knowledge at the time of *Plessy v. Ferguson*, this finding [that segregation had a detrimental effect upon African American children] is amply supported by modern authority." One of the studies the court cited reported that children of both races, when shown both a white and a black doll, picked the white doll as the one they would like to play with, and the one that was "nice." Remarkably, even most of the black children picked the black doll as the one that "looked bad."

The ruling in *Brown v. Board of Education* met with massive resistance in the Southern states. When the governor of Arkansas dispatched the state's National Guard to block the admission of black students to Little Rock's public schools, President Dwight Eisenhower ordered over one thousand federal troops to Little Rock in 1957 after the governor refused to obey a court injunction against blocking the admission of black students. When the Little Rock school board thereafter petitioned the federal court for a delay in implementing school desegregation, the Supreme Court unanimously rejected its request in *Cooper v. Aaron* (1958). That decision came after a special summer session of the court, resulting in a unanimous opinion signed by each of the nine justices, the only time in the court's history when this was done. Ruling that "The interpretation of the Fourteenth Amendment enunciated by this Court in the Brown case is the supreme law of the land, and [Article] VI of the Constitution makes it of binding effect on the States 'any Thing in the Constitution or Laws of any State to the Contrary notwithstanding.'" As such, "no state legislator or executive or judicial officer can war against the Constitution without violating his undertaking to support it."

Cooper v. Aaron failed to end Southern resistance to desegregation of its schools. For the next twenty years, the Supreme Court was presented with a number of schemes to block public school integration, including closing all schools and setting up a dual school system. These efforts were uniformly unsuccessful. In addition, in order to enforce desegregation orders, the Supreme Court ruled in *Swann v. Charlotte-Mecklenburg County Board* (1971) that mandatory busing could be ordered to facilitate desegregation.

The unparalleled success of the NAACP and other civil rights organizations over these twenty years only ended with the Supreme Court's decision in *Milliken v. Bradley* (1974). There, the Supreme Court refused to order integration of the Detroit public schools on a regional basis with suburban schools because only the Detroit schools were deemed to be segregated as a matter of law.

During the 1960s, the Supreme Court effectively repudiated its nineteenth-century decisions striking down legislation protecting equal access to public accommodations and safeguarding voting rights. The court first had occasion to examine the constitutionality of the Civil Rights Act of 1964. With respect to public accommodations, Title II of that legislation provided that "all persons shall be entitled to the full and equal enjoyment of the goods, services, facilities, privileges, advantages, and accommodations of any place of public accommodation . . . without discrimination or segregation on the ground of race, color, religion, or national origin." In *Heart of Atlanta Motel, Inc. v. United States* (1964), the majority opinion distinguished the prior precedent of the *Civil Rights Cases* (1883), ruling that the legislation at issue there broadly proscribed all discrimination without limiting the proscriptions of the act to enterprises directly and substantially affecting interstate commerce. Here, by contrast, such a limitation was imposed, and was therefore found to be constitutional under the Commerce Clause. In a second case, announced the same day, the court ruled that even a local restaurant with a small capacity was subject to the ban on discrimination in public accommodations because of the interstate travelers who frequented the restaurant (*Katzenbach v. McClung* [1964]).

With respect to elections, the court upheld the Voting Rights Act of 1965 in *South Carolina v. Katzenbach* (1966). That act prohibited the use of literacy tests and other similar qualifications for five years in those voting districts in which fewer than half of those of voting age had voted in 1964; suspended any new voting regulations in those districts without federal approval; and permitted the use of federal examiners or registrars to list those applicants who were qualified to vote. The court rejected the argument that the act exceeded the powers of Congress under its prior, nineteenth-century precedents. Relying upon, and emphasizing, the pervasive and long-standing history of voting discrimination in the Southern states, the court found that the Voting Rights Act was constitutional because it "was designed by Congress to banish the blight of racial discrimination in voting, which has infected the electoral process in parts of our country for nearly a century." The court specifically identified several tactics used in the Southern states to bar racial minorities from voting. Those tactics included "grandfather clauses, property qualifications, 'good character' tests, and the requirement that registrants 'understand' or 'interpret' certain matter." Because previous legislation and litigation had been ineffective to address this pervasive discrimination, the court ruled that the remedial legislation was an appropriate congressional response "after enduring nearly a century of systematic resistance to the Fifteenth Amendment."

The Supreme Court next turned its attention to the thorny issue of affirmative action in higher education, exploring whether favoring minority applicants for admission to public colleges and universities violated the Equal Protection Clause. In the early case of *Regents of the University of California v. Bakke* (1978), a sharply divided Supreme Court, by a vote of five to four, held that an admissions program that established a separate admission pool for minority or disadvantaged applicants was unconstitutional, but that it was possible for the medical school involved in that case to take race into account as a factor in future admissions. The decisive vote was that of Justice Lewis Powell. He wrote that attempting to guarantee "some specified percentage of a particular group [be admitted] merely because of its race or ethnic origin," was "facially invalid." Nevertheless, he outlined certain types of programs that would be permissible in considering race in the admissions process. Such programs could, for example, consider race or ethnic background as a "'plus' in a particular applicant's file" so long as the program "treats each applicant as an individual in the admissions process."

The court revisited the issue in two cases involving the admissions processes of the University of Michigan and its law school. In *Grutter v. Bollinger* (2003), the law school's admission process looked at traditional factors such as grade point average, but also considered "soft variables." One of those variables was designed to achieve diversity for the purpose of enriching the education of all those who attended the law school by admitting a "critical mass" of minority students. The majority opinion by Justice Sandra Day O'Connor upheld the admissions process used by the law school by emphasizing the benefits of diversity, rather than remediation of past discrimination, to uphold the consideration of race in the law school's admissions process. She pointed to several amicus briefs filed by businesses and retired military officers "who point to the educational benefits that flow from student body diversity." In a dissenting opinion for four members of the court, Chief Justice Rehnquist contended that the law school's process was really a disguised quota that could not survive strict scrutiny because it was "precisely the type of racial balancing that the Court itself calls 'patently unconstitutional.'"

On the same day it upheld the law school's admissions process in *Grutter*, the Supreme Court struck down the University of Michigan's undergraduate admission process in *Gratz v. Bollinger* (2003). That process utilized a "selection index" under which a score of one hundred points or more resulted in admission. Applicants were entitled to twenty points "based upon his or her membership in an underrepresented racial or ethnic minority group." In an opinion for five members of the Court, Chief Justice Rehnquist found the admissions policy was not "narrowly tailored to achieve the interest in educational diversity that respondents claim justifies their program." Moreover, rather than treating every particular applicant as an individual, as Justice Powell's opinion in *Bakke* required, the process distributed points to every individual who was a member of a minority group without any particularized consideration of that individual. While Justices O'Connor and Breyer agreed that the admissions program was unconstitutional, three dissenters, in separate opinions, would have upheld it. Justice Ginsburg's dissent was particularly notable because of her reliance upon historic discrimination practiced against minority groups. While this has been the principal justification advanced to support special admissions programs in *Bakke*, only Justice Ginsburg relied upon this factor in *Gratz*. She wrote that "The stain of generations of racial oppression is still visible in our society . . . and the determination to hasten its removal remains vital."

The Supreme Court, under Chief Justice Roberts in the twenty-first century, has had occasion to decide a number of matters involving these and other civil rights issues, generally applying a more exacting standard of review than in previous cases. This has resulted in the court striking down several measures designed to eradicate discrimination against minorities. The matters that have come before the court for decision include school assignment issues, the scope of permissible affirmative-action initiatives in education and employment, and the validity and application of certain provisions of the Voting Rights Act.

SCHOOL ASSIGNMENT ISSUES

In *Parents Involved in Community Schools v. Seattle School District No. 1* (2007), the court reviewed public school district student assignment plans from Seattle, Washington, and Louisville, Kentucky. In one of his earliest opinions on the court, Chief Justice Roberts delivered a plurality opinion on behalf of Justices Thomas, Scalia, and Alito in which he characterized the plans at issue as "rel[ying] upon an individual student's race and assigning that student to a particular school, so that the racial balance at the school falls within a predetermined range based on the racial composition of the school district as a whole." Emphasizing that the standard of strict scrutiny applies when the government makes decisions based on race, Chief Justice Roberts noted that the use of race must be "'narrowly tailored' to achieve a 'compelling' state interest." Since there never had been a judicial finding of de jure segregation in Seattle, and Louisville's desegregation decree had been dissolved years before, there was no justification for utilizing a racial standard to remediate the effects of past potential discrimination. The plurality also ruled that the interest in achieving diversity in higher education was not sufficient to uphold a plan that looked at race alone. Chief Justice Roberts concluded that "*The way to stop discrimination on the basis of race is to stop discriminating on the basis of race.*"

In a concurring opinion, Justice Clarence Thomas emphasized that "*racial imbalance is not segregation*," that there was no demonstrated danger in the school district of "resegregation," and that racial balancing in public school assignments could only be utilized to remedy past de jure segregation.

Justice Anthony Kennedy cast the fifth and deciding vote to strike down the school assignment plans, but he did not join in all of Chief Justice Roberts's opinion. He dismissed the use of the colorblind constitutional model as controlling, reasoning that "in the real world, it is regrettable to say, it cannot be a universal constitutional principle." Justice Kennedy also noted that he believed diversity could be a "a compelling educational goal a school district may pursue," and contended that school authorities were not required to "accept the status quo of racial isolation in schools," a conclusion he believed to be "profoundly mistaken." Despite these concerns, he found these school districts to have improperly considered race as the controlling factor. He wrote that "Crude measures of this sort threaten to reduce children to racial chits valued and traded according to one school's supply and another's demand."

Justice John Paul Stevens delivered a dissenting opinion that criticized the court for retreating from *Brown v. Board of Education*, accusing the court of having "changed significantly" since 1968. He charged that "It is my firm conviction that no Member of the Court that I joined in 1975 would have agreed with today's decision."

A more reasoned dissenting opinion was delivered by Justice Stephen Breyer, joined by Justices Stevens, Souter, and Ginsburg. This seventy-seven-page opinion contended the majority ruling was inconsistent with *Brown v. Board of Education*, and that four basic considerations justified the student assignment plans before the court. These were a prior history of segregation or litigation about segregation in both school districts; the court's prior desegregation precedent, which supported the use of "compulsory race-conscious measures to combat segregated schools"; the narrowly tailored plans aim to implement the compelling state interest of "diversity in public primary and secondary schools"; and the threat posed by the majority decision, which posed the "risk of a return to school systems that are in fact (though not in law) resegregated."

The public reacted favorably to the decision in the *Seattle School District* cases, with some 71 percent of the American public agreeing that "public schools may not consider an individual's race when deciding which students are assigned to specific schools." Only 24 percent disagreed with this statement. Nevertheless, the multiple opinions showed a significant disagreement among the justices then on the court, and a differently constituted court would have occasion to revisit these issues in the context of affirmative-action programs utilized in public higher-education admissions processes, as is discussed later in this chapter.

THE PRE-CLEARANCE PROVISIONS OF THE VOTING RIGHTS ACT OF 1965

Employing the powers granted it by Section 2 of the Fifteenth Amendment, Congress enacted the Voting Rights Act of 1965 to safeguard the rights of African Americans to vote. As noted previously, the Act had three major provisions, one of which (the pre-clearance provision), prohibited the use of any new regulations affecting voting in the covered jurisdictions (mainly the states of the old Civil War Confederacy) unless the regulations were first approved by either the attorney general of the United States or by a three-judge district court. In *South Carolina v. Katzenbach* (1966), the Supreme Court upheld the Act as a constitutional exercise of congressional power based upon what it found to be repeated denials of the rights of African Americans to vote, with states employing tactics the court described as "an invidious and pervasive evil which has been perpetuated in certain parts of our country through unremitting and ingenious defiance of the Constitution" and which constituted "nearly a century of systematic resistance to the Fifteenth Amendment."

The Voting Rights Act of 1965 was extended several times, most recently in 2006, when it was extended for twenty-five years to 2031. Despite the passage of nearly fifty years since enactment of the original legislation, the pre-clearance provisions still applied to the original jurisdictions covered by the Act. This temporal disparity gave rise to several constitutional challenges to the Voting Rights Act. One such challenge was made by a municipal utility district in Texas, and that challenge came before the Supreme Court in *Northwest Austin Municipal Utility District Number One v. Holder* (2009).

In an opinion for eight members of the court, Chief Justice Roberts noted that the preclearance provision "imposes substantial 'federalism costs'" by authorizing "federal intrusion into sensitive areas of state and local policymaking." As such, "These federalism costs have caused Members of this Court to express serious misgivings about the constitutionality of [the preclearance provisions]." Moreover, "Things have changed in the South. Voter turnout and registration rates now approach parity. Blatantly discriminatory evasions of federal decrees are rare. And minority candidates hold office at unprecedented levels." The majority opinion also indicated that by differentiating between states, the Act was at variance with "our historic tradition that all the States enjoy 'equal sovereignty.'"

To these general considerations, Chief Justice Roberts added the key fact that the Voting Rights Act "coverage formula is based on data that is now more than 35 years old, and there is considerable evidence that it fails to account for current political conditions." As such, "The Act's preclearance requirements and its coverage formula raise serious constitutional questions."

Rather than resolve these questions, the eight-member majority chose instead to conclude the plaintiff district was eligible to seek a "bailout" under the provisions of the Act. The court chose this path in order "to avoid the unnecessary resolution of constitutional questions," which it characterized as "difficult."

In a separate opinion concurring in the judgment, but dissenting in part, Justice Thomas stated he would hold that the preclearance provision "exceeds Congress' power to enforce the Fifteenth Amendment." He noted that states had both "autonomy" and "primary authority" over matters relating to voting. Moreover, there was a "lack of current evidence of intentional discrimination with respect to voting," and the Fifteenth Amendment, in Justice Thomas's view, required an actual denial of the right to vote "on account of" race, color, or prior condition of slavery.

Based on these factual and legal considerations, Justice Thomas concluded that "Punishment for long past sins is not a legitimate basis for imposing a forward-looking preventative measure that has already served its purpose."

As Thomas Goldstein of the SCOTUS blog has aptly put it, Chief Justice Roberts's opinion represented "a model for his philosophy of judicial minimalism." Goldstein saw the approach taken by the chief justice as having afforded Congress an opportunity to correct the temporal disparity presented by pre-clearance provisions that were based on decades-old statistical data.[2]

THE STATES AS EQUAL SOVEREIGNS ON VOTING MATTERS

When Congress failed to act to address the problems identified in the *Northwest Austin* opinion, the issue came before the Supreme Court again four years later, in *Shelby County, Alabama v. Holder* (2013). In that case, the court struck down the coverage formula as unconstitutional. In the opinion of the court written by Chief Justice Roberts and joined by Justices Scalia, Kennedy, Thomas, and Alito, the majority held that the pre-clearance coverage formula was justified in 1966 based upon the history of pervasive discrimination in the covered jurisdictions, but that "history did not end in 1965," and "things have changed dramatically" in the ensuing years. Citing data found in the 2006 Congressional Reports dealing with the reauthorization of the Voting Rights Act, the majority opinion documented a huge gain in black voting in the covered jurisdictions between 1965 and 2004, with little gap between white and black voters. As such, "Coverage today is based on decades-old data and eradicated practices."

The majority pointed out that in the *Northwest Austin* opinion, eight members of the court had agreed that the preclearance provisions imposed "substantial federalism costs" and were inconsistent with the "historical tradition that all the States enjoy equal sovereignty." Moreover, the majority in that case had stated that the Voting Rights Act "imposes current burdens and must be justified by current needs."

Quoting from an earlier Supreme Court opinion, Chief Justice Roberts noted that "the Framers of the Constitution intended the States to keep for themselves, as provided in the Tenth Amendment, the power to regulate elections." Moreover, there is "equal sovereignty" among the separate states, and each is "equal in power, dignity and authority." Under the Voting Rights Act, however, there is "a disfavored subset of States." This classification cannot be justified by a history of past discrimination alone because the Fifteenth Amendment is "not designed to punish for the past; its purpose is to ensure a better future."

The "fundamental problem" with the congressional reauthorization of the Voting Rights Act was that "Congress did not use the record compiled to shape a coverage formula grounded in current conditions. It instead reenacted a formula based on 40-year-old facts having no logical relation to the present day." Because flaws in the coverage formula were the cause of the constitutional infirmity, the court invalidated only the coverage formula under Section 4(b) of the Voting Rights Act, and it did not rule on the pre-clearance requirement of Section 5 for covered jurisdictions. Thus, that pre-clearance requirement could stand (pending future challenges) if the coverage formula were properly amended.

In a separate concurring opinion, Justice Thomas would have gone further by striking down Section 5 as well. In his view, the logic of the majority opinion also compelled the invalidation of the pre-clearance requirement given the significant changes in black voter turnout, registration, and office holding in the covered jurisdictions, and the absence of the pervasive discrimination that had existed in the past in those jurisdictions.

In a dissenting opinion, Justice Ginsburg, joined by Justices Breyer, Sotomayor, and Kagan, emphasized the fact that Congress had made a determination, "based on a voluminous record, that the scourge of discrimination was not yet extirpated." As such, the key issue on appeal was whether the Supreme Court or Congress should decide if the pre-clearance provisions of the Voting Rights Act should remain in effect. Justice Ginsburg emphasized that Congress held "extensive hearings" in 2006 and was authorized by the Fifteenth Amendment to enact "appropriate legislation" to enforce its provisions. Moreover, under the storied precedent of *McCulloch v. Maryland* (1819), Congress could adopt "all means which are appropriate, which are plainly adapted to that end."

Under this authority, Congress properly reauthorized the Voting Rights Act in the dissenters' view, because pre-clearance was required due to the existence of a variety of new and "subtler second-generation barriers to majority voting," including such practices as "racial gerrymandering" and at-large voting. That these discriminatory practices were still endemic in the covered jurisdictions was shown, in the view of the dissenters, by the fact that more than seven hundred voting changes were blocked by the pre-clearance process as discriminatory between 1982 and 2006. Moreover, where a covered jurisdiction truly had no problems with ongoing discrimination, Congress provided a "bail out" procedure.

Justice Ginsburg went on to contend that, standing by itself, the history of Alabama's racism justified keeping Shelby County under the preclearance requirement: "Alabama's sorry history of [Section] 2 violations alone provides sufficient justification for Congress' determination in 2006 that the State should remain subject to [Section] 5's preclearance requirement."

Finally, the dissenters took issue with the contention that all states are equal in sovereignty, contending instead that that principle is limited to the terms on which states were admitted to the Union.

Although the opinion of the court in *Shelby County* clearly permitted Congress to enact a revised coverage formula for pre-clearance that is based on current conditions, the decision set off a firestorm of protest among Democrats and the liberal media. President Obama, for example, indicated he was "deeply disappointed" by the ruling, while the *New York Times*, in its lead editorial the following day, termed the decision "An Assault on the Voting Rights Act," "another damaging and intellectually dishonest ruling," and a decision in which "The Roberts Court kills a vital enforcement section, punting it back to a paralyzed Congress." Even more strident was Andrew Cohen, writing on TheAtlantic.com, on June 28, 2013. His view was that the opinion of the Court was "as lamentable as *Plessy* or *Dred Scott*," and represented "the legal sanctification of an ugly movement that has brought America a new generation of voter suppression laws."

CHANGES IN VOTING RULES

Given the significant recent increase in claims that the rights of minority citizens to vote have been unlawfully limited in varied ways, litigation regarding voting rights has continued, with particular emphasis placed upon new legislation or regulations that may have the purpose or effect of restricting minority voting. The controversy relating to these new laws accelerated after the presidential election of 2020, when the incumbent president, Donald Trump, repeatedly claimed the election had been stolen from him by laws that had expanded the ability to vote but, in his view, enabled election fraud. Republican legislators in several states soon enacted new laws that restricted the time, place, or matter of voting, targeting such practices as unlimited absentee voting and ballot harvesting, where one person gathered and submitted ballots cast by multiple voters. These new laws were challenged immediately, with claims of racial bias in their enactment. The new president, Joseph Biden, and many progressives and liberals characterized such laws as a return to the "Jim Crow" laws of the nineteenth century. The litigation that ensued has been filed against jurisdictions covered by the Voting Rights Act, but has not been limited to them.

The Supreme Court was soon brought into this fray, reviewing a challenge to two laws enacted in Arizona by the Republican legislature in that state. In *Brnovich v. Democratic National Committee* (2021), the Supreme Court upheld both laws against a challenge brought under section 2 of the Voting Rights Act. The first law disqualified any ballot cast by a voter if it was cast in the wrong precinct, while the second law prohibited ballot harvesting, permitting mail-in ballots to be collected only by an election official, a mail carrier, or members of the voter's family or household, as well as by a voter's caregiver.

Section 2(a) of the Voting Rights Act prohibits laws that result in a denial or abridgment of the right to vote on account of race or color. In determining whether a change in voting rules results in such a denial or abridgment, Section 2(b) explicitly requires consideration of "the totality of circumstances" surrounding the enactment of a new law. To make out a violation, proof was required under the act demonstrating that "the political processes leading to nomination or election in the State or political subdivision are not equally open to participation" by minority voters "in that its members have less opportunity than other members of the electorate to participate in the political process and to elect representatives of their own choice."

In an opinion for six members of the court, Justice Alito concluded that "the core of [section] 2(b) is the requirement that voting be 'equally open.'"

Since the statute expressly requires consideration of "the totality of circumstances," Justice Alito suggested that "several important circumstances" should be considered to address this requirement. "First, the size of the burden imposed by the challenged voting rule is highly relevant," but "Mere inconvenience cannot be enough to demonstrate a violation." Second, "the degree to which a voting rule departs from what was standard practice" at the time when section 2 was amended is relevant. Third, "The size of any disparities in a rule's impact on members of different racial or ethnic groups is also an important factor to consider," but "very small differences should not be artificially magnified." Fourth, a court must consider "the opportunities provided by the State's entire system of voting when assessing the burden imposed by a challenged provision." This requires an examination of "other available means" of voting. Fifth, another important factor is "the strength of the state interest served by a challenged voting rule." The majority indicated that this list of five circumstances was not "exhaustive."

Other factors, such as those considered under Title VII and Fair Housing Act models, were ruled to be "unhelpful" in section 2 cases. Thus, use of disparate impact or necessity models would invalidate neutral voting regulations with long histories and would also "transfer much of the authority to regulate election procedures from the States to the federal courts."

Here, considering the totality of circumstances, Arizona's laws were held to pass muster under section 2. The disqualification of a ballot cast in the wrong precinct is reasonable given the amount of information given to a voter regarding his or her polling place. Moreover, that rule did not lead to any significant racial disparities in Arizona, since members of minority groups had their ballots disqualified only about 1 percent of the time compared to .5 percent for non-minority voters.

Arizona's law prohibiting ballot harvesting was also ruled reasonable given the multiple avenues voters have to submit their ballots, including by mailing, by using an early ballot drop box, or by using an authorized election official's office, as well as by dropping off their ballots at any polling place or voting center on Election Day. Moreover, special provisions are made for those who are unable to use an early voting system, such as those suffering from illness or disability. In addition, there was no statistical evidence showing a disparate impact on minority voters of the ballot harvesting requirement. Even if such an impact had been shown, the state was justified by its "compelling interest in preserving the integrity of the election process" in banning ballot harvesting, which has been documented by the Federal Election Reform Commission to lead to vote-buying schemes and other fraud and abuse.

Justice Kagan filed a vigorous dissenting opinion, which was joined by Justices Breyer and Sotomayor. Describing the Voting Rights Act as one that "marries two great ideals: democracy and racial equality," she criticizes the majority for "undermin[ing] Section 2 and the right it provides." Justice Kagan accused the majority of "writ[ing] its own set of rules, limiting Section 2 from multiple directions," giving "a cramped reading to broad language."

After reviewing the historical background of the Voting Rights Act and criticizing the court for striking down the Section 5 coverage formula in the *Shelby County* decision, the dissenting opinion turned to the language of Section 2. Justice Kagan argued that its text "requires courts to eradicate voting practices that make it harder for members of some races than of others to cast a vote, unless such a practice is necessary to support a strong state interest." Moreover, Section 2 focuses on "effects," not intent. The statute thus requires the plaintiff to prove a "statistically significant racial disparity in electoral opportunities."

Turning to the majority opinion, the dissenters contended that the factors identified in Justice Alito's majority opinion are "mostly made-up," and are at odds with the language of Section 2. Among other deficiencies, the majority overemphasizes the state interest factor, requiring only a showing that the interest is a reasonable one.

In the Arizona case, the dissenters contended that both voting restrictions should have been struck down because of their effects. To begin with, the out-of-precinct voting rule followed by Arizona was a "national outlier," with Arizona in some past elections accounting for one-third of all discarded votes in the country. In addition, statistical evidence demonstrated that the rule impacted more heavily on minority voters in 2016, with minority voters twice as likely in that year's election to have their ballots discarded than whites. Second, the ballot harvesting rule should have been stricken because it made it more difficult for Native Americans to vote. Justice Kagan pointed out that most members of the Native American community had no mail delivery or local post office and necessarily relied on third parties to submit their ballots. Moreover, any state interest in prohibiting ballot harvesting was minimal because Arizona had made it a felony for anyone to tamper with a ballot, and no case had ever been filed charging such tampering involving ballot collection.

The reaction to the court's ruling was mixed, but mostly critical, especially among progressives and liberals. President Biden stated that "the court has now done severe damage" to the Voting Rights Act, both in *Brnovich*, with respect to section 2, and also in its prior ruling on section 5. He argued that "we should be fully enforcing voting-rights laws, not weakening them." The *New York Times* editorial board headline similarly proclaimed that "The Supreme Court Abandons Voting Rights," arguing that the six conservative justices in the majority "have given a free pass to state legislatures to discriminate." It pointed out that in 2021, "28 laws restricting voting have passed in 17 states."

Other commentators saw the ruling in a more positive light. The *Wall Street Journal*, for example, had as its editorial headline "The Court Bolsters Voting Rights." It contended that "The Justices are strengthening the Voting Rights Act by establishing parameters for lower courts to prevent its political abuse."

Litigation over restrictions on voting is likely to continue despite the *Brnovich* ruling. The Biden administration, through Attorney General Merrick Garland, announced in June 2021, prior to the decision in *Brnovich*, that it will target changes in voting rules that limit minority voting, and bring suit where appropriate. It brought suit against the State of Georgia, principally contesting the validity of changes made to absentee voting that prohibited the distribution of unsolicited absentee ballots by election officials and limited the number of drop boxes for returning those ballots. The suit noted that more than 29 percent of black voters used absentee ballots, compared to less than 24 percent of white voters, in the 2020 presidential election.

AFFIRMATIVE ACTION IN STUDENT ADMISSIONS

One of the most controversial aspects of race-related litigation has been the provision of racial preferences afforded to members of designated minority groups identified by public colleges and universities. Students who did not fall within a designated minority group, and were denied admission to such colleges or universities, have challenged such preferences as violative of the Fourteenth Amendment. The Supreme Court has generally rejected such challenges in deeply divided opinions.

The *Grutter* and *Gratz* decisions discussed above predated the Roberts court, and they provided the rule of decision in higher-education admissions for ten years. Then, on a new challenge by a rejected student applicant, the court once again took up the question in *Fisher v. University of Texas at Austin* (2013). There, the Supreme Court declined to overturn the court's five-to-four precedent in *Grutter v. Bollinger* (2003), despite previous suggestions that it might do so.

Justice Kennedy's opinion for seven of the eight members of the court who participated in the *Fisher* decision held that the lower courts had failed properly to consider whether the University of Texas at Austin had applied the "narrow tailoring" required by *Grutter*, under which the university was required to conduct a "searching examination" to "ensure that each applicant is evaluated as an individual and not in a way that makes an applicant's race or ethnicity the defining feature of his or her application." Moreover, the university must prove that the use of race is "necessary" to achieve the benefits of diversity, and it is "the Judiciary's obligation to determine" if this it has done so and "whether a university could achieve sufficient diversity without using racial classifications." Here, the lower courts failed to conduct this "searching examination," and the case was therefore returned to the appeals court to "assess whether the University has offered sufficient evidence that would prove that its admissions program is narrowly tailored to obtain the educational benefits of diversity."

Significantly, Justice Kennedy indicated that the three prior decisions on racial classifications in education—including *Gratz*, and *Grutter*—were "take[n] . . . as given for purposes of deciding this case." As Justice Scalia pointed out in his one-paragraph concurring opinion, that was because the student who challenged the university program had not asked that *Grutter* be overruled.

Fisher represented a further example of the often-utilized approach of the court under Chief Justice Roberts to avoid broad decisions on constitutional questions where narrower grounds existed on which to decide a case. Nevertheless, the holding of *Grutter* regarding the educational benefits of diversity remained controversial, as it continues to remain today.

It is notable that Justice Thomas wrote a twenty-page concurring opinion in which he explained why he would overrule *Grutter* and "hold that a State's use of race in higher education admissions decisions is categorically prohibited by the Equal Protection Clause." On the other hand, Justice Ginsburg penned the sole dissent in *Fisher*, explaining why she believed the University of Texas admissions program was constitutional. She noted that the "lingering effects of 'an overtly discriminatory past' [and] the legacy of 'centuries of law-sanctioned inequality'" could be considered in assessing the constitutional permissibility of a race-based classification in university admissions.

On remand from the Supreme Court in *Fisher*, the Fifth Circuit chose again to hold, by a two-to-one vote, that the University of Texas' admissions approach was constitutional. The Supreme Court granted certiorari to review that decision, and upheld the University of Texas' approach the second time around in *Fisher v. University of Texas* (2016) ("*Fisher II*").

CONSIDERATION OF STUDENT DIVERSITY

In *Fisher II*, the Supreme Court found the admissions practices of the University of Texas to be constitutional. Those practices included admission of anyone who scored in the top 10 percent of their class at a Texas high school, plus admission of additional applicants who were evaluated based on two constructs. For this latter group, which totaled some 25 percent of the entering class, the admissions staff first utilized an "Academic Index" of SAT scores and high school academic performance. Next, they utilized a "Personal Achievement Index," which was characterized as a "holistic review" of multiple factors, one of which was race.

The case was decided after the death of Justice Scalia, and the vote was four to three, with Justice Kagan recused. In the majority opinion, written by Justice Kennedy, the court reaffirmed that an admissions program at a public university is constitutionally evaluated under a standard of strict scrutiny. For such a program to satisfy that standard, a university has the burden of proving the existence of a compelling interest, a permissible purpose, use of a classification that is necessary to accomplish the purpose, and the narrow tailoring of the use of race to accomplish that purpose, including satisfying the burden to demonstrate that race-neutral alternatives were insufficient to do so. While the burden is on the university to demonstrate the existence of these factors, a university's determination that educational benefits would flow from implementing its admission program "is, in substantial measure, an academic judgment to which some, but not complete, judicial deference is proper."

The compelling interest relied upon by the University of Texas to justify its affirmative action program was its goal of conferring on its students "the educational benefits that flow from student body diversity." The majority emphasized that deference was appropriate in this case because the university had conducted extensive studies in revising its admissions program to respond to earlier challenges made against previous programs, that there was no claim of bad faith by the university in devising the new program, and that the university had supported the use of its admission criteria by "a reasoned, principled explanation." It held that the university's admission program was therefore constitutional, and that the petitioner had failed to show that she was denied equal treatment when her application was denied.

The use of race as a "subfactor" in the Personal Achievement Index was found to be permissible in this case because no other alternative was considered workable, and the petitioner had not identified any reasonable alternative. Moreover, the majority characterized the consideration of race as only a "factor of a factor of a factor." In addition, the new program had significantly raised minority students' participation in the student body, increasing African

American admissions by over 50 percent and Hispanic admissions by almost 100 percent.

While upholding the University of Texas' admission program, the majority emphasized that the university must continually reevaluate its admission standards to take changed circumstances into account.

In a fifty-one-page dissenting opinion, Justice Alito, joined by Chief Justice Roberts and Justice Thomas, criticized the holding, emphasizing that the university had failed to identify any specific compelling interest, but had only advanced an amorphous description of the students it considered as needed to enrich the diversity of the student body. As such, the dissenters believed the university had failed to meet the strict scrutiny burden of proving the existence of a clear compelling interest that was implemented by an admissions program narrowly tailored to serve that interest.

Justice Alito contended that rather than race being simply a "factor of a factor of a factor," the applicant's race was identified on the front of every admissions file and, in the judgment of the dissenters, race "pervades every aspect of [the] admissions process."

The dissenters went on to challenge every aspect of the university's justifications for considering race, pointing out that the university had been unable to define what the necessary "critical mass" of minority students was. With respect to the specific factors raised by the university in justification, Justice Alito evaluated claims it made based on demographics, classroom diversity, interracial diversity, and feelings of loneliness and isolation by prior minority students. On demographics, he argued that if the goal of the university was to match the minority percentage of the state as a whole, that would be racial balancing, and therefore unconstitutional. On classroom diversity, he noted that the university had been unable to define what level of classroom diversity was sufficient, and that there was no showing that the new approach to admissions would facilitate such diversity. With respect to interracial diversity, he pointed to prior contentions by the university that the Top 10 Percent program had resulted in the admission only of poor students from minority communities, and that more privileged minority students were needed to satisfy the goal of interracial diversity. In Justice Alito's view, "This is affirmative action gone wild." Concerning the argument that previous minority students felt lonely and isolated, Justice Alito noted that this was based only on anecdotal stories, and that no number of students so affected was ever given by the university. Finally, by relying upon the numerical increase of minority students under the new admissions program to justify that program, the dissenters described this approach as "a simple racial census," and further pointed out that the new admissions approach discriminated against Asian American students.

The dissenters concluded that even if a generic interest in attaining the educational benefits of diversity was constitutionally permissible, there was no narrow tailoring of the use of race by the University of Texas to achieve such benefits. Better alternatives were available in the view of the dissenters, and the most preferable alternative would be a "race-blind, holistic review that considers the applicant's unique characteristics and personal circumstances."

As the law stood after *Fisher II*, universities could claim generic and amorphous interests in student diversity to justify the use of race as a factor in achieving such diversity. This goal of achieving a diverse student body is now generally accepted not only by universities, but also, as demonstrated in the briefing of several cases, by the military and by several prominent corporations. Given the court's ruling, and the acceptance of the diversity goal by some important sectors of American society, to the extent that *Fisher II* remains controlling, all a university needs to do to justify an admissions program that utilizes race as a factor is to conduct detailed studies, identify a broad interest in student diversity, and relegate race to one of several factors in a new admissions program. Moreover, the conclusion of the court that deference should be accorded to a university's determination where there is a "reasoned, principled explanation" of its use of race to achieve student diversity will likely be triggered by implementing such studies.

Despite its acceptance by elite organizations and the military, the public is not on board with considering race in public college admissions. A Gallup poll conducted between June 29 and July 2, 2016, indicated that such colleges should admit applicants based solely on merit, with 70 percent of those polled taking this view. Only 26 percent believed that colleges should take the applicants' race and ethnicity into account in order to promote diversity on the campus. Disapproval of considering race as a major factor in admissions was shared by all ethnic groups. Thus, only 4 percent of whites, 17 percent of African Americans, and 26 percent of Hispanics felt that race and ethnicity should be a major factor in admissions. Significantly, there was no significant difference in these views between the general public and those Americans who felt they were most familiar with college admissions processes.

These public perceptions, when added to the closeness of the vote in *Fisher II*, the participation of only seven justices in deciding that case, the retirement of Justice Kennedy, the death of Justice Ginsburg, and the addition of Justices Gorsuch, Kavanaugh, and Barrett to the court, gave the court an opportunity to reconsider its earlier rulings on the use of a diversity goal to justify racial preferences in public university admissions. It took this opportunity in two cases challenging the admissions practices of Harvard College and the University of North Carolina. See *Students for Fair Admissions, Inc. v. President & Fellows of Harvard College* et al., Nos. 20–1199 and 21–707

(2022) These cases were argued in 2022, but not yet decided when this book went to press.

VOTER ELIMINATION OF AFFIRMATIVE ACTION IN STUDENT ADMISSIONS

Following the Supreme Court decisions in *Gratz* and *Grutter*, Michigan voters amended that state's constitution to prohibit the use of race-based preferences as part of the admissions process for state universities. By a six-to-two vote, with Justice Kagan not participating in the decision, the Supreme Court held that the judiciary lacked the power to set aside such laws. There was no opinion of the court, and the majority delivered four separate opinions, with three justices in the majority concurring only in the result.

Justice Kennedy's plurality opinion, which was joined by Chief Justice Roberts and Justice Alito, emphasized that the case was not about the constitutionality or the merits of race-conscious admissions policies in higher education. The plurality noted that "This case is not about how the debate about racial preferences should be resolved. It is about who may resolve it."

The plurality characterized the adoption of the constitutional amendment by Michigan voters as one that "exercised their privilege to enact laws as a basic exercise of their democratic power." As such, "Michigan voters used the initiative system to bypass public officials who were deemed not responsive to the concerns of a majority of the voters with respect to a policy of granting race-based preferences that raises difficult and delicate issues." In Justice Kennedy's view, "First Amendment dynamics would be disserved if this Court were to say that the question here at issue is beyond the capacity of the voters to debate and then to determine."

Opinions concurring in the judgment were delivered by Justices Scalia and Breyer, but the most striking and controversial opinion was the fifty-eight-page dissenting opinion authored by Justice Sotomayor, who was joined only by Justice Ginsburg. Justice Sotomayor devoted much of her opinion to an explication of the so-called political-process doctrine, a doctrine that Justices Scalia and Thomas indicated should be overruled, and one that the plurality watered down as both unsupported in precedent and as raising "serious constitutional concerns." As Justice Sotomayor formulated it, the political-process doctrine provides that "governmental action deprives minority groups of equal protection when it (1) has a racial focus, targeting a policy or program that 'inures primarily to the benefit of the minority' . . . and (2) alters the political process in a manner that uniquely burdens racial minorities' ability to achieve their goals through that process." Concluding that the Michigan constitutional amendment violated both prongs of this test, Justice Sotomayor argued that "majority rule is not without limit" under the Constitution, and that courts must "vigilantly polic[e] . . . the political process to ensure that the majority does not use other methods to prevent minority groups from partaking in that process on equal footing."

In the most publicized passages of her opinion, Justice Sotomayor proclaimed that "Race matters" for several reasons, including a "long history of racial minorities . . . being denied access to the political process," and "persistent racial inequality in society," an inequality "that cannot be ignored and that has produced stark socioeconomic disparities." Moreover, "Race matters because of the slights, the silent judgments that reinforce that most crippling of thoughts; 'I do not belong here.'"

Finally, Justice Sotomayor spent several pages of her dissenting opinion pointing out the virtues of "diversity in institutions of higher education," accusing her colleagues of "how little [they] understand about the reality of race in America."

In a brief concurring opinion, Chief Justice Roberts took issue with Justice Sotomayor's dissenting opinion, characterizing it as "expounding its own policy preferences in favor of taking race into account in college admissions." In his view, racial preferences could themselves have the "debilitating effect" of reinforcing doubts regarding whether a student "belongs," and good-faith disagreements regarding racial preferences can exist. As such, it "does more harm than good to question the openness and candor of those on either side of the debate."

Given the holding that voters may ban race-based admission programs in state universities and colleges, the court has empowered voters to have their say on such programs, legitimatizing a citizen's brake on perceived excesses enforced by public institutions of higher learning in this area.

AFFIRMATIVE ACTION IN EMPLOYMENT DECISIONS

Questions of the propriety under the Constitution of race-based affirmative-action programs in employment have been the subject of much litigation and have become another area of significant public controversy. One such litigation that reached the Supreme Court before most of the current justices had been confirmed involved the rights of competing candidates in public safety employment for promotion.

In *Ricci v. DeStefano* (2009), the Supreme Court reviewed the legality under Title VII of the Civil Rights Act of 1964 of a decision by the City of New Haven, Connecticut, to discard the results of examinations administered to city firefighters seeking promotions to lieutenant and captain because of the racially disparate results of those examinations. Thus, while some minority firefighters who took the examinations passed, the nineteen positions available for promotion went to the seventeen whites and two Hispanics who received the highest scores.

The City of New Haven's Charter required that a merit system be utilized for promotions and that only the most qualified receive promotions. The examinations in question were objective and consisted of two parts. A written examination was weighted at 60 percent, while an oral examination was weighted at 40 percent. Both examinations were designed by an out-of-state company specializing in the field, and both parts of the tests were objective. Moreover, an independent African American expert validated the entire examination process. Despite these facts, the city threw out the test results because of the racial disparity between white and minority candidates in their scores.

The Supreme Court reversed the decision of the Second Circuit, which had upheld the city's decision. In an opinion by Justice Kennedy, the court decided the case based upon the statutory provisions of Title VII, and declined to reach the separate constitutional question of whether the disparate impact provisions of that statute were consistent with the Fourteenth Amendment guarantee of Equal Protection. This was another example of the court's use of judicial minimalism and was consistent with the approach taken in the first *Fisher* decision and in *Northwest Austin Municipal Utility District* decision. Nevertheless, in a concurring opinion, Justice Scalia observed that the majority opinion merely "postpones the evil day" when the court would have to decide the constitutional question.

Under Title VII, Justice Kennedy held that the city had wrongly discarded the results of the examinations. He noted that "the City made its employment decision because of race. The City rejected the test results solely because the higher scoring candidates were white." The action of the city was wrong in Justice Kennedy's analysis because remedial action to redress discrimination is only appropriate where there is a "strong basis in evidence" supporting the necessity of taking such action. There was no such basis here because the city made its determination based on "raw racial results." Discarding test results required the city to demonstrate either that the examinations were not job-related or that there was a less discriminatory alternative available to the city. Since the record below did not show either, the city had improperly withheld promotions from the candidates who received the highest scores on the examinations.

In a concurring opinion, Justice Alito pointed out that the city's decision was made under racial pressure. He noted that an African American minister close to the mayor who had attacked the test results had previously threatened a race riot during the murder trial of a black man accused of murdering a white man.

In a dissenting opinion for herself, and for Justices Stevens, Souter, and Breyer, Justice Ginsburg began by noting that "context matters." Here, there had been a history of prior "pervasive" racial discrimination in New Haven, as well as a "legacy of racial discrimination" in firefighting in that city. She additionally noted that approximately 60 percent of New Haven residents were either black or Hispanic.

The dissenting opinion focused upon the use of a written component in the promotion examinations. Justice Ginsburg noted that written examinations were not sufficiently "practical," and that one other Connecticut city, Bridgeport, consequently weighted the oral portion of its promotion examinations heavier than the written because the oral examinations were more practical. The dissent characterized New Haven's heavy reliance on the written portion of the examinations as "a questionable practice, to say the least." Rather than utilize written examinations, Justice Ginsburg emphasized that alternatives were available to the city, including assessment tests, which put the firefighters in real-life situations to gauge their reactions and competence.

The *Ricci* decision graphically illustrates the difficult decisions governmental entities must make in employment-related decisions where test results lead to racial disparities among the applicants. The approach suggested by the dissenters has been chosen by many entities as the easy way out, in order to avoid accusations of racial discrimination, but the assessment approach itself suffers from possible subjectivity in assessing the qualifications of the applicants. In any event, the court will ultimately need to decide whether Title VII's disparate impact standard is itself unconstitutional because it yields results impermissibly based on race.

NOTES

1. The Supreme Court's extensive precedent on issues of racial discrimination is discussed at length in chapters 2 and 9 of *Shaping America*, supra, with particular emphasis on the historical context of those decisions.

2. Tom Goldstein's analysis of judicial minimalism appears in his SCOTUS blog commentary, "Analysis: Supreme Court invalidates Section 5's Coverage Scheme," June 22, 2009.

Chapter 6

The Right to Bear Arms

The Second Amendment provides that "A well regulated Militia, being necessary to the security of a free State, the right of the people to keep and bear Arms, shall not be infringed." The proper interpretation of this provision has generated significant public controversy, particularly in light of the numerous mass shootings in schools and public places all across the country from California and Colorado to Connecticut, Ohio, and Virginia, and to Texas and Florida. In each of the years 2020 through 2022, there were over six hundred mass shootings, a term that encompasses shootings in which four or more people were injured or killed. In the first three weeks of 2023, moreover, an additional sixty-nine people were killed in thirty-nine separate mass shootings across the country.

Against this background of increasing incidences of gun violence, there have been numerous and consistent demands by both Democratic Party leaders and the public at large calling for further restrictions on who may own a gun, what types of firearms can be banned, and what restrictions can be placed on ownership and use. On the other side, organizations such as the NRA and many politicians from both parties defend a broad right to keep and bear arms, including by carrying firearms in public. In the face of these developments, the Supreme Court has eviscerated its prior precedent and reinvigorated the protections afforded by the Second Amendment to individual gun owners not in a militia.

The eighteenth- and nineteenth-century cases did not address any of the basic issues relating to the scope of the Second Amendment, including who and what is protected by its provisions. The earliest case that considered such issues was *United States v. Miller* (1939). In a unanimous decision, the Supreme Court in that case upheld against a Second Amendment challenge a federal conviction for transporting a short-barreled shotgun in interstate commerce. *Miller* concluded that "in the absence of any evidence tending to show that possession or use of a 'shotgun having a barrel of less than eighteen inches in length' at this time has some reasonable relationship to the preservation or efficiency of a well regulated militia, we cannot say that the Second Amendment guarantees the right to keep and bear such an instrument."

After a gap of nearly seventy years following its decision in *Miller*, the Supreme Court revisited the Second Amendment protections, deciding several key issues, including whether the amendment protects an individual right to bear arms, what type of weapons are protected, and whether its prohibitions apply to the states. Despite several opportunities to do so, however, it initially declined, over several dissents, to decide whether the amendment protects the right to carry arms in public for self-defense, whether it prohibits imposing a multiday waiting period to obtain a firearm, or whether it protects a citizen applicant for a gun permit from having to show he or she has a "justifiable need to carry a handgun." In 2022, the court finally decided some of these issues.

THE INDIVIDUAL RIGHT TO BEAR ARMS

In *District of Columbia v. Heller* (2008), the Supreme Court was called upon to interpret the scope of the right to "keep and bear Arms" protected by the Second Amendment. Although the prefatory clause of the amendment refers to "militia," the court held that the amendment "guarantees the *individual* right to possess and carry weapons in case of confrontation," and that the right was not limited by that clause. In a majority opinion by Justice Scalia, which was joined by four other justices, the reference to "militia" was read "not [to] limit" the right to bear arms, but only to "announce . . . a purpose."

Given this interpretation, the court held unconstitutional District of Columbia laws that completely banned the private possession of handguns in the home, and also mandated that any firearms permitted to be kept at an individual's home must be unloaded and disassembled, or rendered inoperative by trigger lock or other device.

There were two dissenting opinions, the first by Justice John Paul Stevens, and the second by Judge Stephen Breyer. Both dissenting opinions were joined by Justices Stevens, Breyer, Souter, and Ginsburg, all of whom are no longer on the court. In the dissenters' view, the Second Amendment, in the words of Justice Breyer's dissenting opinion, only "protects militia-related, not self-defense related, interests." The dissenters relied heavily upon the Supreme Court's prior opinion in *United States v. Miller* (1939).

The majority dismissed the ruling in *Miller*, contending that the inapplicability of the Second Amendment in that case stemmed from the fact that "the *type of weapon at issue* was not eligible for Second Amendment protection."

All the opinions in *Heller* recognized that the right protected by the Second Amendment, whatever its scope, was subject to limitations. Justice Scalia, for example, noted that the right "is not unlimited," and that the majority opinion should not be taken "to cast doubt on long-standing prohibitions on possession of firearms by felons and the mentally ill, or laws forbidding the carrying of firearms in sensitive places such as schools and government buildings, or laws imposing conditions and qualifications on the commercial sale of arms," a list he noted was not "exhaustive."

In reaching their respective conclusions regarding the proper scope of the Second Amendment right to keep and bear arms, both Justice Scalia's majority opinion and Justice Stevens's dissenting opinion focused on the historical record at the time of the adoption of the Second Amendment. Indeed, the majority opinion manifests Justice Scalia's "textualism" approach, which he explained in his 1997 book, *A Matter of Interpretation: Federal Courts and the Law.* As applied to constitutional provisions, this approach focuses upon the original meaning of the constitutional text, not any current meaning. Indeed, Justice Scalia's majority opinion begins its analysis with the text of the Second Amendment, relies upon "other leading documents of the founding era," and cites an amicus briefed by professors of Linguistics and English to support his reading of the text. By contrast, in discussing what standard of review should be used to determine if a firearms regulation passes constitutional muster, Justice Breyer's dissenting opinion calls for "an interest-balancing inquiry," contending that "a court, not a legislature, must make the ultimate constitutional conclusion, exercising its 'independent judicial judgment' in light of the whole record to determine whether a law exceeds constitutional boundaries." Justice Scalia rejected this approach, calling it "judge empowering." He observed that "a constitutional guarantee subject to future judges' assessments of its usefulness is no constitutional guarantee at all. Constitutional rights are enshrined with the scope they were understood to have when the people adopted them, whether or not future legislatures or (yes) even future judges think that scope is too broad."

This tension between Justice Scalia's majority opinion and Justice Breyer's dissenting opinion demonstrates that the proper method of discerning the existence or scope of constitutional rights still divides the Supreme Court, and that neither the textualists, nor the exponents of a "living Constitution," have ended their debate on this issue at the Supreme Court. Significantly, however, the confirmations of Justices Gorsuch, Kavanaugh, and Barrett have strengthened the textualist presence on the court. Nevertheless, even if textualism is ultimately adopted as the proper approach for interpreting constitutional rights, a resort to history will not always be conclusive. Indeed, in the *McDonald* majority opinion, discussed immediately below, Justice

Alito conceded that the historical record review in *Heller* left "room for disagreement."

SECOND AMENDMENT APPLICATION TO THE STATES

In *McDonald v. Chicago* (2010), a divided Supreme Court held, by a five-to-four margin, that the Second Amendment right to keep and bear arms applied fully to the states. The case involved local Illinois ordinances that effectively banned possession of handguns in the home. The court struck down these ordinances as unconstitutional under the Second Amendment, reaffirming what it referred to as "the central holding" of its prior Second Amendment decision in *Heller*. The core of that holding was that "the Second Amendment protects the personal right to keep and bear arms for lawful purposes, most notably for self-defense within the home."

While many law professors, both conservative and liberal, as well as the parties to the case, relied heavily upon the Fourteenth Amendment Privileges or Immunities Clause to analyze the issue presented, the court chose instead to utilize the so-called selective incorporation approach it had previously used in determining whether provisions of the Bill of Rights applied to the states. The court adopted this approach because the Privileges or Immunities Clause had previously been restrictively construed by the court in the *Slaughterhouse Cases* (1873). Despite urgings by the parties and amici to overrule that decision, the majority opinion by Justice Alito held that the court would "decline to disturb" the *Slaughterhouse* decision.

Justice Thomas, who joined the majority opinion, also wrote a separate, lengthy concurring opinion indicating he believed that the *Slaughterhouse Cases* were wrongly decided, and that he would use the Privileges or Immunities Clause instead of selective incorporation to resolve the issue presented. In his view, the right to keep and bear arms was protected as a privilege of United States citizenship. He repeated his view on the Privileges or Immunities Clause in *Timbs v. Indiana* (2019), in which a unanimous court held that the Eighth Amendment's Excessive Fines Clause was an incorporated protection applicable to the states under the Due Process Clause of the Fourteenth Amendment. Justice Thomas concurred in the judgment in *Timbs*, and Justice Gorsuch wrote a concurring opinion, citing Justice Thomas's opinion in *McDonald*, and noting that "As an original matter, I acknowledge, the appropriate vehicle for incorporation may well be the Fourteenth Amendment's Privileges or Immunities Clause, rather than, as this Court has long assumed, the Due Process Clause."

In determining that the Second Amendment right to keep and bear arms applied to the states, the *McDonald* court ruled that the Second Amendment right was "fundamental . . . to ordered liberty," as required under the selective incorporation approach. Justice Alito's opinion noted that the right was fundamental, particularly in the context of the handgun possession ban put in place by the ordinances in question, because individual self-defense was "the central component" of the Second Amendment.

The majority opinion exhaustively reviewed the history of both the Second Amendment and the Fourteenth Amendment, as well as English law and legal commentaries, following the approach taken in Justice Scalia's majority opinion in *Heller*. In his dissenting opinion for himself, Justice Ginsburg, and Justice Kagan, Justice Breyer cited eight articles by historians who considered the *Heller* decision "flawed," contending that the historical record did not support an individual right to keep and bear arms. Justice Breyer warned that relying upon historians was dangerous for "nonexpert judges" to do in rendering their decisions, particularly because the historians themselves often "strongly disagree." Significantly, Justice Alito conceded that there was "certainly room for disagreement about *Heller*'s analysis of the history of the right to keep and bear arms."

In two dissenting opinions, one by Justice Stevens and the other by Justice Breyer, arguments were made that principles of federalism required that decisions on restricting the possession or use of guns were better made at the local level, giving deference to local preferences and varying approaches tailored to local conditions. The majority rejected this approach, finding that the right in question to keep and bear arms was a fundamental one, and thus could not be abridged by state or local governments.

After *Heller* and *McDonald*, significant questions still remained regarding the power of federal, state, or local governments to regulate the sale, possession, or use of firearms. In *Heller*, for example, Justice Scalia specifically noted that the Second Amendment right "is not unlimited," citing such "long-standing prohibitions on the possession of firearms by felons and the mentally ill, or laws forbidding the carrying of firearms in sensitive places such as schools and government buildings, or laws imposing conditions and qualifications on the commercial sale of arms." Indeed, Justice Scalia noted that this list was not "exhaustive." As such, the permissibility of any future regulations on the sale, possession, and use of firearms is unclear, particularly where the regulation does not impact on the possession or use of handguns by individuals. The right to purchase and possess a gun for self-defense seems secure, especially in light of the *Caetano* decision discussed immediately below.

Six years after the court ruled that the Second Amendment fully applied to the states, it strongly emphasized that it meant what it said. In *Caetano v. Massachusetts* (2016), it summarily reversed the criminal conviction of a Massachusetts woman for possessing a stun gun. In upholding her conviction, the Massachusetts Supreme Judicial Court had held that the Second Amendment did not extend its protections to stun guns for three reasons. First, stun guns were not in common use when the Second Amendment was enacted. Second, stun guns were held to be dangerous per se and unusual. Third, stun guns were found not to be readily adaptable to military use.

The Supreme Court granted certiorari, and summarily vacated the conviction in a unanimous per curiam opinion, without even hearing oral argument. In one and a half pages, it rebutted the three prongs of the Massachusetts court's reasoning, noting that (1) *Heller* clearly stated that the Second Amendment applied to arms not in existence when the amendment was enacted, (2) the dangerous per se and unusual argument fell for the same reason, and (3) *Heller* also rejected the argument that "only those weapons useful in warfare are protected."

In a concurring opinion, Justice Alito augmented these points, setting forth the domestic violence backdrop that led to Ms. Caetano purchasing the stun gun. Joined by Justice Thomas, he reasoned that "the pertinent Second Amendment inquiry is whether stun guns are commonly possessed by law-abiding citizens for lawful purposes *today*," and concluded that "stun guns are widely owned and accepted as a legitimate means of self-defense across the country." As such, the categorical ban imposed by Massachusetts violated the Second Amendment. Indeed, in his view, "If the fundamental right of self-defense does not protect Caetano, then the safety of all Americans is left to the mercy of state authorities who may be more concerned about disarming the people than about keeping them safe."

Despite the court's forceful ruling in *Caetano*, litigation attempting to limit or eliminate an individual's right to bear arms has continued. This is not surprising given the increasing frequency of mass shootings and the well-financed organizations contending on both sides of the issue. Gun-rights advocates will continue to seek to eliminate restrictions on what type of weapons may be sold, on what restrictions may be imposed on purchasers or sellers, and on where and when weapons may be carried. By contrast, organizations seeking to enact gun-control measures will continue to seek to extend limits in each of these areas.

CARRYING FIREARMS IN PUBLIC, TRANSPORTING THEM, AND MULTIDAY WAITING PERIODS

One issue that has been the subject of significant litigation is whether the Second Amendment grants a right to carry firearms in public. The Supreme Court declined over several terms to decide this issue despite the existence of conflicting decisions by both federal and state courts. Dissenting from one denial of review on this issue, Justice Thomas, joined by Justice Gorsuch, called on the court to decide this issue as "one of national importance" (*Peruta v. California* [2017]). Thomas pointed out that twenty-six states had asked the court to resolve this issue, and that five federal courts of appeals and three of the highest state courts had reached conflicting decisions on it as of 2017. He concluded the court should not "stand by idly while a State denies its citizens that right, particularly when their very lives may depend on it."

Justice Thomas noted that state courts as early as the mid-nineteenth century had recognized the right to openly carry firearms in public, and that the *Heller* decision, in defining "bear arms," stated that it included the ability to "carry [firearms] upon the person or in the clothing or in a pocket." The dissent concluded that "I find it extremely improbable that the Framers understood the Second Amendment to protect little more than carrying a gun from the bedroom to the kitchen." This was particularly so because the *Heller* court emphasized that self-defense was "the *central component* of the [Second Amendment] right itself." Justice Thomas concluded that "The Court's decision to deny certiorari in this case reflects a distressing trend: the treatment of the Second Amendment as a disfavored right."

Justice Thomas raised the same concerns regarding his perception of the disfavored status of Second Amendment rights in his dissent from the denial of review in *Silvester v. Becerra* (2018). In that decision, the Ninth Circuit had ruled that a mandatory ten-day waiting period to obtain a firearm did not violate the Second Amendment. He pointed out that, by contrast, the court would likely review a ten-day waiting period for a woman seeking an abortion (having earlier struck down a twenty-four-hour waiting period for an abortion), or a waiting period before racist speech could be published.

While the court did avoid reviewing several Second Amendment cases before 2019, a rash of school shootings in 2018 might have stimulated the court to review new bans on Second Amendment rights that emerged from the controversy resulting from these incidents. Those incidents have mobilized significant protests and resulted in multiple calls for the enactment of more restrictive firearms regulations. Thus, in early 2019, the court granted review in *New York State Rifle & Pistol Association v. New York*, Docket No. 18–280, *cert. granted* January 22, 2019. In that case, the petitioners attacked a ban imposed by New York City on "transporting a licensed, locked and unloaded handgun to a home or shooting range outside city limits." The issue presented was whether such a ban was "consistent with the Second Amendment, the commerce clause, and the constitutional right to travel."

After the Supreme Court accepted the case for review, the New York authorities in that case argued that the dispute had been mooted by the subsequent passage of laws repealing the original law. In a remarkable amicus brief, five Senate Democrats supported the New York position, but went even further, arguing that the Supreme Court's integrity would be compromised and legislative reprisals, including restructuring of the court, possibly taken, if the court decided the case on the merits, especially if it ruled that the New York law was unconstitutional.

The Supreme Court, on April 27, 2020, ruled by a six-to-three margin that the case was moot. It vacated the judgment and remanded the case to the Second Circuit Court of Appeals for further appropriate proceedings.

In a dissenting opinion written by Justice Alito, and joined by Justices Gorsuch and Thomas, the argument was made that the case was not moot, and that the New York law was unconstitutional. Indeed, Justice Alito commented that "This is not a close question. The answer follows directly from *Heller*." Justice Alito also pointedly noted the comments by the Senate Democrats in their "prominent" amicus brief.

While Justice Kavanaugh agreed the case was moot, he nevertheless indicated that he "share[d] Justice Alito's concern" that lower courts, at both the federal and state level, were not "properly applying" the rulings in *Heller* and *McDonald*, and that the court therefore "should address that issue soon," pointing out that there were several petitions pending before the court involving Second Amendment issues.

Despite Justice Kavanaugh's urging that the court should address the issue "soon," the court denied review of several Second Amendment cases again in 2020. Once again, Justice Thomas, joined this time in part by Justice Kavanaugh, protested the refusal to grant review in one such case. *Rogers v. Grewal* (June 15, 2020) involved a challenge to a New Jersey law that required an applicant for a gun permit to demonstrate "a justifiable need to carry a handgun." Justice Thomas accused the court of a "decade-long failure to protect the Second Amendment," and pointed out that the *Rogers* case gave the court "the opportunity to provide guidance on the proper approach for evaluating Second Amendment claims; acknowledge that the Second Amendment protects the right to carry in public; and resolve a square Circuit split on the constitutionality of justifiable-need restrictions on that right." He noted that it had been more than ten years since the court's prior substantive rulings on the scope of the Second Amendment, and that many of the lower courts, in his view, "have resisted our decisions in *Heller* and *McDonald*."

As such, "Whatever one may think about the proper approach to analyzing Second Amendment challenges, it is clearly time for us to resolve the issue."

The court did finally grant review of another Second Amendment case (*New York State Rifle & Pistol Association v. Corlett* [2021]). Recaptioned as *New York State Rifle & Pistol Association v. Bruen* (2022), it raised the issue of whether, or under what conditions, individuals may be permitted to carry a firearm in public. The New York law required an applicant to show "proper cause" to do so, including demonstrating a "special need for self-protection distinguishable from that of the general community." The New York law differed from laws in forty-three other states that require licensing but provide that a license "*shall* issue" under certain conditions, including firearms training and a check of medical health records. By contrast, the New York law stated only that such a license "*may* issue" under the conditions noted above.

In a majority opinion written by Justice Thomas for six members of the court, New York's restrictions on the right to carry handguns in public were struck down as violative of the Second and Fourteenth Amendments because those amendments "protect an individual's right to carry a handgun for self-defense outside the home."

Initially, in a very significant ruling, the majority rejected the test followed by several courts of appeal. Those courts mandated a two-part test, focusing first on the history of restrictions on gun ownership and use, and second, on a means-end scrutiny, balancing the rights of gun owners against governmental interests. The Supreme Court majority, by contrast, ruled that the "text, as informed by history" is the proper standard, and that "the text controls." A means-end balancing test, utilizing a standard of intermediate scrutiny, is improper because the Second Amendment itself provided the necessary balancing of interests. The text of the Second Amendment establishes a right to "keep and *bear* arms." The use of the word "bear" "naturally encompasses public carry." And restrictions on that right must pass the strict scrutiny standard of review.

In the view of the majority, there are "two relevant metrics" to determine the constitutionality of governmental restrictions on public carry. These are "whether modern and historical regulations impose a comparable burden on the right of armed self-defense, and . . . whether that regulatory burden is comparably justified." In sum, "the government must affirmatively prove that its firearms regulation is part of the historical tradition that delimits the outer bounds of the right to keep and bear arms."

In a lengthy portion of the majority opinion, Justice Thomas then reviewed the history regarding restrictions on public carry from English law to the end of the nineteenth century and beyond. He concluded that most of these restrictions did not burden the public carrying of firearms, but were aimed instead at concealed weapons, "unusual or unlawful weapons," or weapons that were used "to terrorize the people." As to the nineteenth-century bans on carrying guns imposed in the territories, Justice Thomas contended that they affected only a few people, were based on the unusual circumstances existing in the territories, and were never tested in court. Moreover, the important history of Reconstruction confirmed that "public carry for self-defense remained a central component of the protections that the Fourteenth Amendment secured for all citizens."

In conclusion, the majority ruled that the public understanding of the propriety of imposing restrictions on public carry was the same in 1791 and 1868, and that it was not appropriate to rely on English history, which was ambiguous in any event, or post-enactment history, which must not be given "more weight than it can rightly bear."

Significantly, all the other conservative justices except Justice Gorsuch chose to write separate opinions indicating that the constitutionality of many other restrictions were not affected by the Opinion of the Court. Justice Alito pointed out that the majority opinion did not decide who may buy firearms, the requirements to do so, or "the kinds of weapons that people may possess." Joined by Chief Justice Roberts, Justice Kavanaugh concluded that the majority opinion does not prohibit licensing requirements, noting the forty-three states that have "shall issue" laws imposing reasonable restrictions on the right to carry arms in public. He also reaffirmed the *Heller* observations that Second Amendment permits a "variety" of gun regulations. Finally, Justice Barrett pointed out that the majority opinion does not decide how post-ratification practice bears on the original meaning of the Second Amendment, or whether primary reliance should be placed upon the Second or Fourteenth Amendment understanding where, unlike in this case, there was a difference in understandings.

Justice Breyer wrote a dissenting opinion, joined by Justices Sotomayor and Kagan. As Justice Alito noted disapprovingly in his concurring opinion, the dissenting opinion starts off by recounting, over most of nine pages, many episodes of gun violence in America. Turning to the merits, Justice Breyer attacked the majority opinion on several points.

First, he criticized the majority for not letting an evidentiary record be developed in the lower court to show "how the law has actually been applied on the ground." For example, while the majority claimed the law imposed "demanding requirements," *amici*, including the American Bar Association and the City of New York, contended that the law was "flexible" in application.

Second, Justice Breyer pointed out that the "means-end" approach rejected by the majority was used by virtually every federal circuit court of appeals. Moreover, contrary to the majority's suggestion that only the

Second Amendment was being subjected to such a standard, the dissenters pointed out that the same or similar approach was used by the court on First Amendment free-speech and free-exercise claims, as well as in cases involving equal protection and Fourth Amendment claims.

Third, the six other states that employ a "may issue" approach to gun licensing are, like New York, "densely populated urban areas [which] face different kinds and degrees of dangers from gun violence than rural areas." This explains why stricter licensing laws are appropriate in such jurisdictions.

Fourth, the majority's exclusive reliance on history adopts an approach that could be difficult for judges to apply, especially where historians disagree. For example, some linguistic experts filed an amicus brief purporting to show that the phrase "bear arms" was almost exclusively used historically in a military context. Moreover, reliance on history is problematic given "modern-day circumstances that [the Framers] could not have anticipated."

Fifth, after reviewing at length the historical laws, Justice Breyer contended that Justice Thomas's summary of the historical evidence was faulty, since it ignored the "700-year Anglo-American tradition of regulating the public carriage of firearms in general, and concealed or concealable firearms in particular."

Where does this leave the court on firearms regulation? This much can be said. *Heller* established an individual right to keep and bear arms, and *McDonald* decided that this right applied to state regulation. *New York State Rifle* protected the individual's right to carry a firearm in public, subject to reasonable regulations. As noted in the opinions themselves, and especially in the concurring opinions joined by four conservative justices in *New York State Rifle*, many questions nevertheless remain unanswered regarding what constitutional restrictions can be placed upon gun ownership or use. These include, among several others, whether AK47s and firearms other than handguns and stun guns (see *Caetano*) can be prohibited, whether "red flag" laws are constitutional, and whether minimum-age requirements can be imposed on the purchase of a firearm.

Chapter 7

Cruel and Unusual Punishment

The Eighth Amendment bans the infliction of "cruel and unusual punishments." These four words are not self-explanatory, and they raise numerous issues regarding their proper application. One notable feature of the court's recent decisions in this area has been a relatively muted response to decisions that have radically changed and eviscerated historical understandings of the relatively limited application of this constitutional ban. While some politicians and conservative commentators have criticized these decisions, little coverage has been given to them by the media, and public protests are absent.

The earliest cases in which the court addressed the meaning of "cruel and unusual punishments" involved the *methods* of execution prescribed for capital crimes. These cases concluded that "Punishments are cruel when they involve torture or a lingering death." See, for example, *In re Kemmler* (1890) (execution by electrocution is not cruel). Over time, the court has greatly expanded its view of what is cruel and unusual.

The Supreme Court shifted from reviewing the methods of execution to considering the *severity of the punishments* inflicted in the pivotal case of *Weems v. United States* (1910). In that case, a sentence of fifteen years' imprisonment "at hard and painful labor" imposed upon a government official convicted of falsifying public documents was held by a plurality of the court to violate the Eighth Amendment. Justice Joseph McKenna concluded, after reviewing prior case law and the writings of constitutional scholars, that "punishments come under the condemnation of the Bill of Rights, both on account of their degree and kind." He wrote that the amendment, "in the opinion of learned commentators, may be . . . progressive, and is not fastened to the obsolete, but may acquire meaning as public opinion becomes enlightened by a humane justice." In dissent, future Chief Justice Edward White, joined by Justice Oliver Wendell Holmes, criticized McKenna's interpretation, which, in White's view, was "repugnant to the natural import of the language employed in the clause." In the dissenters' view, the Eighth

Amendment looked at the modes of punishment, not at the "degree of severity" imposed by the sentence.

The Supreme Court gradually extended the reasoning of the plurality opinion in *Weems* to a number of punishments, concluding, for example, that depriving a soldier who had deserted from the army of his American citizenship constituted a cruel and unusual punishment (*Trop v. Dulles* [1991]). In that case, the court reasoned that the Cruel and Unusual Punishments Clause "must draw its meaning from the evolving standards of decency that mark the progress of a maturing society."

Most notably, the court repeatedly in the 1970s and 1980s also placed a number of limitations on the imposition of the death penalty. In *Furman v. Georgia* (1972), the court went so far as to hold that the death penalty, as then determined throughout the entire country, was unconstitutionally imposed because of the failure to instruct judges and juries with appropriate guidelines before imposing the penalty. In *Gregg v. Georgia* (1976), the court then ruled that a Georgia procedure that divided the trial of a defendant subject to capital punishment into two phases was an appropriate way to determine whether the punishment of death was permissible. In phase one, the guilt or innocence of the defendant is determined. Should the defendant be found guilty, a second phase is scheduled to determine those circumstances that should be taken into account as mitigating or aggravating factors before any decision can be made to impose the death penalty. This has become the national standard employed to date in all capital punishment trials.

The approach of the Supreme Court to determining issues relating to cruel and unusual punishments continues to evolve. Over a hundred years later, the majority of the Supreme Court currently takes the "progressive" approach of Justice McKenna, while a vocal minority would follow the textualist approach of Justices White and Holmes. Unlike the court's textualist approach to the Second Amendment in *Heller*, the Supreme Court has treated questions under the Eighth Amendment very differently, fundamentally following the approach of *Weems* by emphasizing the court's independent judicial judgment to construe the operative phrase,"cruel and unusual punishments," in harmony with developing public consensus. Utilizing this approach, the Supreme Court in the twenty-first century has construed the Eighth Amendment in several noteworthy cases involving criminal sentencing, holding that the amendment limits the ability of judges to impose certain criminal sentences, with two justices even suggesting that imposition of the death penalty itself might constitute the infliction of a cruel and unusual punishment.

LIFE WITHOUT PAROLE FOR JUVENILES FOR CRIMES NOT INVOLVING HOMICIDE

The Supreme Court significantly expanded the scope of the Eighth Amendment's Cruel and Unusual Punishments Clause in *Graham v. Florida* (2010). There, by a six-to-three vote, the court held that the clause prohibited imposing a sentence of life imprisonment without the possibility of parole on a juvenile offender who had committed a non-homicide crime. *Graham* involved a burglary committed by a juvenile who was sixteen years old at the time of the crime, and the court concluded that he and other juveniles sentenced to life imprisonment could not constitutionally be deprived of the opportunity to obtain parole, but must instead have "some realistic opportunity to obtain release."

In reaching their conclusion, the majority followed the two-pronged approach set down in the prior decision in *Roper v. Simmons* (2005).[1] They first looked at the objective indicia of state laws and practices involving the imposition of life sentences without parole on juveniles, and then invoked the court's independent judgment as to the constitutionality of imposing such a punishment. With respect to the first factor, while the court noted that some thirty-seven states permitted the imposition of such a sentence, the majority chose instead to emphasize the fact that a sentence of life imprisonment without the possibility of parole was rarely imposed upon juveniles. Pointing out that there were only 129 prisoners serving such a sentence at the time of its decision, the majority concluded that there was a "consensus against its use."

Turning to the exercise of its independent judgment, the court relied upon amicus briefs filed by the American Medical Association and the American Psychological Association to conclude that the brains of juveniles are less mature, and that juveniles are more capable of change than adults are. As such, from a "moral standpoint," juveniles had "limited culpability," and it was not constitutionally permissible to deprive them of a chance for parole based upon the development of their character during their imprisonment.

The majority also pointed out that only eleven countries in the world permitted the imposition of a life sentence without the possibility of parole upon juveniles, and that in practice only two countries (the United States and Israel) actually imposed such sentences. Given the storm of opposition to the majority's citation to world practices in its *Roper* opinion, the *Graham* majority noted that world practice "does not control our decision" and is "not dispositive," but it is also "not irrelevant."

Chief Justice Roberts filed a concurring opinion in which he agreed that the imposition of a life sentence without the possibility of parole on the sixteen-year-old defendant before the court was unconstitutional.

Nevertheless, he criticized the majority for imposing a strict and categorical rule prohibiting the use of such a punishment in all cases involving juveniles.

In a dissenting opinion that was joined by Justices Scalia and Alito, Justice Thomas emphasized that in its more recent Eighth Amendment decisions, the court had previously emphasized that "death is different," but was now extending the reasoning applied in death penalty cases to other sentences. Moreover, Justice Thomas noted that the majority opinion assumed courts were more capable of making moral judgments then were legislatures. But legislators, he noted, can hold hearings and are in a better position to balance the respective interests on such questions of sentencing than courts are.

The dissenters also noted that the only relevant evidence of a consensus on the issue of sentencing is found in state legislation, and that the consensus with respect to imposing sentences of life imprisonment without the possibility of parole on a juvenile was clearly in favor of the propriety of such sentences, given the thirty-seven states that permitted it. Moreover, the fact that such sentences were *rarely* imposed in practice did not mitigate against the possibility of such a sentence *ever* being imposed.

Justice Thomas then turned to the exercise of the court's independent judgment, criticizing the reliance in the majority opinion upon psychological research. He noted there is a difference between a "fleeting symptom" of "transient" antisocial behavior by a juvenile, on the one hand, and a "lifelong pattern" or "life-course-persistent style" of such behavior, on the other hand, and that juries are capable of making such determinations based on the evidence presented in a particular case.

LIFE WITHOUT PAROLE FOR JUVENILES FOR HOMICIDE

The Supreme Court further extended its cruel and unusual punishments jurisprudence in *Miller v. Alabama* (2012), in which the court held, in a five-to-four decision, that even in the case of homicide, imposition of a sentence of life imprisonment without the possibility of parole on a juvenile is not constitutionally permissible in the absence of an individualized sentencing process. *Miller* involved the disposition of two cases, both involving fourteen-year-old defendants who had been convicted of murder and sentenced to life imprisonment without the possibility of parole.

In her majority opinion, Justice Kagan concluded that the Eighth Amendment requires both "individualized sentencing for defendants facing the most serious penalties" and punishment that is proportional to the crime. In reviewing the cases, she concluded there were "two strands of precedent" that interpreted the proportionality requirement. The first line of cases invalidated any sentence under which there was a mismatch between the defendant's culpability and the severity of the punishment imposed. Here, "children are constitutionally different from adults for purposes of sentencing," because of their "diminished culpability and greater prospects for reform." In reaching this conclusion, the majority relied, as had the majority in *Graham*, on articles and studies from "science and social science."

The second strand of precedent relied upon by the majority had ruled that capital punishment may never be mandatory. The *Miller* majority extended this to sentences that imposed life imprisonment without the possibility of parole. As in *Graham*, *Miller* concluded that such a sentence resembled the death penalty, at least in the context of juvenile defendants, and should be treated in the same manner. Having reviewed the prior cases, Justice Kagan's opinion for the majority concluded that "the confluence of these two lines of precedent leads to the conclusion than mandatory life-without-parole sentences for juveniles violates the Eighth Amendment."

Justice Kagan dismissed the fact that some twenty-eight states and the federal government mandated a sentence of life imprisonment without the possibility of parole for homicides. In her opinion, these legislative enactments did not represent any "objective indicia" of a community consensus on the acceptability of that punishment being imposed upon juveniles across the board. Instead, she contended that the court was not absolutely *barring* the imposition of such a punishment in all cases involving juveniles. Instead, the majority was only requiring that juveniles faced with the possibility of such a sentence be afforded a process of individualized sentencing.

Finally, the majority explicitly noted that while it was not categorically barring the imposition upon a juvenile convicted of homicide of a sentence of life imprisonment without the possibility of parole, nevertheless "we think appropriate occasions for sentencing juveniles to this harshest possible penalty will be uncommon." *Miller* thus holds that such a sentence may not mandatorily be imposed upon a juvenile convicted of homicide, and that juveniles must instead receive an individualized consideration of their particular circumstances before sentencing.

The majority opinion generated three vigorous dissents written respectively by Chief Justice Roberts for himself and Justices Scalia, Thomas, and Alito; by Justice Thomas, joined by Justice Scalia; and by Justice Alito, also joined by Justice Scalia.

Chief Justice Roberts pointed out first that a sentence of life imprisonment without the possibility of parole imposed upon a juvenile was not "unusual" because there were 2,500 juveniles in the United States then serving such a sentence for homicides they had committed. Second, the court's prior reliance on the existence of "objective indicia" of a community consensus also militated against the decision made by the majority since a majority of states as well as the federal government imposed the same penalty for juvenile murderers. Thus, unlike the case presented in *Graham*, a sentence of life imprisonment without the possibility of parole imposed upon a juvenile was not “exceedingly rare.” The chief justice next noted that *Graham* and prior decisions had relied heavily upon the fact that murder was different in kind than other crimes, but the court majority was now abandoning that distinction, as well as equating life imprisonment without parole with the death penalty. Finally, Chief Justice Roberts concluded that the majority opinion in *Miller* represented a “further judicial displacement of the legislative role in prescribing punishments for crime.”

Justice Thomas’s dissenting opinion took issue with many of the court’s prior decisions on what constituted “cruel and unusual punishments,” contending (mirroring Justices White and Holmes) that the Eighth Amendment was concerned only with the “character of the punishment,” rather than the process of imposing a sentence. He also echoed the point made by Chief Justice Roberts that the prior decisions of the court had emphasized that the death penalty was different in kind from other punishments, and should continue to be treated as *sui generis*.

Justice Alito’s dissenting opinion was particularly harsh on the majority, accusing it of having “discarded” the “pretense” of “heeding” a state legislative consensus as being “objective indicia” of what constituted acceptable punishment, because the majority effectively “overrules . . . [the] legislative judgments” of twenty-eight states and the federal government. Justice Alito also noted that the court’s Eighth Amendment case law had now become “entirely inward looking,” resting almost exclusively upon the court’s independent judgment as to the acceptability of any particular sentence.

In *Montgomery v. Louisiana* (2016), with the same four dissenters, the court ruled that *Miller* was to be applied retroactively. Speaking for the majority, Justice Kennedy ruled that *Miller* announced a new “substantive rule of constitutional law” that must be retroactively applied. However, in a six-to-three ruling authored by Justice Kavanaugh, the court refused to go further to require the sentencing judge to make an separate factual finding of permanent incorrigibility, or in the alternative, provide an explanation on the record with an “implicit finding” of permanent incorrigibility. In the case before the court, the sentencing judge recognized he had discretion in imposing a sentence, but nevertheless concluded that a life sentence without parole was appropriate. No more was required (*Jones v. Mississippi* [2021]).

While the majority justices in *Montgomery* stated that extending parole eligibility to juvenile offenders would not “impose an onerous burden on the States,” in reality the impact of the decisions in *Graham*, *Miller*, and *Montgomery* is enormous. In the Commonwealth of Pennsylvania alone, for example, some five hundred juveniles (three hundred from Philadelphia) were serving life sentences without the possibility of parole in 2012, and each of those sentences had to be reviewed. By October 2016, the Philadelphia district attorney (since indicted and convicted, on his guilty plea, on corruption charges) had extended only sixty-five offers of parole. One incarcerated convict had already served sixty-three years in prison for two murders he had committed when he was fifteen years old. He was offered a plea deal that would have made him eligible for parole, but he declined, insisting instead that he be released immediately. In other counties in Pennsylvania, judges adopted a variety of approaches, including ordering immediate releases and reducing sentences to time served without conducting any hearing. Ultimately, the Supreme Court of Pennsylvania ruled there was a presumption against imposing a life-without-parole sentence and that the prosecution was now required to prove beyond a reasonable doubt that the particular defendant was incapable of rehabilitation.[2]

Reviewing these decisions from the viewpoints of appropriate judicial review and proper exercise of the Supreme Court's powers, the minimization of the legislative judgments of both a majority of states and of the federal government as to the acceptability of a sentence imposing life imprisonment without the possibility of parole, combined with a heightened application of the court's "independent judgment," raise serious questions as to the point at which the court will cease to provide a subjective review of legislatively approved sentences. Finally, the court's heavy reliance upon "science and social science" to back its conclusions opens it to accusations that it is cherry-picking the literature to find articles and studies that support its subjective conclusions. In the area of its Eighth Amendment jurisprudence, the court may fairly be characterized as exercising what Justice Byron White once called "raw judicial power."

INTELLECTUAL DISABILITIES THAT AFFECT SENTENCING

This choice to exercise the court's raw power in determining constitutionally permissible methods of criminal punishment continued in *Hall v. Florida* (2014), the fourth Eighth Amendment decision decided since 2009. In that case, the Supreme Court reviewed the evidence required to impose capital punishment where the defendant makes a claim that he or she was intellectually disabled. This was necessary because the Supreme Court had previously ruled in *Atkins v. Virginia* (2002) that the Eighth Amendment prohibited execution of a person suffering from an intellectual disability.

The Florida law at issue in *Hall* defined *intellectual disability* "to require an IQ test score of 70 or less." By a five-to-four margin, the court held that

"This rigid rule . . . creates an unacceptable risk that persons with intellectual disability will be executed, and thus is unconstitutional." In his majority opinion, Justice Kennedy noted that the Florida rule "takes an IQ score as final and conclusive evidence of a defendant's intellectual capacity, when experts in the field would consider other evidence." In Hall's case, the key IQ measurement came in at seventy-one although in prior scores in tests taken over some forty years, his IQ ranged between 60 and 80.

Considering the objective indicia prong utilized to assess whether a punishment is cruel and unusual, Justice Kennedy contended that only a maximum of nine states had laws comparable to the Florida rule, while forty-one other states either barred capital punishment or permitted additional evidence to be presented on the issue of intellectual disability. Much of the majority opinion, however, went beyond the objective indicia provided by state legislation in favor of the court's independent judgment. This, in turn, was "informed by the views of medical experts," which, although not determinative, nevertheless represented "informed assessments." Reviewing the conclusions of professional associations and other experts, including "clinical definitions of intellectual disability," Justice Kennedy noted that they visualize IQ as a range, rather than as a fixed number. As such, these expert assessments, in the majority's view, support "the Court's independent assessment that an individual with an IQ test score 'between 70 and 75 or lower' . . . may show intellectual disability by presenting additional evidence regarding difficulties in adaptive functioning."

As in the prior cases, the dissenters would have none of this. In an opinion by Justice Alito, they attacked the majority for an overreliance on "professional societies, most notably the American Psychiatric Association." In view of the dissenting justices, "what counts are our society's standards—which is to say, the standards of the American people—not the standards of professional associations, which at best represent the views of a small professional elite." In addition, since such professional associations often change their views, "tying Eighth Amendment law to these views will lead to instability and continue to fuel protracted litigation."

The dissenters also criticized the majority opinion for its analysis of state law under the objective indicia prong. Justice Alito argued there was no actual consensus among the states on the IQ score issue presented in the case. In reality, the states that had considered the issue were nearly evenly split. Moreover, it was not fair to include states that had abolished the death penalty in the calculation because that "says nothing about how that State would resolve the evidentiary problem of identifying defendants who are intellectually disabled." Given the lack of any consensus, the dissenters concluded that "we have no basis for holding that Florida's method contravenes our society's standards of decency."

In the wake of the *Hall* decision, we can expect that lawyers representing death row inmates will now contend that new psychological and social science research requires that even the IQ range of 70 to 75 identified in the *Hall* majority as the trigger for permitting additional evidence on the issue of intellectual disability is itself too restrictive. Thus, to the extent that such authorities are relied upon, they—not the courts—ultimately become the adjudicator of what is cruel and unusual.

THE DEATH PENALTY

In *Glossip v. Gross* (2015), prisoners on death row in Oklahoma challenged the use of the drug midazolam, the first of three drugs employed to execute inmates in that state, claiming that the drug "creates an unacceptable risk of severe pain." Five justices, in an opinion written by Justice Alito, first found the prisoners had failed to show that the risk of harm from the use of midazolam was substantial as compared to "a known and available method of execution." In addition, and as an independent ground for the ruling, the majority held that the prisoners had failed to demonstrate that midazolam was ineffective to prevent severe pain, and thus failed to meet the standard of proof required to obtain a preliminary injunction to halt the use of the challenged drug.

While four justices dissented in two separate opinions, the dissenting opinion of Justice Breyer, who was joined by Justice Ginsburg, was most noteworthy because it explicitly called on the court to decide "whether the death penalty violates the Constitution." In doing so, he was questioning the court's prior opinion in *Gregg v. Georgia* (1976), where the court ruled that "the punishment of death does not invariably violate the Constitution." Concluding that "I believe it highly likely that the death penalty violates the Eighth Amendment," he listed "three fundamental constitutional defects" in the administration of the death penalty. First, the death penalty is "cruel" because innocent people have been executed. Second, it is cruel because it is imposed arbitrarily, that is, without "reasonable consistency," and its imposition even varies from county to county within states that permit capital punishment. Third, it is cruel because it is imposed only after "excessive delays," which average some eighteen years after a death sentence is imposed, during which time prisoners on death row are typically placed in solitary confinement, which Justice Breyer describes as "dehumanizing," for twenty-two hours or more a day.

The death penalty is also "unusual," in Justice Breyer's view, because "in the last two decades, the imposition and implementation of the death penalty have increasingly become unusual," and "most places within the

United States have abandoned its use." Thus, "30 States have either formally abolished the death penalty or have not conducted an execution in more than eight years," nine other states conducted less than five executions in that time period, and three of the remaining eleven states accounted for 80 percent of all executions nationally in 2014.

In a concurring opinion, Justice Scalia responded to "Justice Breyer's plea for judicial abolition of the death penalty." He noted that the Eighth Amendment itself, in providing that no person shall be "deprived of life" without due process of law, recognizes that the death penalty is not cruel and unusual per se. Justice Scalia further accused Justice Breyer of "[r]edefining 'cruel' to mean 'unreliable,' 'arbitrary,' or causing 'excessive delays,' and 'unusual' to include a 'decline in use.'" As such, the Breyer dissent is simply "a white paper devoid of any meaningful legal argument." He then addresses each of the points advanced by Justice Breyer, contending that "his argument is full of internal contradictions and (it must be said) gobbledy-gook."

While only two of the justices in *Glossip* explicitly questioned whether the imposition of capital punishment is itself cruel and unusual, the reasoning advanced by Justice Breyer is faithful to part of the analytic framework utilized by a majority of the court in prior Eighth Amendment cases by examining the objective indicia of actual incidences of use of the punishment. What the Breyer analysis omits is reference to the court's independent judgment, an inquiry that has been given increasingly greater prominence in the Eighth Amendment determination. Giving the chipping away of permissible punishments under the Eighth Amendment by the court in the twenty-first century, however, it is possible that the Supreme Court may exercise that independent judgment in the future to find capital punishment violative of the Constitution in a future case, although the confirmations of Justices Gorsuch, Kavanaugh, and Barrett lessen that possibility. If that possibility should nevertheless occur, the court will have rejected the explicit words of the Fifth Amendment, which, as Justice Scalia pointed out, recognizes that a person may be "deprived of life" so long as he or she is afforded "due process of law."

One final note: in considering how the Roberts court has been interpreting the Eighth Amendment, it is useful to consider the warning Justice McKenna gave in the *Weems* opinion. Even though he favored a "progressive" approach to determining what constituted "cruel and unusual punishments," and although he found the amendment must adapt to what he called "the ever-changing requirements of our national life," he nevertheless cautioned that this approach "essentially depend[s] upon the fact that this court, while never hesitating to bring within the powers granted, or restrained by the limitations created, all things generically within their embrace, has also incessantly declined to allow general words to be construed so as to include subjects not within their intendment."

NOTES

1. *Roper v. Simmons* is discussed in *Shaping America*, supra, 260–62.
2. *Commonwealth of Pennsylvania v. Batts*, No. 45 MAP 2016 (June 26, 2017).

Chapter 8

Property Rights

TAKINGS

One of the key provisions of the Constitution protecting property owners is contained in the final clause of the Fifth Amendment. It provides that "nor shall private property be taken for public use, without just compensation." By upholding the actions of private parties taking others' private property for commercial uses, the court's expanded understanding of this provision has come under intense criticism, as noted further below.

"Takings" are of two principal forms. On the one hand, the government can physically acquire private property as, for example, when a homeowner's house is acquired to facilitate the construction of the new highway. Takings can also be accomplished through governmental regulations restricting an owner's ability to use his own property. These are often referred to as "regulatory takings." An example of such takings was before the Supreme Court in *Lucas v. South Carolina Coastal Council* (1992). There the court required a local government to pay just compensation to the owner of two beachfront lots where it rezoned such properties to prohibit construction of any permanent structures on them. *Lucas* had spent nearly a million dollars to acquire the two lots, so that the economic harm inflicted on him by the rezoning was particularly severe. Where regulations have a lesser impact on the affected property owners, the court has followed a more "flexible" approach. See *Penn Central Transportation Co. v. New York City* (1978) ("balancing factors such as the economic impact of the regulation, its interference with reasonable investment-back expectations, and the character of the government action").

One of the most controversial takings decisions of the Supreme Court was delivered in *Kelo v. City of New London* (2005). In their book, *The Dirty Dozen* (2008), Robert A. Levy and William Mellor put the *Kelo* decision in their list of twelve Supreme Court cases that "radically expanded government and eroded freedom."[1] In that case, the Supreme Court upheld a physical taking under which the governmental authority permitted seizure of homes for the purpose of permitting a developer to build a multi-use complex on the acquired lands. The objecting landowners pointed to the Fifth Amendment's requirement that private property be taken "for public use," arguing unsuccessfully that the transfer of their property to a private developer to construct a commercial project did not qualify as such a use. The Supreme Court rejected their argument, ruling that even though the property would not used by the public, the public *use* requirement was at base only a requirement that there be a public *purpose* for the acquisition. It therefore ruled that the development plans satisfied that requirement.

Kelo generated intense opposition. In one reaction, nine states adopted constitutional amendments to limit eminent-domain takings under the public use/public purpose requirement, and the court was severely criticized in many media sources.

In its most recent takings decision, *Cedar Point Nursery v. Hassid* (2021), the Roberts court reviewed the constitutionality under the Takings Clause of a California regulation that granted labor organizations the right to "take access" to an agricultural employer's property to solicit support for unionization. In a six-to-three decision, the court ruled that the regulation constituted a "*per se* physical taking." Where such takings occur, the majority noted it has required compensation in such cases because "The Government must pay for what it takes."

Writing for six members of the court, Chief Justice Roberts explained that "The access regulation appropriates a right to invade the growers' property and therefore constitutes a *per se* physical taking." This was because "The right to exclude is 'is one of the most treasured' rights of property ownership." Reviewing prior precedent, the chief justice concluded that "The upshot of this line of precedent is that government-authorized invasions of property—whether by plane, boat, cable, or beachcomber—are physical takings requiring just compensation."

Responding to the contention that treatment of the access regulation as a per se physical taking erodes the distinction between trespass and taking, Chief Justice Roberts explained that "our holding does nothing to efface the distinction between trespass and taking. Isolated physical invasions, not undertaken pursuant to a granted right of access, are properly assessed as individual torts rather than appropriations of a property right."

In what Chief Justice Roberts described as a "thoughtful opinion," Justice Breyer in dissent asked whether the access regulation physically appropriated the growers' property or merely regulated their property rights. He concluded on behalf of three justices that the regulation simply "regulates the employers' right to exclude others." In support, Justice Breyer contended that prior precedent involving regulations that provided nonpermanent rights of access were held to be takings only if they go "too far." Many ordinary regulations, such as those authorizing government inspections, permit temporary entry onto a property owner's land and are reasonable restrictions on property rights. The regulation at issue was designed by the California law to "ensure peace in the agricultural fields by guaranteeing justice for all agricultural workers and stability in labor relations." Rather than adopt "a new broad rule," the dissent concluded the court should have followed the rule adopted in prior precedent, and employed the flexible test of the *Penn Central* decision to assess the validity of the access regulation.

Once again, we have a decision in which the Roberts court arguably changed the law, here by contracting the circumstances under which regulatory authorities can authorize temporary invasions of a private property without paying just compensation. The standard adopted by the majority will inevitably lead to further challenges of the governmental power to do so where any physical invasion of a property is authorized.

NOTE

1. Robert A. Levy and William Mellor, *The Dirty Dozen: How Twelve Supreme Court Cases Radically Expanded Government and Eroded Freedom* (New York: Sentinel, 2008), 158–68, 220–21.

Chapter 9

The Commerce Clause and the Taxing Power

Article I, Section 8, of the Constitution grants Congress the powers "To lay and collect Taxes," and "To regulate Commerce with foreign Nations, and among the several states, and with the Indian Tribes." The evolution of the court's interpretation of the Commerce Clause provides an excellent example of how the court goes about changing constitutional law.

Through the long presidency of Franklin Roosevelt and continuing during the tenures of the Democrat presidents who succeeded him, the Commerce Clause became the cornerstone for the expansion of the power of the federal government through the enactment of remedial legislation. The Commerce Clause was particularly important in supporting congressional power to regulate almost all facets of our daily lives, promoting and validating regulatory legislation in a myriad of areas touching, even so lightly, on interstate commerce. We saw this in the discussion above of the *Heart of Atlanta Motel* and *McClung* cases, which found congressional power under the Commerce Clause to support legislation in the Civil Rights Act of 1964 guaranteeing access to public accommodations to all, even though the prior decisions in the *Civil Rights Cases* (1883) had struck down similar legislation that was not tethered to a connection with interstate commerce.

In reaction to this vast expansion of the federal government, conservative scholars and Republican politicians focused on limiting the application of the Commerce Clause. This cause gained traction under the presidencies of Ronald Reagan and George H. W. Bush, especially with their appointments of Chief Justice Rehnquist and Justices Scalia and Thomas. Populist movements have continued to this day to seek to limit big government through such vehicles as the Tea Party and other, more radical groups. These groups were galvanized by the presidency of Donald Trump and his call to "Make America Great Again."

The court's long history interpreting the Commerce Clause dates back two hundred years to Chief Justice John Marshall's opinion in *Gibbons v. Ogden* (1824), which made broad pronouncements regarding the breath of congressional power under the Commerce Clause. In the nineteenth and early twentieth centuries, however, Marshall's observations regarding the capacious scope of the Commerce Clause were often neutralized by conservative court rulings narrowing the application of the clause. In *United States v. E.C. Knight Co.* (1895), for example, the Supreme Court ruled that the Sherman Antitrust Act could not be utilized to prohibit a merger among sugar producers that would have permitted them to control 98 percent of the market. The majority ruled that prohibiting monopoly fell within the ambit of state regulatory authority and distinguished between commerce and manufacture. Chief Justice Melville Fuller wrote for eight members of the court that "Commerce succeeds to manufacture, and is not part of it. The power to regulate commerce is the power to prescribe the rule by which commerce shall be governed, and is a power independent of the power to suppress monopoly." A similar ruling was made in *Hammer v. Dagenhart* (1918), where the court ruled that Congress did not have the power to ban the shipment over state lines of products produced by child labor since, once again, that labor was part of manufacturing, and not part of commerce.

The Supreme Court made an abrupt change in the cases it decided in the mid-twentieth century under both the Commerce and Taxing Clauses. In the early years of the New Deal, when the Roosevelt administration enacted several pieces of legislation to combat the economic collapse caused by the Great Depression, the court adhered to its prior conservative decisions. In the controversial case of *Schechter Poultry Corp. v. United States* (1935), for example, the court held that the criminal convictions of local slaughterhouse operators for violations of the Live Poultry Code for the New York metropolitan area could not stand, even though that code had been adopted as a code of fair competition under the Roosevelt administration's National Industrial Recovery Act. In the majority opinion, Chief Justice Charles Evans Hughes distinguished between direct and indirect impacts on interstate commerce, ruling that such transactions as those involved in the case remained within the domain of state power. Indeed, the court unanimously ruled that if transactions that only had an indirect effect upon interstate commerce could be regulated by Congress under the Commerce Clause, "there would be virtually no limit to the federal power, and for all practical purposes, we should have a completely centralized government."

A similar ruling was made in *United States v. Butler* (1936) to strike down a tax imposed on processors of farm goods that was designed to fund payments to farmers to limit their crops under the New Deal's Agriculture Adjustment Act. There the court held, in a six-to-three decision, that regulating agriculture production fell within the province of the states and using the taxing power to regulate agricultural production would permit "the regulation of all industry throughout the United States."

These restricted views of the Commerce and Taxing Clauses had a short lifespan. In *NLRB v. Jones & Laughlin Steel Corp.* (1937), the court changed course and upheld the Wagner Labor Act, ruling that the Commerce Clause could support congressional legislation regulating employment, as applied to a large international steel business with ten thousand employees in Pennsylvania, because the intrastate activities there had a "close and substantial" relationship to interstate commerce. Subsequently, the court employed a "substantial effects" test to uphold congressional legislation under the Commerce Clause, including regulating agriculture, establishing a social security system, and imposing fair labor standards. Indeed, *United States v. Darby* (1941), in the course of upholding the enactment of the Fair Labor Standards Act under the Commerce Clause, overruled *Hammer v. Dagenhart*. This drastic turnabout by the Supreme Court in its interpretation of the Commerce Clause was catalyzed by the ability of President Franklin Roosevelt to ultimately appoint eight members of the court.

The most extreme application of the substantial effects test came in the notorious case of *Wickard v. Filburn* (1942). There, the court held that congressional power under the Commerce Clause permitted it to penalize a farmer for growing wheat on his own land for his personal consumption because the amount he grew violated the quota established by the Agricultural Adjustment Act.

One of the major goals of the conservative movement in the later years of the twentieth century, and continuing today, is to impose restrictions on the power of Congress to legislate under the Commerce Clause, in order to curtail the nearly unlimited power for Congress to regulate wide swaths of the economy and personal conduct, as exemplified by the *Wickard* opinion. It was not until the last decade of the twentieth century that a more conservative court was able to impose some restrictions on congressional power under the Commerce Clause.

Thus, in *United States v. Lopez* (1995), the court struck down a federal law that prohibited the knowing possession of a firearm in a school zone. In a majority opinion by Chief Justice Rehnquist, the court concluded that the law was defective because Congress failed to limit its reach by imposing any jurisdictional element tied to interstate commerce. Moreover, in the view of the majority, the law was not supported by any congressional findings demonstrating that the activity at issue substantially affected interstate commerce. Finally, the legislation failed because it attempted to regulate noncommercial activity, unlike the New Deal cases.

The Supreme Court built upon the *Lopez* precedent in *United States v. Morrison* (2000). That decision, in a five-to-four opinion, struck down the 1994 Violence Against Women Act, despite the fact that that legislation only became law after four years of hearings, and contained extensive findings, including the necessity for a federal civil remedy to address gender-related violence. Chief Justice Rehnquist's opinion of the court concluded that "The Constitution requires a distinction between what is truly national and what is truly local." As such, "we accordingly reject the argument that Congress may regulate noneconomic, violent criminal conduct based solely on that conduct's aggregate effect on interstate commerce." Otherwise, Congress could regulate any type of crime, including murder, invading the traditional police power of the states to criminalize such conduct.

Despite the limitations placed upon congressional power under the Commerce Clause enunciated in *Lopez* and *Morrison*, a third decision seemed to indicate a retreat from those rulings. In *Gonzales v. Raich* (2005), six members of the court joined an opinion that the federal Controlled Substances Act was a valid enactment under the Commerce Clause, and could therefore be used to prohibit the use of home-grown marijuana for personal medical purposes even where such use was permitted by California state law. Justice John Paul Stevens relied on past precedent in the majority opinion, noting that "our case law firmly establishes Congress' power to regulate purely local activities that are part of an economic 'class of activities' that have a substantial effect on interstate commerce." Stevens relied heavily upon *Wickard v.Filburn* in his opinion. Three justices dissented, but Justice Scalia joined the majority.

THE CONSTITUTIONALITY OF THE AFFORDABLE CARE ACT

The limits of congressional power under the Commerce Clause reached the Supreme Court again seven years later in one of the most controversial decisions of the twenty-first-century court. In *National Federation of Independent Business v. Sebelius* (2012), the Supreme Court ruled on the constitutionality of two key provisions of the Patient Protection and Affordable Care Act, popularly known as the Affordable Care Act or "Obamacare." Unlike *Lopez* and *Morrison*, *National Federation* involved commercial conduct, namely congressionally mandated purchases of health insurance.

At issue on the appeal was the constitutionality of two key provisions of the ACA—the so-called Individual Mandate, and the Medicaid Expansion. The former required all individuals in the country to purchase a minimum level of health insurance coverage; if they refused to do so, they were required to pay a "shared responsibility payment" or "penalty" to the Internal Revenue

Service. This payment was required to be "assessed and collected in the same manner" as a tax penalty. The Medicaid Expansion provision required state governments to increase both the scope and the number of individuals to be covered by the federal Medicaid program. If the state failed or refused to implement this expansion, the Affordable Care Act provided that it could lose *all* federal Medicaid funds.

With respect to the Individual Mandate, the court found, by separate five-to-four decisions, that the mandate exceeded congressional powers under both the Commerce Clause and the Necessary and Proper Clause, but was authorized under the taxing power. The ruling under the Commerce and Necessary and Proper Clauses came in two separate opinions, the first by Chief Justice Roberts speaking only for himself, and the second in a separate opinion authored jointly by Justices Scalia, Kennedy, Thomas, and Alito.

THE INDIVIDUAL MANDATE AND THE COMMERCE AND NECESSARY AND PROPER CLAUSES

Chief Justice Roberts noted that the constitutionality of the Individual Mandate presented a novel question because there had not been any prior attempt by Congress to "compel individuals not engaged in commerce to purchase an unwanted product." Such a power was inconsistent with the plain language of Article 1, Section 8, relating to the regulation of commerce because "The power to *regulate* commerce presupposes the existence of commercial activity to be regulated." Moreover, the chief justice continued, the court's own precedents under the Commerce Clause required the existence of some *activity* to support the power to enact legislation under the authority of that clause. For example, in *Wickard v. Filburn*, the farmer was engaged in the activity of growing wheat. By contrast, if Congress was permitted to require people "to *become* active in commerce by purchasing a product," this "would open a new and potentially vast domain to congressional authority." Vesting such power in Congress would "fundamentally [change] the relation between the citizen and the Federal Government," by changing the federal government from "one of enumerated powers" to one with unlimited power. But, Chief Justice Roberts concluded, "That is not the country the Framers of our Constitution envisioned."

Chief Justice Roberts also concluded that Congress was not authorized by the Necessary and Proper Clause to enact the Individual Mandate. While Congress argued that such a mandate was authorized under that clause to ensure the efficacy of "a comprehensive scheme of economic regulation," the chief justice concluded that Congress must first be able to identify an enumerated power that formed the basis for it to legislate in the area, but it had failed to do so here. In addition, even if the Individual Mandate was deemed "necessary" to implement a comprehensive legislative solution, it still would not be "proper" because it "would work a substantial expansion of federal authority." Moreover, Congress was incorrect in arguing that the court's earlier decision in *Gonzales v. Raich* (2005) supported its power to enact the Individual Mandate because there was no claim of an independent power to regulate in that case.

While Chief Justice Roberts's opinion was the first of the several opinions reported, it represented only his views on the constitutionality of the Individual Mandate under the Commerce and Necessary and Proper Clauses. In a separate opinion jointly authored by Justices Scalia, Kennedy, Thomas, and Alito, this plurality of four provided a separate analysis of those issues. The joint opinion noted that "The proposition that the Federal Government cannot do everything is a fundamental precept." In their view, the court's prior cases taught that "the Commerce Clause, even when supplemented by the Necessary and Proper Clause, is not *carte blanche* for doing whatever will help achieve the ends Congress seeks by the regulation of commerce." For example, *Wickard* did not support the Individual Mandate because there was actual activity by the farmer in that case. *Raich* was irrelevant because Congress was not entering a "broad new field" of regulation in that case, and there was no other option available to address the problem of homegrown marijuana. Here, by contrast, Congress had other available options to address the so-called free rider problem of those individuals who did not purchase health care insurance until they were seriously ill as, for example, by surcharging them for that delay.

The joint opinion also concluded that non-purchasers of health insurance were "not participants" in the healthcare market. As such, "If Congress can reach out and command even those furthest removed from an interstate market to participate in the market, then the Commerce Clause becomes a font of unlimited power," or in Hamilton's words, "the hideous monster whose devouring jaws . . . spare neither sex nor age, nor high nor low, nor sacred or profane." Moreover, "If all inactivity affecting commerce is commerce, commerce is everything," and "if every person comes within the Commerce Clause power of Congress to regulate by the simple reason that he will one day engage in commerce, the idea of a limited Governmental power is at an end." Finally, upholding the power of Congress to impose such mandates "would alter the accepted constitutional relation between the individual and the National Government."

Four justices dissented from the ruling that neither the Commerce Clause nor the Necessary and Proper Clause were sufficient to authorize Congress to enact the Individual Mandate. In an opinion by Justice Ginsburg, for herself and for Justices Breyer, Sotomayor, and Kagan, Chief Justice Roberts's opinion was attacked as giving a "crabbed reading" of the Commerce Clause, which "harks back to the era in which the Court routinely thwarted Congress' efforts to regulate the national economy in the interest of those who labor to sustain it."

The dissenting justices contended that Supreme Court precedent emphasized that the scope of congressional power under the Commerce Clause focused on "practical" considerations including "actual experience." Moreover, the case law "was guided by two familiar principles." These were that Congress had power to regulate economic activities "that substantially affect interstate commerce," and that "we owe a large measure of respect to Congress when it frames and enacts economic and social legislation." Thus, if Congress has a "rational basis" in concluding that an activity substantially affects interstate commerce, and there is a "reasonable connection" between the regulatory means chosen and the legislative goal sought to be achieved, the court should not interfere with those judgments. In the area of healthcare, the dissenters believed it was "beyond dispute" that "Congress had a rational basis for concluding that the uninsured, as a class, substantially affect interstate commerce," and thus could be compelled to purchase health insurance.

Chief Justice Roberts's contention that the Individual Mandate required an individual "to become active in commerce by purchasing a product" was rejected on the grounds that any individual was "virtually certain" to consume healthcare in the next one to five years, and thus was effectively in the market either now or would be imminently. The dissenters also argued that *Wickard* was precedent for the Individual Mandate because its effect was to "compel farmers to purchase wheat in the open market."

The dissenters also addressed the view that the power of Congress under the Commerce Clause would "know no limits" if the Individual Mandate were upheld. First, they stressed the "unique attributes" of the healthcare market, including the fact that "everyone" is active in that market. Second, the dissenters identified "a significant free-riding problem" that would result in the absence of a mandate requiring all individuals to purchase health insurance. Third, the dissenters saw "the democratic process" as imposing a non-legal but "formidable check on congressional power" since "purchase mandates are likely to engender political resistance," as was the case with the Affordable Care Act Mandate itself.

Justice Ginsburg's opinion contended that the Necessary and Proper Clause also authorized the Individual Mandate because it was an integral part of a comprehensive statutory scheme regulating economic activity, and was therefore "necessary." It was also "proper" because it acted directly upon individuals. As such, the contention that it offended principles of federalism and state sovereignty was misplaced. Moreover, the health insurance problem has a "national dimension," and "Far from trampling on States' sovereignty, the [Act] attempts a federal solution for the very reason that the states, acting separately, cannot meet the need."

THE INDIVIDUAL MANDATE AND THE TAXING POWER

The Supreme Court next turned to the separate question of whether the taxing power provided a constitutional basis on which the Individual Mandate could be upheld. By a five-to-four vote, Chief Justice Roberts, joined by Justices Ginsburg, Breyer, Sotomayor, and Kagan, held that it did.

Chief Justice Roberts's opinion on the taxing power issue was divided into two parts. In the first part, speaking solely for himself, he pointed out that the government in its Commerce Clause argument had contended the mandate was a regulation requiring individuals to purchase health insurance. By contrast, in this portion of the argument, "the Government asks us to read the mandate not as ordering individuals to buy insurance, but rather as imposing a tax on those who do not buy that product." The chief justice noted that "it is well-established that if a statute has two possible meanings, one of which violates the Constitution, courts should adopt the meaning that does not do so." Moreover, the case law established that the interpretation advanced to support the constitutionality of the Individual Mandate need only be one that was "fairly possible."

The second section of Chief Justice Roberts's opinion represented the views of the five-justice majority. This majority opinion noted that the description in the Affordable Care Act of the payment as a "penalty" rather than a "tax" was not determinative. Here, given that the requirement to pay was found in the Internal Revenue Code; was to be assessed and collected "in the same manner as taxes"; and was expected to raise four billion dollars a year by 2017, this "financial penalty . . . may reasonably be characterized as a tax." While admitting the payment was intended to influence individual conduct, this was immaterial because "taxes that seek to influence conduct are nothing new." Moreover, "Upholding the individual mandate under the Taxing Clause . . . does not recognize any new federal power. It determines that Congress has used an existing one."

In their joint opinion, Justices Scalia, Kennedy, Thomas, and Alito vigorously dissented from the holding that the payment required from those who refused to purchase health insurance could constitutionally be treated as a tax. They contended that "The provision challenged under the Constitution is either a penalty or else a tax," and that the two are "mutually exclusive." Moreover, "The issue is not whether Congress had the *power* to frame the minimum coverage provision as a tax, but whether it *did* so."

In the dissenters' view, based on their review of the case law, taxes represent enforced contributions to provide for the support of government, while penalties are exactions imposed by statute as punishments for unlawful acts. In addition, "we have never held—*never*—that a penalty imposed for violation of law was so trivial as to be in effect a tax." Thus the only question presented was "quite simply, whether the exaction here is imposed for violation of the law." In the dissenters' view, "It unquestionably is."

After a detailed review of the statutory framework and the contentions of the Government, the dissenters concluded that "to say that the Individual Mandate merely imposes a tax is not to interpret the statute but to rewrite it." Indeed, it was noted several times in the Senate Hearing on her nomination to the Supreme Court that this was essentially the position taken by then-professor Amy Coney Barrett in an article when she criticized Chief Justice Roberts for "push[ing] the Affordable Care Act beyond its plausible meaning to save the statute."

THE MEDICAID EXPANSION

The court next turned to the second major issue presented on appeal. This was whether the conditions imposed on the states under the so-called Medicaid Expansion were constitutional. By a seven-to-two majority, the court found it was unconstitutional to attempt to force the states, on penalty of losing all federal Medicaid monies, to expand Medicaid as dramatically as required by the Affordable Care Act.

The justices in the seven-person majority wrote two separate opinions. The first opinion was written by Chief Justice Roberts, and joined by Justices Breyer and Kagan; the second was a joint opinion on behalf of Justices Scalia, Kennedy, Thomas, and Alito. Both opinions emphasized that the Medicaid Expansion offended core principles of federalism, including the independent sovereignty of the States.

Chief Justice Roberts's opinion noted that the Spending Clause contained in Article I, Section 8, granted Congress the power to provide federal funds to the states while conditioning any such grant on states "taking certain actions that Congress could not require them to take." Nevertheless, since legislation enacted under the Spending Clause is viewed "much in the nature of a *contract*," it follows that "The legitimacy of Congress's exercise of the spending power 'thus rests on whether the State voluntarily and knowingly accept the terms of the 'contract.'" The willingness of a state to accept the conditions imposed on receipt of a federal grant is paramount to ensure "the status of the States as independent sovereigns in our federal system." Thus, Congress may use its spending power to incentivize States to implement federal policy, but when "pressure turns into compulsion," then "the legislation runs contrary to our system of federalism."

The Roberts opinion identified a second factor that barred the Federal Government from forcing States to implement a federal program. Exercising such coercion "would threaten the political accountability key to our federal system" by subjecting state officials to public disapproval, while insulating from such disapproval "the federal officials who devised the regulatory program."

The central problem with the Affordable Care Act was that Congress did not "simply refus[e] to grant the new funds to States that will not accept the new conditions," but instead "also threatened to withhold those States' existing Medicaid funds." Rather than encouraging the States to accept the expansion, Congress used "a gun to the head" approach because a noncompliant state would lose all its Medicaid funds. Such a loss would be financially significant, since "Medicaid spending accounts for over 20 percent of the average State's total budget." Moreover, the Medicaid Expansion "accomplishes a shift in kind, not merely in degree," and that shift would place significant additional financial burdens on the states. That is because Medicaid was originally designed to cover only four categories: "the disabled, the blind, the elderly, and needy families with dependent children." By contrast, the expansion under the Affordable Care Act transformed Medicaid into a program "to meet the healthcare needs of the entire non-elderly population with income below 133 percent of the poverty level."

The separate, joint opinion of Justices Scalia, Kennedy, Thomas, and Alito reemphasized many of the same points made in Chief Justice Roberts's opinion. The joint opinion again emphasized that "the annual federal Medicaid subsidy is equal to more that one-fifth of the [average] State's expenditures." Consequently, Congress's "formidable power" to attach conditions to federal grants to the States, "if not checked in any way, would present a grave threat to the system of federalism created by our Constitution." Indeed, "[T]he Spending Clause power, if wielded without concern for the federal balance, has the potential to obliterate distinctions between national and local spheres of interest and power by permitting the Federal Government to set policy in the most sensitive areas of traditional state concern, areas which otherwise would lie outside its reach."

The joint opinion also pointed out that Congress realized that States could not practically refuse to go along with the Medicaid Expansion because Congress failed to devise "a backup scheme so that the most vulnerable groups in our society, those previously eligible for Medicaid, would not be left out in the cold." However, "nowhere in the over 900-page Act is such a scheme to be found." As such, "Congress never dreamed that any State would refuse to go along with the expansion of Medicaid. Congress well understood that refusal was not a practical option."

While the joint opinion, as well as the opinion of Chief Justice Roberts, found the Medicare Expansion unconstitutional, the two opinions differed on whether the entire Affordable Care Act should be invalidated. Justices Ginsburg and Sotomayor noted their concurrence in the judgment announced in Chief Justice Roberts's opinion for three members of the court, thus forming a majority to hold that the rest of the Act could stand. This result was based upon the existence of a severability clause, and the determination, in the words of Chief Justice Roberts' opinion, that the majority was "confident that Congress would have wanted to preserve the rest of the Act."

By contrast, Justices Scalia, Kennedy, Thomas, and Alito concluded that the entire Act had to be invalidated. Since they had found that both the Individual Mandate and the Medicaid Expansion were unconstitutional exercises of powers Congress did not possess, the authors of the joint opinion concluded after a careful review of how the Affordable Care Act was structured, that Congress would not have wished the Act to stand in the absence of these two key provisions.

Although seven members of the court held that the Medicare Expansion was unconstitutional, Justices Ginsburg and Sotomayor dissented on this point. They began by noting that "The spending power conferred by the Constitution, the Court has never doubted, permits Congress to define the contours of programs financed with federal funds." Moreover, when Congress wished to expand coverage, it "could have recalled the existing legislation, and replaced it with a new law making Medicaid as embracive of the poor as Congress chose." In this context, the issue before the court on the Medicaid Expansion "is essentially this: To cover a notably larger population, must Congress take the repeal/reenact route, or may achieve the same result by amending existing law?" In the dissenters' view, "A ritualistic requirement that Congress repeal and reenact spending legislation in order to enlarge the population served by a federally funded program would advance no constitutional principle and would scarcely serve the interests of federalism."

The dissenters additionally noted that Congress had amended the Medicaid program on more than fifty occasions since 1965, and that some of these amendments added significant numbers of beneficiaries, including classes of pregnant women and of children up to eighteen years of age. Given this history, it was incorrect for the chief justice to treat the Medicaid Expansion as "an entirely new program" since, in reality, "it simply reaches more of America's poor than Congress originally covered."

ANALYSIS: TRIUMPH OR DEFEAT FOR THE NEW FEDERALISM?

For conservatives, libertarians, and Tea Party members, "Obamacare" became a principal symbol of an excessive and intrusive federal government whose power needed to be curbed. Public opinion at large supported opposition to the Affordable Care Act at the time the court rendered its judgment, with a slim majority of Americans consistently expressing views against it prior to the Supreme Court's decision. In a blitzkrieg-like assault, some twenty-six states and numerous private parties brought suit to invalidate the Affordable Care Act, targeting the Individual Mandate. While legal scholars and members of Congress ridiculed the attacks on the Mandate as baseless in light of what they perceived to be a nearly unlimited federal power to legislate under the Commerce Clause, the Supreme Court recognized the importance and novelty of the issues presented by scheduling six hours of oral argument over three days. On the appeal, a cadre of conservative scholars and lawyers, including Georgetown University law professor Randy Barnett and former solicitor general Paul Clement, developed arguments that ultimately prevailed under the Commerce Clause, but fell one vote short (that of the chief justice) under the Taxing Power, in the attempt to have the Individual Mandate struck down as an unconstitutional.

Since Chief Justice John Roberts was popularly viewed as an integral part of the Supreme Court's conservative wing, his vote to uphold the Individual Mandate under the Taxing Clause was viewed as apostasy by conservatives. Indeed, rumors circulated shortly after the decision was announced that Roberts had originally agreed with the four justices who wrote the joint opinion but changed his mind thereafter. The rumors (none of which were substantiated with evidence admissible in any trial court) went on to contend that Justice Kennedy lobbied the chief justice for a month in an unsuccessful attempt to have him change his mind, and that the four other conservative justices were bitterly angry with Roberts.

Why, then, did Chief Justice Roberts vote to uphold the Individual Mandate and the Affordable Care Act? While many explanations have been advanced, there are two that deserve special consideration. First, many legal scholars and members of the popular media have compared Roberts's efforts in *National Federation* to those of Chief Justice John Marshall in *Marbury v. Madison*. In both cases, an incumbent president was victorious in the appeal; Thomas Jefferson defeated Marbury's attempt to obtain a judicial commission, while Barack Obama's signature legislative accomplishment was upheld. Moreover, in both cases, the chief justices established important principles of law: Marshall established the right of judicial review over congressional enactments, while Roberts limited the scope of the Commerce Clause in his discussion of the Individual Mandate, and vindicated state sovereignty and principles of federalism in obtaining seven votes to invalidate the Medicaid Expansion.

Second, legal scholars, including law professor Jonathan Adler, have argued that the approach taken by Chief Justice Roberts in *Sebelius* reflected his overall approach of judicial minimalism, an approach we have seen in the discussions above of such decisions as *Northwest Austin Municipal Utility District*, *Fisher v. University of Texas at Austin*, and *Ricci v. DiStefano*. Adler sees Roberts's efforts as attempting to "lessen the role of the Court in the nation's politics."[1]

By voting as he did, Chief Justice Roberts was able to protect the institutional integrity of the Supreme Court, as John Marshall had done in *Marbury*. Had the Affordable Care Act been invalidated by a narrow five-to-four vote orchestrated by a conservative majority, the Supreme Court would have become a major talking point in the 2012 presidential election. President Obama had already famously denounced the court over its *Citizens' United* decision discussed above, and he would surely have intensified his attacks on the court had the Affordable Care Act been struck down.

Despite the overall outcome in *National Federation*, conservatives, libertarians, and Tea Party members (as well as the conservative justices on the Supreme Court) should be satisfied with the significant victories they obtained for the New Federalism. To begin with, the limits placed by the court on the Commerce Clause beginning in *Lopez* and *Morrison*, but cut back on in *Raich*, were reinvigorated by forbidding Congress to use that Clause to mandate citizens to engage in any particular activity. In addition, the strong ruling in favor of state sovereignty on the Medicare Expansion was a major victory. As Chief Justice Roberts stated in his opinion, "In the typical case, we look to the States to defend their prerogatives by adopting 'the simple expedient of not yielding' to federal blandishments when they do not want to embrace the federal policies as their own. . . . The States are separate and independent sovereigns. Sometimes they have to act like it."

REWRITING THE AFFORDABLE CARE ACT TO IMPLEMENT ITS GOALS

Three years after *National Federation*, the Affordable Care Act came before the Supreme Court once again. *King v. Burwell* (2015) dealt not with constitutional issues, but rather with statutory interpretation. The underlying issue was whether tax credits extended to poorer individuals to enable them financially to buy insurance were available to residents of states in which a

Federal Exchange for health insurance transactions had been established. The question arose because the Act provided for tax credits only for those eligible taxpayers who had enrolled through "an Exchange established by the State."

In an opinion for six members of the court, Chief Justice Roberts ruled that the tax credits were available for those who purchased through a Federal Exchange. In reaching this conclusion, and to the great consternation of the three dissenters, he relied upon the underlying purposes of the Affordable Care Act, rather than upon its (clear) text.

The chief justice began his opinion by reviewing prior unsuccessful efforts at the state level to provide for widespread health insurance coverage. Noting that several early efforts had failed in the 1990s, he observed that there was a breakthrough in the state health insurance law enacted in Massachusetts in 2006. Roberts noted that the Massachusetts Plan had three key elements: state regulation of the insurance market; the requirement that all people purchase health insurance or pay a penalty (the "coverage mandate"); and the provision of tax credits for those who could not otherwise afford to buy health insurance. The majority opinion then observed that the Affordable Care Act followed an approach similar to that of Massachusetts, including a coverage mandate and the provision of tax credits for lower-income individuals.

Turning to the text of the Affordable Care Act, the majority noted that it required an "Exchange" to be created in each state and provided for tax credits to be afforded to eligible taxpayers if they enrolled in health insurance through "an Exchange established by the State." In practice, however, thirty-four states chose not to establish any Exchange, and the federal government stepped in to provide one in each of those states. The federal government was authorized to take this action under another provision of the Act, which directed it to establish "such Exchange" if the state did not do so. Significantly, some 87 percent of the individuals who purchased health insurance through a Federal Exchange—totaling about eight million people—fell into the income groups for which tax credits were designed to be available. As such, a ruling that such tax credits were only available for purchases through a State Exchange would endanger the access of those individuals to health insurance.

Chief Justice Roberts initially rejected the argument that deference was owed to the interpretation of the Internal Revenue Service, which had promulgated a rule making the tax credits available for purchases through either a Federal or State Exchange. The majority found that the IRS rule was not entitled to deference because there was no evidence that Congress wished to delegate such an important issue to the discretion of an agency.

Roberts and the majority went on to rule that the phrase, "an Exchange established by the State," was ambiguous, and represented one of the "more than a few examples of inartful drafting" in the legislation, which the chief justice concluded "does not reflect the type of care and deliberation that one might expect of such significant legislation." There was therefore a need to read the provision within the context in which the phrase was used, and against the broader structure of the Act. After reviewing the entire structure of the Act, the majority concluded that if tax credits were limited to State-created Exchanges, the "death spiral" which had been experienced in the states which attempted to broaden the availability of health insurance to their residents in the 1990s would be experienced once again. This would result because the individuals who could not purchase insurance without the tax credits would be exempted from the coverage mandate, and the whole purpose of the Affordable Care Act would fail. Such a result could not be countenanced because "Congress passed the Affordable Care Act to improve health insurance markets, not to destroy them," and "A fair reading of legislation demands a fair understanding of the legislative plan."

Significantly, particularly in light of the dissenting opinion, the majority admitted that the arguments to restrict tax credits to those purchasing through a State Exchange based on the plain meaning of the text "are strong," but nevertheless, "the context and structure of the Act compel us to depart from what would otherwise be the most natural reading of the pertinent statutory phrase."

Not surprisingly, Justice Scalia, joined by Justices Thomas and Alito, penned a scathing dissent. He began by characterizing the majority opinion as reading the legislation to provide that an "'Exchange established by the State' . . . means [an] 'Exchange established by the State or the Federal government.' That is of course quite absurd." Indeed, "Words no longer have meaning if an Exchange that is *not* established by a State is 'established by the State.'" In Justice Scalia's view, the majority forces "normal rules of interpretation" to "yield to the overriding principle of the present Court: The Affordable Care Act must be saved."

The dissenters acknowledged and agreed that legislation must be interpreted in light of the "whole law," and that "Context always matters." Nevertheless, this principle is only to be used as "a tool for understanding the terms of the law, not an excuse for rewriting them." As such, "Statutory design and purpose matter only to the extent they help clarify an otherwise ambiguous provision." Moreover, prior case law indicated that is not proper to "revise legislation . . . just because the text as written creates an apparent anomaly."

Turning to the structure of the Act itself, Justice Scalia pointed out that several of its provisions do, in fact, distinguish between the establishment of State and Federal Exchanges, and that the phrase "established by the State" appears some seven times in the Act, indicating that it was not a simple drafting error in the provision being interpreted by the court. As such, the approach taken by the majority, in Justice Scalia's view, is simply "interpretive jiggery-pokery," a British phrase that refers to deceitful or dishonest behavior.

The dissenters next pointed out that the Constitution in Article I, Section 1, confers "All legislative powers" upon Congress, not upon the courts. Thus, if there is an anomaly or a mistake in legislation as written, it is up to Congress to amend the legislation to conform it to its supposed intent. Given that the majority justices ruled in such a way as to effectively rewrite the Act, Justice Scalia suggested that "We should start calling this law SCOTUScare."

In concluding his dissenting opinion, Justice Scalia noted, after reviewing multiple "somersaults of statutory interpretation" regarding provisions of the Affordable Care Act, that "the cases will publish forever the discouraging truth that the Supreme Court of the United States favors some laws over others, and is prepared to do whatever it takes to uphold and assist its favorites."

As was the case with his vote in *National Federation*, Chief Justice Roberts's vote to "save" the Affordable Care Act in *King v. Burwell* was subjected to considerable analysis by various commentators who questioned why he went to such lengths to save the Act, since it was quite obvious that the plain meaning of the provision at issue was in fact ignored, even though the chief justice explicitly said that the argument to follow it was "strong." On the one hand, some suggested that the chief justice was cowed into submission once again by President Obama, who (in remarks that were repeatedly televised) characterized the case as an "easy" one, and criticized the court for agreeing even to consider it. A more likely explanation is that the court may have been reluctant to interpret the statute in such a way as to deprive eight million lower-income people of access to health insurance. This appeared to be a realistic possibility given the Obama administration's claims that it had no backup plan to provide insurance to these individuals if the court made tax credits unavailable to those who purchased their health insurance on a Federal Exchange. This problem was exacerbated further by the fact that the Republican opposition to "Obamacare" had been largely negative, and that the Republican leadership had been unable to come up with a concrete plan acceptable to all of its factions to address such a ruling in such a way as to preserve health insurance for those who would be affected by the ruling.

In these circumstances, the chief justice chose to save the Act rather than to implement its plain language. He was reduced to evidencing contempt for Congress by referring to its serial "inartful drafting" of the legislation, going so far as to take a veiled slap at Nancy Pelosi, the Democratic leader in the House of Representatives, by referring in the majority opinion to a 1940s cartoon that featured a senator saying (as Pelosi later similarly remarked regarding the Affordable Care Act) that "We'll just have to pass it to find out what it means."

FINDING LACK OF STANDING TO PRESERVE THE AFFORDABLE CARE ACT

The Affordable Care Act came before the court for the third time in *California v. Texas* (2021). Joined by seventeen other states and two individuals, Texas argued that the elimination of the penalty/tax (by reducing it to zero) under the Act's minimum essential coverage requirement removed the constitutional basis relied upon in the court's initial ruling for the law's enactment, rendering it an unconstitutional exercise of congressional power.

Despite the force of this argument, as shown by Justice Alito's thirty-four-page dissenting opinion, seven members of the court rejected this latest challenge on the grounds that each of the appellants lacked standing. Only Justice Gorsuch joined the dissenting opinion.

Justice Breyer's majority opinion for six members of the court ruled that the individual plaintiffs lacked standing because, even though the Act mandated them to obtain health coverage, there was no way of enforcing the Act against them because "With the penalty zeroed out, The IRS can no longer seek a penalty from those who fail to comply." The state plaintiffs also lacked standing because their argument that the states incurred additional costs because of the requirements of the Act had no causal relationship to the minimum essential coverage requirement. Justice Breyer explained that "The programs to which the state plans point offer their recipients many benefits that have nothing to do with the minimum essential coverage provision." As such, "The state plaintiffs have failed to show that the challenged minimum essential coverage provision, without any prospect of penalty, will harm them by leading more individuals to enroll in these programs." The states' argument that they incurred additional costs because of added enrollment in state health plans because of the Act was also rejected. Once again, the majority ruled that such added costs could not fairly be attributed to the minimum essential coverage requirement. In sum, the objectors "fail to show a concrete, particularized injury fairly traceable to the defendants' conduct in enforcing the specific statutory provision they attack as unconstitutional."

Concurring, Justice Thomas noted that while "There is much to commend" in Justice Alito's dissenting opinion, the plaintiffs' position suffered from a "fundamental problem . . . —they have not identified any unlawful action that has injured them." Thus, "Although this Court has erred twice before in cases involving the Affordable Care Act, it does not err today."

Pointing to "the daunting problem of a 'tax' that does not tax," Justice Alito accused the court in dissent of "simply duck[ing] the issue." He pointed to several prior decisions of the court that permitted standing in comparable circumstances. Here, the states had standing in his view because the Act "saddles them with expensive and burdensome obligations, and those obligations are enforced by the Federal Government." Moreover, the Act imposed "ongoing financial costs of complying with [its] reporting requirements." If those obligations cannot be severed from the individual mandate, then "the government cannot lawfully enforce those obligations against the States," making their standing clear.

On the merits, Justice Alito opined that reduction of the tax to zero meant that "the mandate cannot be sustained under the taxing power. As a result, it is clearly unconstitutional, and to the extent that the provisions of the ACA that burden the States are inextricably linked to the individual mandate, they too are unenforceable." He argued that the reporting and other requirements were so linked because "All the opinions in [the original case] acknowledged the central role of the individual mandate's tax or penalty," and the Act itself describes the individual mandate as "*essential* to creating effective health insurance markets."

NOTE

1. Jonathan H. Adler, "Judicial Minimalism, The Mandate, and Mr. Roberts," ssrn.com/abstract= 2169933, 2. See also Paul M. Barrett, "Opening Remarks: John Roberts, CEO," *Bloomberg Businessweek*, July 9–15, 2012, 7.

Chapter 10

Same-Sex Marriage

Under principles of federalism enshrined in the Constitution, the power to legislate is divided between the states and the federal government. Under that division, matters relating to family law, including marriage, generally fall within the province of the states. Thus, states may impose restrictions on who may marry and whom they may marry, including limitations based on the age of the parties and their kinship ties. They also can prohibit bigamy and other relationships involving multiple parties. Unless there is a violation of the Constitution, states are free to impose these restrictions. Such a violation was found in *Loving v. Virginia* (1967), where the court unanimously held that a ban on interracial marriages violated both the Equal Protection and Due Process Clauses of the Fourteenth Amendment. *Loving* ruled that marriage was a fundamental right. The Supreme Court subsequently ruled that a state could not prohibit a party from remarrying because he failed to pay court-ordered child support (*Zablocki v. Redhail* [1979]).

Marriages between people of the same sex were banned by all of the states before 2003, when Massachusetts became the first state to legalize same-sex marriage. When Minnesota's law banning marriage between people of the same sex was challenged in 1971, it was upheld by the Minnesota Supreme Court. An appeal to the Supreme Court of United States was dismissed, without an opinion, "for want of a substantial federal question" in *Baker v. Nelson* (1972). Such a dismissal has precedential value and is binding on all lower courts, both state and federal. The disposition in *Baker* also suggests that as of 1972, attacks on legislation prohibiting same-sex marriage were seen as close to frivolous.

In a remarkable and sudden change in public opinion, a large majority of the populace is now in favor of recognizing a right of same-sex couples to marry. That this shift was sudden is demonstrated by the fact that there was not a majority in favor of same-sex marriage in any state as recently as 2004. Indeed, a *New York Times* December 21, 2003, poll reported that 61 percent of the American public was opposed to legalizing same-sex marriage, and that

55 percent even favored a constitutional amendment to limit marriage to a man and a woman. What explains this rapid change, in part, is the emergence of powerful and well-funded gay-rights organizations that made compelling arguments as to how discrimination against gay and lesbian people caused emotional harm, as, for example, by not allowing a gay partner to visit her would-be spouse in the hospital.

Despite the ruling in *Baker*, legislation banning same-sex marriage became increasingly under attack, and some twelve states and the District of Columbia permitted people of different sexes to marry by 2015. Nevertheless, thirty-two states then banned same-sex marriage, either by popular vote or by constitutional amendment. Given this disparity, proponents of same-sex marriage enlisted the aid of two prominent lawyers, the liberal David Boies and the conservative Ted Olsen, to go to court to argue in favor of a constitutional right to same-sex marriage. They were successful in doing so in the lower courts, initially increasing the number of states that approved same-sex marriage to thirty-six, mainly by court rulings.

Several of these rulings were appealed to the Supreme Court, and the court resisted at first making any broad constitutional ruling. Ultimately, however, a sharply divided Supreme Court declared that same-sex couples had a constitutional right to marry.

STANDING TO LITIGATE MARRIAGE ELIGIBILITY ISSUES

In 2013, on the last day of the Supreme Court term, the court decided two cases involving the constitutionality of measures taken by federal and state authorities to prohibit same-sex marriages. In the first case, the court avoided the constitutional issue by finding that the appellants lacked Article III standing, while in the second appeal, the court issued an opinion upholding certain rights of same-sex persons whose marriages were legal under the controlling state law, and striking down the federal Defense of Marriage Act. Both cases were decided on five-to-four votes, but with different combinations of justices in the majority and on the dissents.

Hollingsworth v. Perry (2013) presented the issue whether the Equal Protection Clause prohibited the State of California from defining marriage exclusively as the union of a man and a woman. In an opinion by Chief Justice Roberts, a five-member majority comprised of the chief justice and Justices Scalia, Ginsburg, Breyer and Kagan, held that the proponents of Proposition 8, the initiative measure that banned same-sex marriages in California, lacked standing to appeal from a ruling finding that the initiative was unconstitutional, even where the state officials who were proper parties declined to appeal the adverse ruling.

The majority reasoned that the proponents had not been ordered to do, or to refrain from doing, anything and that they "had no 'direct stake' in the outcome of their appeal." In addition, the court had "never before upheld the standing of a private party to defend the constitutionality of a state statute when state officials have chosen not to," and "We decline to do so for the first time here."

The four dissenters joined an opinion by Justice Kennedy, who contended the proponents did have standing to appeal because they had "gone to great lengths to convince voters to enact an initiative," and both had "a stake in the outcome and the necessary commitment to provide zealous advocacy." Indeed, in the view of the dissenters, "There is much irony in the Court's approach to justiciability in this case. A prime purpose of justiciability is to ensure vigorous advocacy, yet the Court insists upon litigation conducted by state officials whose preference is to lose the case."

That the standing ruling was influenced by a desire not to rule prematurely on the constitutionality of restricting same-sex marriage is obvious on many levels, including the first sentence of Chief Justice Robert's opinion of the court, which recites that "The public is currently engaged in an active political debate over whether same-sex couples should be allowed to marry." To curtail that ongoing debate through a broad ruling binding on all states would have subjected the court to the same type of criticism that followed its decision in *Roe v. Wade* (1973) on what restrictions could constitutionally be imposed on a woman's right to choose to have an abortion.

A CONSTITUTIONAL RIGHT TO SAME-SEX MARRIAGE

Section 3 of the federal Defense of Marriage Act defined "marriage" for purposes of more than one thousand federal laws to exclude same-sex partners from those laws' benefits and burdens. By a five-to-four margin, with the opinion of the court authored by Justice Kennedy, the court held that this provision of DOMA was unconstitutional under the Fifth Amendment as applied to same-sex spouses whose marriages were lawful under the applicable state law.

Justice Kennedy's majority opinion is a curious and confusing mix of concepts of federalism, equality, and dignity, and it fails clearly to enunciate the standard against which laws relating to same-sex marriage should be measured. Initially, his opinion contains significant strands of federalism. For example, the majority opinion characterizes the states as possessing an "historic and essential authority to define the marital relation," and criticizes DOMA as departing from the "history and tradition of reliance on state law to define marriage." It further recites that "the State's power in defining the marital relation is of central relevance in this case quite apart from principles of federalism."

Justice Kennedy went on to invoke concepts of human dignity and equality repeatedly throughout the majority opinion. In referring to those states which have permitted same-sex marriage, he stated that "the State acted to give [same-sex couples'] lawful conduct a lawful status. This status is a far-reaching legal acknowledgment of the intimate relationship between two people, a relationship deemed by the State worthy of dignity in the community equal with all other marriages. It reflects both the community's considered perspective on the historical roots of the institution of marriage and its evolving understanding of the meaning of equality." The majority opinion also relied on Justice Kennedy's opinion in *Lawrence v. Texas* (2003), which was decided exactly ten years earlier and struck down criminal prosecutions for same-sex sodomy.[1] As in *Lawrence*, the majority opinion refers to a "stigma" DOMA places on same-sex spouses: "The avowed purpose and practical effect of the law here in question are to impose a disadvantage, a separate status, and so a stigma upon all who enter into same-sex marriages made lawful by the unquestioned authority of the States." Indeed, the majority opinion sees DOMA as a statute which "writes inequality into the entire United States Code," including "laws pertaining to Social Security, housing, taxes, criminal sanctions, copyright, and veterans' benefits." As such, "DOMA's principal effect is to identify a subset of state-sanctioned marriages and make them unequal."

Justice Kennedy found that DOMA creates a "second-tier marriage" for gay people and "demeans the couple, whose moral and sexual choices the Constitution protects [citing *Lawrence v. Texas*], and whose relationship the State has sought to dignify. And it humiliates tens of thousands of children now being raised by same-sex couples."

Based on this mix of protected equality, human dignity, and federalism, the court held that DOMA "is in violation of the Fifth Amendment." Significantly, however, the opinion closes by explicitly noting that "This opinion and its holding are confined to . . . lawful marriages" entered into in states that recognize same-sex marriage.

The majority opinion generated three dissenting opinions. Chief Justice Roberts initially noted that "without some more convincing evidence that the Act's principal purpose was to codify malice, and that it furthered *no* legitimate government interests, I would not tar the political branches with the brush of bigotry." Roberts went on to underline the limited scope of the holding, noting that "The Court does not have before it, and the logic of its opinion does not decide, the distinct question whether the States, in the exercise of their 'historic and essential authority to define the marital relation,' . . . may continue to utilize the traditional definition of marriage." Moreover, in his view, that state power to define the marital relation "will come into play on the other side of the board in future cases about the constitutionality of state marriage definitions."

Justice Scalia wrote a blistering critique of the majority opinion and its impact in a separate dissenting opinion, joined by Justice Thomas. Initially, those justices and the Chief Justice would have found a lack of standing in the congressional representatives who were defending DOMA when the executive branch refused to do so. On the merits, Justices Scalia and Thomas criticized the vague nature of the majority opinion's rulings, noting that "The opinion does not resolve and indeed does not even mention what had been the central question in this litigation: whether, under the Equal Protection Clause, laws restricting marriage to a man and a woman are reviewed for more than mere rationality." Indeed, in the words of Justice Scalia, "The sum of all the Court's nonspecific hand-waving is that this law is invalid (maybe on equal-protection grounds, maybe on substantive-due-process grounds, and perhaps with some amorphous federalism component playing a role) because it is motivated by a 'bare . . . desire to harm' couples in same-sex marriages."

Justice Scalia also predicted that the majority opinion would not be limited in its future application, starkly proclaiming that "I promise you this: The only thing that will 'confine' the Court's holding is its sense of what it can get away with." Moreover, "In my opinion . . . the view that this Court will take of state prohibition of same-sex marriage is indicated beyond mistaking by today's opinion. As I have said, the real rationale of today's opinion, whatever disappearing trail of its legalistic argle-bargle one chooses to follow, is that DOMA is motivated by 'bare . . . desire to harm' couples in same-sex marriages. How easy it is, indeed how inevitable, to reach the same conclusion with regard to state laws denying same-sex couples marital status."

In support of his argument as to the future impact of the majority opinion, Justice Scalia looked back at the history of *Lawrence v. Texas*. Citing the next to last sentence of the *Windsor* majority opinion limiting its application to lawful marriages, Justice Scalia complained that "I have heard such 'bald, unreasoned disclaimer[s]' before."

Finally, Justice Scalia contended that the decision whether to permit same-sex marriages should be left to the political process. He stated that "We might have covered ourselves with honor today, by promising all sides of this debate that it was theirs to settle and that we would respect their resolution. We might have let the People decide."

A third dissenting opinion was written by Justice Alito, who stated that in his view "The Constitution does not guarantee the right to enter into a same-sex marriage. Indeed, no provision of the Constitution speaks to the issue." As such, in the current case, the proponents of same-sex marriage are seeking an "innovation not from a legislative body elected by the people, but from unelected judges."

Justice Alito stated that "judges have cause for both caution and humility" in approaching this issue because "At present, no one—including social scientists, philosophers, and historians—can predict with any certainty what the long-term ramifications of widespread acceptance of same-sex marriage will be. And judges are certainly not equipped to make such an assessment."

In the closing paragraphs of his opinion, Justice Alito stated that "To the extent that the Court takes the position that the question of same-sex marriage should be resolved primarily at the state level, I wholeheartedly agree. I hope that the Court will ultimately permit the people of each State to decide this question for themselves. Unless the Court is willing to allow this to occur, the whiffs of federalism in the today's opinion of the Court will soon be scattered to the wind."

Following the *Windsor* decision, lower federal courts nearly unanimously read it the way Justice Scalia predicted they would, with several circuit and multiple district courts striking down state laws banning same-sex marriages. At the federal appellate level, after *Windsor*, only the Sixth Circuit upheld state laws which limited marriage to the union of one man and one woman. The "whiffs of federalism" in Justice Kennedy's opinion completely dissipated, failing to respect the electorates or legislatures of those states which had chosen to foreclose same-sex marriages. Finally, the Supreme Court put to rest any lingering doubts regarding the constitutionality of bans on same-sex marriage when it reversed the Sixth Circuit in *Obergefell v. Hodges* (2015).

In *Obergefell*, the court held that there was a fundamental constitutional right for same-sex couples to marry based upon the Due Process and Equal Protection Clauses of the Fourteenth Amendment. The vote was five to four; the justices were sharply divided; and each of the four dissenters wrote a dissenting opinion.

THE MAJORITY OPINION.

In the majority opinion, Justice Kennedy wrote that the Constitution promises liberty to all people to enable them "to define and express their identity." That liberty, as protected by the Due Process Clause, "extend[s] to certain personal choices central to individual dignity and autonomy, including intimate choices that define personal identity and beliefs." This includes "the right to marry," which the Supreme Court had recognized in prior decisions to be "fundamental under the Due Process Clause." The right to marry is fundamental because marriage promises "nobility and dignity to all persons," and has "centrality . . . to the human condition."

Justice Kennedy identified four principles and traditions which, in the view of the majority, supported the conclusion that the right to marry was fundamental. First, "the right to personal choice regarding marriage is inherent in the concept of individual autonomy." Second, "the right to marry is fundamental because it supports a two-person union unlike any other in its importance to the committed individuals." Third, "it safeguards children and families and thus draws meaning from related rights of childrearing, procreation, and education." Indeed, children of same-sex couples will feel stigmatized if their parents are not allowed to marry because they will feel that their families are "somehow lesser." Fourth, "marriage is a keystone of our social order," and numerous benefits are tied to it.

Given these principles and traditions regarding the fundamental nature of the right to marry, the majority concluded that "It demeans gays and lesbians for the State to lock them out of a central institution of the Nation's society." Since same-sex couples now "ask for equal dignity in the eyes of law," Justice Kennedy noted that "The Constitution grants them that right," and, as such, "The Court now holds that same-sex couples may exercise the fundamental right to marry."

Justice Kennedy's opinion relied heavily upon a substantive due process approach, citing cases such as *Pierce v. Society of Sisters* (1925) and *Meyer v. Nebraska* (1923).[2] He also based the ruling upon the Equal Protection Clause, finding it interlocks with the Due Process Clause, with the two acting synergistically, based upon prior decisions, to recognize a connection between liberty and equality. Because gay and lesbian couples are treated differently than heterosexual couples, this unconstitutionally "serves to disrespect and subordinate them."

Responding to the contentions that same-sex marriage had not been recognized historically, Justice Kennedy replied that marriage as an institution "has evolved over time," including the decline of arranged marriages and the recognition of greater rights for women. In addition, the treatment of homosexuality has also changed, discarding in 1973 the psychiatric community's classification of it as a mental disorder. Moreover, the original intent of those who drafted the Bill of Rights and the Fourteenth Amendment is not determinative, because "When new insight reveals discord between the Constitution's central protections and a received legal structure, a claim to liberty must be addressed." Finally, responding to the dissenters, the majority ruled that there was no need to wait for "further legislation, litigation, and debate" because "The dynamic of our constitutional system is that individuals need not await legislative action before asserting a fundamental right."

Further responding to several of the dissenting opinions which raised the specter of discrimination against religious groups that continued to oppose same-sex marriage, the majority opinion recited that the view that marriage is "a gender-differentiated union of man and woman" is held "in good faith by reasonable and sincere people here and throughout the world." Moreover, "Many who deem same-sex marriage to be wrong reach that conclusion based on decent and honorable religious or philosophical premises, and neither they nor their beliefs are disparaged here." As such, these individuals have a First Amendment right to "advocate" and "teach" against same-sex marriage: "it must be emphasized that religions, and those who adhere to religious doctrines, may continue to advocate with the utmost, sincere conviction that, by divine precepts, same-sex marriage should not be condoned. The First Amendment ensures that religious organizations and persons are given proper protection as they seek to teach the principles that are so fulfilling and so central to their lives and faiths, and to their own deep aspirations to continue the family structure they have long revered. The same is true of those who oppose same-sex marriage for other reasons."

THE DISSENTING OPINIONS

The ruling that same-sex couples have a fundamental constitutional right to marry met with four vigorous dissents. The dissenters advanced seven principal points. First, the question of who may marry is a matter for decision by the states, but five justices, in violation of the principle of judicial restraint, usurped the rights of the people in the thirty-two states that had voted to ban same-sex marriage. Second, the ruling cut off the ongoing political debate in the several states regarding whether same-sex marriage should be permitted, in the course of which debate eleven states and the District of Columbia had approved same-sex marriage, while other states had rejected it. Third, no Supreme Court precedent supported a due process liberty right to same-sex marriage, because liberty under that clause only embraces rights which were deeply rooted in the country's history and tradition, whereas same-sex marriage was first recognized in this country in 2003 by judicial decision in Massachusetts. Fourth, legitimatizing same-sex marriage may lead to the further degrading of the traditional marriage model in which a mother and father procreate and raise children in a lifelong relationship, and some states may reasonably wish to promote this model. Fifth, defining same-sex marriage as a fundamental right was premature in any event since it constitutes a new model of marriage recognized in the United States for the first time little more than a decade ago, and its long-term effects on society and on children raised in such relationships is presently unknown. Sixth, the recognition of same-sex marriage as a constitutional right threatens religious liberty by explicitly granting opponents the right only to teach or advocate opposition to same-sex marriage, while remaining silent on whether they may exercise their opposition by action. Seventh, the language of the majority opinion effectively labeled opponents of same-sex marriage as bigots, which serves only to hamper continuing public debate and to impede free speech, despite the fact that the majority opinion purports to preserve the opponents' free speech rights.

In his dissenting opinion, Chief Justice Roberts questioned "Just who do we think we are?" In his view, the real question presented to the court was "*who decides* what constitutes 'marriage'?" and "Five lawyers" in the majority opinion were "Stealing this issue from the people." Those five justices had chosen to close the "vibrant debate" regarding same-sex marriage to "enact . . . their own vision of marriage as a matter of constitutional law." But "Closing debate tends to close minds." The chief justice noted that Justice Ginsburg herself had earlier criticized *Roe v. Wade* as having been "heavy-handed judicial intervention," which was "difficult to justify and appears to have provoked, not resolved, conflict."

Chief Justice Roberts further noted that "this Court is not a legislature," but that the majority was second-guessing the wisdom of legislation banning same-sex marriage that had been passed in many states. In his judgment, "The fundamental right to marry does not include a right to make a State change its definition of marriage," and "The people of the state are free to expand marriage to include same-sex couples, or to retain the historic definition." Indeed, marriage historically has been based upon a "vital need: ensuring that children are conceived by a mother and father committed to raising them in the stable conditions of a lifelong relationship."

Moreover, Chief Justice Roberts contended that the purported fundamental right of same-sex marriage had "no basis in the Constitution or this Court's precedent." Indeed, the solicitor general "expressly disowned" at oral argument any contention that there was a due process basis for same-sex marriage. Previous cases had established that for a liberty right to be designated as fundamental, it must be "rooted in the traditions and conscience of our people." Chief Justice Roberts observed that the "strong medicine of substantive due process" must therefore be administered with judicial restraint, pointing out that the doctrine had previously been abused in such decisions as *Dred Scott v. Sanford* (1857) and *Lochner v. New York* (1905). He distinguished the cases relied upon by the majority, including *Lawrence v. Texas* (2003), as having involved "government intrusion" that was not present in this same-sex marriage context where the petitioners were claiming a right, rather than seeking protection from a punishment. The chief justice further observed that the reasoning of the majority opinion would equally support a fundamental right to polygamy.

Finally, Chief Justice Roberts turned to the question of religious liberty, arguing that the majority opinion "creates serious questions about religious liberty." He questioned whether the results of the opinion would require religious schools to provide housing for married same-sex couples or for religious adoption agencies to place children with same-sex married couples; or whether the opinion would permit the government to revoke the tax exemptions of some religious institutions. In addition, the language of the majority opinion labels opponents of same-sex marriage as bigots.

In closing, Chief Justice Roberts invited same-sex couples to celebrate the decision but "do not celebrate the Constitution. It had nothing to do with it."

In his dissenting opinion, Justice Scalia focused upon two points—threats to the democratic process in the approach taken by the majority, and a repudiation of the federalism interests that had been recognized in the *Windsor* decision two years previously. As a result of the majority opinion, he contended that "my Ruler, and the Ruler of 320 million Americans coast-to-coast, is a majority of the nine lawyers on the Supreme Court." By their approach, they have robbed the people of their most important liberty, "the freedom to govern themselves." The decision cuts off the debate in which some eleven states and the District of Columbia had chosen to permit same-sex marriage, but in which a greater multiple of other states had rejected it. Justice Scalia characterized the majority opinion as a "Judicial Putsch," and as "a naked judicial claim to legislative—indeed, *super*-legislative—power; a claim fundamentally at odds with our system of government." In his view, "A system of government that makes the People subordinate to a committee of nine unelected lawyers does not deserve to be called a democracy." Moreover, the justices of the Supreme Court were hardly a representative body, with each of them at that time having attended either Harvard or Yale Law School, none of them being Protestants, and only one of them coming from the vast territory that constitutes the middle states of this nation.

Justice Scalia then pointed out that the *Windsor* opinion had specifically stated that the area of domestic relations was "a virtually exclusive province of the States," and that all the justices in the majority opinion in *Obergefell* had joined that opinion. Moreover, when the Fourteenth Amendment was ratified in 1868, all the then-existing states provided that marriage was limited to one man and one woman. In Justice Scalia's originalist view, "That resolves these cases," since the fundamental right proclaimed by the majority was rooted in the Due Process Clause of that Amendment.

Justice Thomas's dissenting opinion focused upon three issues: the limits of liberty rights recognizable under substantive due process; disregard of the political process by the majority; and threats to religious liberty from its decision. Justice Thomas argued that due process liberty is "negative liberty," which involves "freedom from physical restraint"; as such, it only reaches "freedom from government action," and does not extend to "entitlement to government benefits." Even such cases as *Loving v. Virginia* (1967) involved criminal sanctions and prohibitions imposed on interracial couples, not an entitlement to benefits.

Justice Thomas next pointed out that the approach taken by the majority subverts the democratic process that, in thirty-two of the thirty-five states that had put the issue to a popular vote, rejected same-sex marriage. As such, the majority opinion "disregards the political process as a protection for liberty."

Next, Justice Thomas observed that "It appears all but inevitable that the two [government and religious institutions] will come into conflict, particularly as individuals and churches are confronted with demands to participate in and endorse civil marriages between same-sex couples." Moreover, the majority opinion makes only "a weak gesture towards religious liberty in a single paragraph." Indeed, that paragraph appears to limit religious liberty to oppose same-sex marriage to teaching, whereas "Religious liberty is about freedom of action in matters of religion generally."

In closing his dissenting opinion, Justice Thomas points out that while the majority relies upon the concept of advancing human dignity, in fact dignity is "innate," not something bestowed by the government, including by the courts.

In the fourth and final dissenting opinion, Justice Alito discussed issues of federalism; the definition of "liberty" under the Due Process Clause; the traditional basis for marriage; and religious liberty and conscience issues. He contended that "Today's decision usurps the constitutional right of the people to decide whether to keep or alter the traditional understanding of marriage," an issue that is to "be decided by the people of each state." By removing that issue from the democratic process, the majority opinion "evidences . . . the deep and perhaps irremediable corruption of our legal culture's conception of constitutional interpretation."

Justice Alito contended that "liberty" under the Due Process Clause only embraced rights that were deeply rooted in the nation's history and tradition. This was not true of same-sex marriage, as no country had recognized it prior to the Netherlands in 2000, and no U.S. state had recognized such a marriage as permissible before Massachusetts did in 2003. As such, the petitioners were seeking a "new right," not one that was "deeply rooted" in American history and tradition.

Justice Alito then turned to an analysis of the claim that same-sex marriage was properly based upon the happiness of the parties. He argued, instead, that the traditional understanding of marriage was one based on procreation within a "lasting unit that has long been thought to provide the best atmosphere for raising children." While he admitted that this traditional understanding had become "frayed," with more than 40 percent of babies being born to unmarried women in recent years, Justice Alito contended that such developments could, in fact, strengthen the view of states opposing same-sex marriage. This was because they could properly "worry that by officially abandoning the older understanding, they may contribute to marriage's further decay." In addition, quoting his dissenting opinion in the *Windsor* case, he noted the long-term consequences of recognizing same-sex marriage were "not now known and are unlikely to be ascertainable for some time to come."

The Alito dissent also argued the majority opinion would be used to "vilify" opponents of same-sex marriage by comparing laws banning same-sex marriage to laws denying equal treatment to African Americans and women. In addition, while the majority claimed to protect rights of conscience, their opinion might result in a situation where "those who cling to old beliefs will be able to whisper their thoughts in the recesses of their homes, but if they repeat those views in public, they will risk being labeled as bigots and treated as such by governments, employers, and school."

ANALYSIS: THE SHORTCOMINGS OF *OBERGEFELL*

As Professor Jonathan Turley (a proponent of same-sex marriage) has observed, the majority opinion "extends the concept of liberty far beyond prior decisions," and its "dignity" underpinnings may encourage enactment of anti-free-speech legislation and regulations such as now exist in Europe and Canada to combat what Justice Kennedy describes as "Dignitary wounds" in the majority opinion.[3] In any event, the majority effectively repudiates prior decisions of the court that held that fundamental rights must be deeply rooted in the traditions and conscience of the people. As the court noted in *Washington v. Glucksberg* (1997), in refusing to recognize a right to assisted suicide, a fundamental right should only be recognized with "the utmost care" so the "liberty" protected by the Due Process Clause is not "subtly transformed into the policy preferences of the Members of this Court." One may reasonably wonder whether the *Glucksberg* holding is itself in jeopardy, given the "dignity" reasoning of the majority. Indeed, Law Professor Josh Blackman has documented how the *Obergefell* majority simply declared the *Glucksberg* precedent inapplicable. In doing so, he concluded that "This utter rejection of tradition, without even the need to feign one, effects a massive shift in the Court's already unbounded substantive due process jurisprudence."[4]

The majority opinion has also been criticized for its repeated references to "new insights" and "enhanced" or "better informed" understandings, an approach that invites recognition and proliferation of new "fundamental rights" based upon periodic and sudden changes in public opinion. With respect to same-sex marriage, for example, public opinion polls as recently as 2003 recorded a majority opposed to its legal recognition.

The dissenting opinions also properly recognize that the approach taken by the majority tears decision-making from the people and confers it upon a court whose members do not reflect the public at large. Such an approach threatens the institutional respect the American people traditionally accorded to the Supreme Court.

A final, and significant, problem posed by the majority decision is that it invites bigotry and retaliation against opponents of same-sex marriage. As discussed above, a number of lawsuits seeking to force businesses to conform to the desires of same-sex couples have already been filed, for example, to compel opponents of same-sex marriage to design wedding cakes celebrating gay marriage, to provide photography services for same-sex weddings, or to lease their facilities for such weddings. Some of these suits have resulted in substantial monetary judgments against the businesses that refused to compromise their religious beliefs. Threats have also been made to sue churches that refuse to perform same-sex marriages. In addition, as Chief Justice Roberts noted in his dissenting opinion, the government admitted at oral argument that "the tax-exemptions of some religious institutions would be in question if they opposed same-sex marriage." Given these developments, persons of faith, as well as religious institutions, are threatened by the majority opinion's explicit recognition of their right only to teach and advocate their positions against same-sex marriage, while not expressly noting the explicit guarantee of the First Amendment for them freely to "*exercise*" their religion through specific *action.*

It is currently unclear what the ultimate outcome of such lawsuits against religiously affiliated organizations and private businesses will be, particularly since the majority opinion in *Masterpiece Cakeshop* avoided deciding the general issue. But one thing is clear: there will be significant and expensive litigation that opponents of same-sex marriage will have to defend, at great financial and personal costs, with media coverage often charging them with bigotry. Such litigation and publicity will be chilling to the free exercise rights of all opponents of same-sex marriage, giving the absence of any specific recognition of the right to take action against the recognition of same-sex marriages, such as by refusing to provide certain services to them, based upon the free exercise of religious beliefs. Whether the majority's recognition of a right to "teach" and "advocate" against same-sex marriage will be sufficient to protect those opponents will require years of litigation to resolve.

On a closing note, opponents of same-sex marriage may take solace, and perhaps comfort, from the observations of Justice Robert Jackson, who was also the chief prosecutor of the Nazi war criminals in the Nuremberg War Crimes Trials. Justice Jackson made an important and apt comment for our purposes in *West Virginia State Board of Education v. Barnette* (1943), a decision that struck down a requirement that students salute the American Flag.[5] In his opinion, he reminded the reader that "If there is any fixed star in our constitutional constellation, it is that no official, higher or petty, can prescribe what shall be orthodox in politics, nationalism, religion, or other matters of opinion or *force citizens to confess by word or act their faith therein*" (emphasis added).

LISTING FEMALE SPOUSES OF BIRTH MOTHERS ON BIRTH CERTIFICATES

Under Arkansas law, the name of a birth mother's male spouse was generally required to appear on a child's birth certificate regardless of his biological relationship to the child. The same law did not require birth certificates to list same-sex female spouses of women who give birth. In *Pavan v. Smith* (2017), the Supreme Court summarily reversed, without even hearing oral argument or requiring full briefing, an Arkansas Supreme Court decision that ruled the Arkansas law was constitutional and was not inconsistent with *Obergefell* because it "centers on the relationship of the biological mother and the biological father to the child, not on the marital relationship of husband and wife." In an unsigned opinion for six members of the Supreme Court of the United States, the majority ruled that this "differential treatment infringes *Obergefell's* commitment to provide same-sex couples 'the constellation of benefits that the States have linked to marriage.'"

The majority pointed out that in the case of opposite-sex couples, the Arkansas law required the birth mother's husband be listed on the child's birth certificate, even when the husband was not the biological father. As such, the state "may not, consistent with *Obergefell*, deny married same-sex couples that recognition."

In a dissenting opinion joined by Justices Thomas and Alito, Justice Gorsuch argued that rational reasons supported a "biology-based birth registration system" that assisted individuals to "determine their biological lineage, citizenship, or susceptibility to genetic disorders." The dissenters also pointed out that the law afforded important exceptions that permitted same-sex couples to be treated the same way as opposite-sex couples. These exceptions included cases of artificial insemination and adoption, where the female spouse of the birth mother could be listed on the birth certificate.

NOTES

1. *Lawrence v. Texas* is discussed in *Shaping America*, supra, 257–60.
2. The *Pierce* and *Meyer* decisions are discussed in *Shaping America*, 145–47.
3. Jonathan Turley, "The Trouble with the 'Dignity' of Same-Sex Marriage," *Washington Post*, July 2, 2015.
4. Josh Blackman, "Obergefell and Tradition," joshblackman.com/blog, April 13, 2017.
5. *West Virginia State Board of Education v. Barnette* is discussed in *Shaping America*, 152–54.

Chapter 11

Abortion

The most striking example of the Supreme Court changing constitutional law came in 2022, when the court overruled *Roe v. Wade* nearly fifty years after it was decided. From the time of the *Roe* decision and continuing persistently through the present, the issue of what constitutional limits on abortion could be imposed has divided the country, as well as the Supreme Court, whose decisions have mostly come in highly divided five-to-four decisions.[1]

Public opinion polls have consistently indicated that most of the population supports a general right to abortion, but subject to significant limitations, including sharply regulating the availability of abortion after the first trimester. Democrats, many women, and some men support a no-limits approach to abortion and would even permit it up to the moment of birth. In the 2022 federal elections, in which the Republican Party was favored to win both houses of Congress, the Democratic Party's reliance on preserving a constitutional right to abortion even after the Supreme Court overruled *Roe v. Wade* was successful in preserving that party's control of the Senate and reducing the Republican Party's victory in taking the House of Representatives to a handful of seats. The Democrats' reliance upon rejecting limits on abortion in favor of a woman's right to choose was dramatically illustrated in Bucks County, Pennsylvania, where *every* Democratic poster on lawns and highways was limited to the one single issue of preserving abortion rights.

The strong emotional appeal to some women of preserving a right to abortion reflects the political force of the feminist movement, and the militant approach taken by its early leaders, including Betty Friedan and Gloria Steinem, as well as those who followed, including presidential candidate and former senator Hillary Clinton. The feminist movement was also nearly successful in passing the Equal Rights Amendment to the Constitution, which was passed by Congress in 1971 and 1972, and thereafter ratified by thirty-five of the thirty-eight states needed to enact a constitutional amendment. Feminism remains a powerful force politically today, particularly in the Democratic Party, and in the general culture as well. Its most visible recent success, together with its influence in the 2022 federal elections, was in energizing the "#MeToo" movement urging women to out their employers who had sexually assaulted or otherwise abused them. The publicity given to such incidents resulted in criminal convictions for such powerful men as movie producer Harvey Weinstein, and the marginalization or "canceling" of several movie stars, including Johnny Depp, who struck back by winning a multimillion-dollar defamation suit against his former wife and accuser.

In *Roe v. Wade* (1973), and the related case of *Doe v. Bolton* (1973), the court ruled, by seven-to-two margins, that a woman has a constitutional right to choose an abortion. Justice Blackmun's majority opinion relied upon the right of privacy, which he declared was "founded in the Fourteenth Amendment's concept of personal liberty and restrictions upon state action." That concept was seen to be "broad enough to encompass a woman's decision whether or not to terminate her pregnancy" "because denial of an abortion by the state would involve imposing a 'detriment . . . upon the pregnant woman'" because giving birth to a child "may force upon the woman a distressful life and future. Psychological harm may be imminent. Mental and physical health may be taxed by child care. There is also the distress, for all concerned, associated with the unwanted child, and there is the problem of bringing a child into a family already unable, psychologically and otherwise, to care for it."

Justice Blackmun ruled that the right of personal privacy "is not unqualified and must be considered against important state interests in regulation." Nevertheless, since the right to choose an abortion is "fundamental," it could only be overcome by showing a compelling state interest in doing so.

To implement its ruling, the majority found a trimester approach to be appropriate in determining what limitations, if any, the state may place upon a woman's right to choose to have an abortion. During the first trimester, "the abortion decision and its effectuation must be left to the medical judgment of the pregnant woman's attending physician." After the first trimester, the state could regulate the abortion procedure only "in ways that are reasonably related to maternal health." Finally, "subsequent to viability, the state in promoting its interest in the potentiality of human life may, if it chooses, regulate, and even proscribe, abortion except where it is necessary, in appropriate medical judgment, for the preservation of the life or health of the mother."

Justice William Rehnquist, who had recently been confirmed to serve on the court, dissented. He pointed out that the traditional test of whether a state law was constitutional was whether it had "a rational relation to a valid state objective." He noted that at the time the Fourteenth Amendment was adopted, at least thirty-six state or territorial laws limited abortion. He also argued the trimester approach "partakes more of judicial legislation than it does of a determination of the intent of the drafters of the Fourteenth Amendment."

Justice Byron White also dissented, contending that the issue of abortion "should be left with the people and to the political processes the people have devised to govern their affairs." Instead, the majority opinion "simply fashions and announces a new constitutional right for pregnant mothers and, with scarcely any reason or authority for its action, invests that right with sufficient substance to override most existing state abortion statutes. The upshot is that the people and legislatures of the 50 States are constitutionally disentitled to weigh the relative importance of the continued existence and development of the fetus, on the one hand, against a spectrum of possible impacts on the mother, on the other hand. As an exercise of raw judicial power, the Court perhaps has authority to do what it does today; but in my view its judgment is an improvident and extravagant exercise of the power of judicial review that the Constitution extends to this court."

The court's decisions in *Roe* and *Bolton* met with vocal criticism, not only from pro-life groups, but also from many academics for its inadequate constitutional reasoning. Moreover, a year before she was nominated to serve on the Supreme Court, future Justice Ruth Bader Ginsburg pointed out in a law review article that *Roe* "halted a political process that was moving in a reform direction," and generated "prolonged divisiveness."

With the appointment of five new justices by presidents Ronald Reagan and George H.W. Bush, as well as the elevation of Justice Rehnquist to chief justice, subsequent decisions on abortion, while maintaining the constitutional right of a woman to choose to undergo an abortion, chipped away at the base of the constitutional right announced in *Roe*, with most decisions rendered thereafter by five-to-four majorities.

Roe survived two major attacks in the 1980s and 1990s. In *Webster v. Reproductive Health Services* (1989), emboldened by the additions of Justices O'Connor, Scalia, and Kennedy to the court, numerous religious groups, multiple states attorneys general, and other interest groups launched a full-scale attack on *Roe*, requesting that it be overruled. *Webster* preserved *Roe* in a five-to-four decision, with Chief Justice Rehnquist rejecting requests by the solicitor general of the United States and many friends of the court to overrule *Roe*, since he noted significant differences between the statute involved in that case and the Missouri statute involved in *Webster*. Indeed, the *Webster* court upheld the provision of the Missouri law that prohibited the use of public employees or facilities, including hospitals, to perform or assist with abortions except where they were necessary to save the woman's life, as well as a separate provision that required a doctor to perform appropriate medical examinations or tests to ascertain if the fetus was viable when the woman was believed to be twenty or more weeks' pregnant. Chief Justice Rehnquist noted the viability testing requirement "permissibly furthers the State's interest in protecting potential human life, and we therefore believe [the statute] to be constitutional."

Despite his decision not to overrule *Roe*, Chief Justice Rehnquist's opinion for himself, Justice White, and Justice Kennedy, concluded that "to the extent indicated in our opinion, we would modify and narrow *Roe* and succeeding cases." He called the "rigid trimester analysis" of *Roe* "a virtual Procrustean bed" that was "unsound in principle and unworkable in practice." Moreover, "The key elements of the *Roe* framework—trimesters and viability—are not found in the text of the Constitution or any place else one would expect to find a constitutional principle. Since the bounds of the inquiry are essentially indeterminate, the result has been a web of legal rules that has become increasingly intricate, resembling a code of regulations rather than a body of constitutional doctrine."

In a separate concurring opinion, Justice Scalia stated he would "more explicitly" overrule *Roe*. He complained that Rehnquist opinion was too piecemeal and that "it thus appears that the mansion of constitutional abortion law, constructed overnight in *Roe v. Wade* must be disassembled doorjamb by doorjamb, and never entirely brought down, no matter how wrong it might be."

Justice O'Connor provided the key vote to preserve *Roe*. In a separate concurring opinion, she expressed her view that a ban on abortions was permissible so long as the nature of the ban did not place an "undue burden" on the woman. Justice O'Connor concluded that the viability testing requirement did not "impose an undue burden on the woman's abortion decision." Nevertheless, she declined to join Chief Justice Rehnquist's opinion because she saw it as effectively overruling *Roe.*

Four justices dissented, with an opinion by Justice Blackmun, joined by Justices Brennan and Marshall, and a separate dissenting opinion written by Justice Stevens. Justice Blackmun's dissenting opinion was angry and almost apocalyptic in its language. In concluding his opinion, he remarked that "for today, at least, the law of abortion stands undisturbed. For today, the women of this nation still retain the liberty to control their destinies. But the signs are evident and very ominous, and a chill wind blows."

The second major assault on *Roe* came in *Planned Parenthood v. Casey* (1992). In the very first paragraph of the lead opinion, the court itself noted that *Casey* represented the sixth time in ten years that the solicitor general of the United States had called for the reversal of *Roe v. Wade.*

At issue in *Casey* were several provisions of the Pennsylvania Abortion Control Act of 1982. One provision established a twenty-four-hour waiting period before a woman could have an abortion, during which time she was to be provided information to permit her to give informed consent to the procedure. The information included the nature of the abortion procedure, the health risks of birth and abortion, the probable fetal age, and the availability of adoption and child support if the fetus was not aborted. Other provisions required that one parent of the minor give informed consent to any abortion for the minor (subject to a judicial bypass procedure), and that a married woman must provide a written statement that she had notified her husband about her intent to obtain an abortion. The first two of these provisions were upheld, with only the husband notification requirement struck down.

In a lengthy joint opinion by Justices O'Connor, Kennedy, and Souter, speaking for five members of the court, the majority ruled that the principle of *stare decisis* ("let it stand") prevented the overruling of *Roe v. Wade.* Proclaiming that "Liberty finds no refuge in a jurisprudence of doubt," that opinion stated that "the essential holding of Roe v. Wade should be retained and once again reaffirmed." The joint opinion noted that despite "reservations any of us may have in reaffirming the central holding of Roe," such reservations "are outweighed by the explication of individual liberty we have given, combined with the force of stare decisis." That individual liberty protected by the Fourteenth Amendment included "personal decisions relating to marriage, procreation, contraception, family relationships, child rearing and education." Such choices are "choices central to personal dignity and autonomy."

The joint opinion indicated that the "rigid" trimester approach of *Roe* was rejected, and that "the line should be drawn at viability, so that before that time the woman has a right to choose terminate her pregnancy." The joint opinion proposed to apply the "undue burden" standard that Justice O'Connor had suggested in *Webster*, but this portion of the opinion did not command a majority of the court. Instead, Chief Justice Rehnquist, joined by Justices White, Scalia, and Thomas, expressly rejected the undue burden standard, advocating instead that "States may regulate abortion procedures in ways rationally related to a legitimate state interest." These justices would have upheld all the Pennsylvania requirements, while Justice Blackmun, in dissent, was in favor of retaining the trimester and strict-scrutiny approaches of *Roe.* He would have invalidated all the challenged provisions of the Pennsylvania law. He reiterated the fear he noted in his *Webster* dissenting opinion, writing that "I fear for the darkness as four Justices anxiously await the single vote necessary to extinguish the light."

Justice Souter, who was joined to form a majority by Justices O'Connor, Kennedy, Blackmun, and Stevens, wrote a lengthy explication of the doctrine of *stare decisis*, concluding that nothing had happened since the decision in *Roe* to change its factual assumptions, or to contest "Roe's central holding, that viability marks the earliest point at which the State's interest in fetal life is constitutionally adequate to justify a legislative ban on non-therapeutic abortions."

In two separate opinions, one by Chief Justice Rehnquist and the other by Justice Scalia, four justices called for the overruling of *Roe v. Wade*. Chief Justice Rehnquist's opinion stated that "We believe that Roe was wrongly decided, and that it can and should be overruled consistent with our traditional approach to stare decisis in constitutional cases." These justices also rejected the undue burden standard as representing "an unjustified constitutional compromise, one which leaves the Court in a position to closely scrutinize all types of abortion regulations despite the fact that it lacks the power to do so under the Constitution." Chief Justice Rehnquist also observed that "a woman's interest in having an abortion is a form of liberty protected by the Due Process Clause, but States may regulate abortion procedures in ways rationally related to a legitimate state interest."

Justice Scalia was much more acerbic in his dissenting opinion. He contended that "The power of a woman to abort her unborn child" is not a liberty protected by the Constitution. This was "because of two simple facts: (1) the Constitution says absolutely nothing about it, and (2) long-standing traditions of American society have permitted it to be legally proscribed." He concluded that "the Imperial Judiciary lives," and "to portray Roe as the statesmanlike 'settlement' of a divisive issue, a jurisprudential Peace of Westphalia that is worth preserving, is nothing less than Orwellian. Roe fanned into life an issue that has inflamed our national politics in general, and has obscured with its smoke the selection of Justices to this Court, in particular, ever since. And by keeping us in the abortion-umpiring business, it is the perpetuation of that disruption, rather than of any Pax Roeana that the Court's new majority decrees." In sum, "We should get out of this area, where we have no right to be, and where we do neither ourselves nor the country any good by remaining."

The Supreme Court did, in fact, "get out of [the abortion] area" for some eight years. But in 2000, it reentered the area to determine the constitutionality of a Nebraska statute that banned the partial-birth abortion procedure. In *Sternberg v. Carhart* (2000), a highly fractured Supreme Court invalidated that statute by five-to-four vote. Eight of the nine justices wrote their own, separate opinion.

The partial-birth abortion procedure was characterized in 1997 by a publication of the American Medical Association as "ethically wrong." Justice Scalia, in dissent, characterized it as "horrible" and "visibly brutal." Justice Thomas's dissenting opinion referred to it as "a procedure that approaches infanticide." Justice Kennedy's dissenting opinion described the procedure at length, concluding that it has "the appearance of a live birth," and that "With only the head of the fetus remaining in utero, the abortionist tears open the skull. . . . The abortionist then inserts a suction tube and vacuums out the developing brain and matter found within the skull." Moreover, "Witnesses report observing the portion of the fetus outside the woman react to the skull penetration."

Writing for a majority of five, Justice Breyer explained that the statute was unconstitutional for two reasons. First, it failed to provide an exception where it was necessary to preserve the woman's health. "Necessary," in the view of the majority, "cannot refer to an absolute necessity or to absolute proof." The necessity requirement, which was set down in *Casey*, was satisfied "where substantial medical authority supports the proposition that banning a particular abortion procedure could endanger women's health." Second, the statute was overbroad, and could be interpreted to cover other abortion procedures. As such, the statute imposed an undue burden on a woman's ability to choose that form of abortion.

Justice Scalia vehemently dissented, comparing the majority's decision to *Dred Scott* and *Korematsu*. He contended that "The method of killing a human child—one cannot even accurately say an entirely unborn human child— . . . is so horrible that the most clinical description of it evokes a shudder of revulsion." As to the undue burden standard utilized by the majority, he characterized it as "a value judgment," which was dependent upon "how much one respects (or believes society ought to respect) the freedom of the woman who gave it life to kill it."

Justice Kennedy saw the majority opinion as misapplying his joint opinion in *Planned Parenthood v. Casey*. He argued in dissent that "*Casey* is premised on the States having an important constitutional role in defining their interests in the abortion debate," and that "States . . . have an interest in forbidding medical procedures that, in the State's reasonable determination, might cause the medical profession or society as a whole to become insensitive, even disdainful, to life, including life in the human fetus."

Justice Thomas began his dissenting opinion by contending that *Roe v. Wade* "was grievously wrong." In his view, the *Stenberg* majority opinion represented "a reinstitution of the pre-*Webster* abortion-on-demand era in which the mere invocation of 'abortion rights' trumps any contrary societal interest."

Chief Justice Rehnquist joined the dissenting opinions of Justices Kennedy and Thomas, and wrote a short dissenting opinion for himself, reiterating his belief that *Casey* was "wrongly decided."

Decided seven years after *Stenberg*, *Gonzales v. Carhart* (2007) marked a significant change in the court's approach to limitations on abortion. There, a bare majority of the Supreme Court upheld the constitutionality of a federal statute that proscribed the use of the same partial birth abortion procedure described in *Stenberg*, except where it was necessary to save the woman's life, because of its "disturbing similarity to the killing of an newborn infant." The federal statute did not provide a health exception, since Congress had found that the partial-birth abortion procedure was never necessary to preserve the health of the woman, and that other abortion options were available to her. *Gonzales* was decided by a five-to-four margin, with the majority opinion written by Justice Kennedy, who was joined by two newly confirmed justices—Chief Justice Roberts and Justice Alito—as well as by Justices Thomas and Scalia.

Justice Kennedy wrote for the majority that "where it has a rational basis to act, and it does not impose an undue burden, the State may use its regulatory power to bar certain procedures and substitute others, all in furtherance of its legitimate interests in regulating the medical profession in order to promote respect for life, including life of the unborn." In the case of the federal statute barring partial-birth abortions, "Congress could . . . conclude that the type of abortion proscribed by the Act requires specific regulation because it implicates additional ethical and moral concerns that justify a specific prohibition." This was because "Congress determined that the abortion methods it proscribed had a 'disturbing similarity to the killing of a newborn infant.'"

As to whether an exception was required where the procedure was necessary to preserve a woman's health, the majority opinion rejected the *Stenberg* approach, which deferred to "substantial medical authority" that believed banning a particular procedure might lead to such a danger. Justice Kennedy reasoned that such an approach "is too exacting a standard to impose on the legislative power . . . to regulate the medical profession." Moreover, when a particular woman had a true medical necessity requiring use of the partial-birth abortion procedure to preserve her health, she would have standing to make a challenge to the statute on an "as-applied" basis. Thus, while the statute was constitutional on its face, it could be challenged in its application to a specific individual woman.

Justice Ginsburg delivered a forceful dissent on behalf of four justices, including Justices Stevens, Souter, and Breyer. She described the opinion of the court as "alarming," and contended that "It blurs the line, firmly drawn in *Casey*, between previability and postviability abortions. And, for the first time since *Roe*, the court blesses a prohibition with no exception safeguarding a woman's health." Justice Ginsburg also argued that the privacy basis relied upon in *Roe* was not the proper focus. Instead, challenges to restrictions on abortion "center on a woman's autonomy to determine her life's course, and thus to enjoy equal citizenship stature."

The dissenters also criticized the majority for invoking "moral concerns," and for employing "an antiabortion shibboleth for which it concededly has no reliable evidence: Women who have abortions come to regret their choices, and consequently suffer from 'severe depression and loss of esteem.'" Such views, they argued, reflect "ancient notions about women's place in the family and under the Constitution—ideas that have long since been discredited."

Justice Ginsburg also characterized references to the fetus as an "unborn child" and as a "baby" as evidencing an unconcealed "hostility to the right *Roe* and *Casey* secured." Moreover, the opinion was argued to be "quite simply, irrational," and "cannot be understood as anything other than an effort to chip away at a right declared again and again by this Court—and with increasing comprehension to its centrality to women's lives." In conclusion, Justice Ginsburg referred to the addition of the new justices to the court, leading, in the view of the dissenters, to a decision that "is hardly faithful to our earlier invocations of 'the rule of law' and the 'principles of *stare decisis*.'"

After *Gonzales*, there was great hope from the pro-life community, and correspondingly great concern from pro-choice advocates, regarding the prospects for additional restrictions being constitutionally placed upon the availability of abortion. Both the hopes and concerns proved unfounded initially, with the Supreme Court returning to its previous vigorous defense of abortion rights in the *Whole Woman's Health* case. There the majority opinion was written by Justice Breyer, who had dissented in *Gonzales v. Carhart.*

Whole Woman's Health v. Hellerstedt (2016) was the first Supreme Court decision related to abortion following *Gonzales v. Carhart. Whole Woman's Health* did not address abortion procedures directly. Instead, its focus was on the constitutionality of a Texas law relating to the regulation of abortion clinics in that state. The two provisions of that law that were challenged in the Supreme Court required, first, that abortion doctors have admitting privileges at a hospital located within thirty miles from their facility, and second, that the facilities themselves meet the minimum standards for ambulatory surgical centers under Texas law. Both these provisions were found to be unconstitutional, by a five-to-three margin, on the grounds that they placed substantial obstacles in the path of women seeking pre-viability abortions and, as such, constituted an undue burden on their access to abortion. Significantly, Justice Breyer's majority opinion repeatedly referenced a risk-benefit type of analysis, under which the burdens imposed on abortion had to be compared to the benefits conferred by the challenged law.

With respect to the requirement for admitting privileges, the court found that the district court record revealed no significant health-related problems experienced under the then-current regulatory regime, which required providers to work out a relationship with doctors with admitting privileges. Similarly, the majority ruled that the surgical center requirement placed an undue burden on women seeking abortions because preexisting Texas law imposed many health and safety requirements, which were both policed and enforced. In addition, the district court further found that abortion was generally safe and indeed "safer . . . than many common medical procedures."

Since both these requirements were found to place significant burdens on women seeking abortions, and the Texas law was found to provide few, if any, benefits, the burdens imposed by the law were found to be undue, and therefore unconstitutional. In support of the conclusion regarding undue burden, the majority pointed out that several abortion clinics had closed after the legislation was enacted, and that the nearest abortion clinic available to many women in the State of Texas was many miles away. For example, the district court found that the number of abortion providers in the state would be reduced from the forty then existing to only seven or eight; that 1.65 million women would be living more than 150 to two hundred miles from an abortion clinic; and that rural women would be particularly disadvantaged because the clinics that would remain would be concentrated in five metropolitan areas. Finally, there were additional findings that the costs of compliance with the new law could be $1 to 1.5 million per abortion clinic, and that some clinics would be unable to comply because of physical size limitations.

Despite the ruling in *Gonzales v. Carhart* that legislative fact-finding was reviewed under an deferential standard, the *Whole Woman's Health* majority held that it was "wrong to equate the judicial review applicable to the regulation of a constitutionally protected personal liberty with the less strict review applicable where, for example, economic legislation is at issue."

Justice Breyer also rejected the argument that the Texas law might "force unsafe facilities to shut down." He dismissed comparisons to the gruesome infanticides in Pennsylvania at the abortion clinic operated by Kermit Gosnell, stating that, while "Gosnell's behavior was terribly wrong . . . there is no reason to believe that an extra layer of regulation would have affected that behavior."

There were two dissenting opinions, one by Justice Thomas for himself alone, and the other written by Justice Alito, and joined by Chief Justice Roberts and Justice Thomas.

Justice Thomas explained that he rejected "the Court's abortion jurisprudence," but went on to point out that, even under the controlling Supreme Court precedents, the majority significantly changed the undue burden standard from that set forth in the previously controlling plurality opinion in *Planned Parenthood of Southeastern Pa. v. Casey*. That opinion recognized a state could use its regulatory power to regulate aspects of abortion procedures "where it has a rational basis to act, and it does not impose an undue burden." Instead of the *Planned Parenthood* standard, the majority imposed a burdens-versus-benefits test not supported by *Planned Parenthood*; suggested that the courts need not defer to the legislature, but instead must independently assess medical justifications restricting abortion in an independent review of the record; and held that a legitimate state interest, standing alone, is not sufficient to justify restrictions placed on abortion. In Justice Thomas's view, this revised undue burden test departs from prior precedent and "looks . . . far more like the strict-scrutiny standard that *Casey* rejected, under which only the most compelling rationales justified restrictions on abortion."

Justice Thomas concluded his dissenting opinion with a lengthy discussion of how the court had confused the applicable standards of review, while simultaneously "transforming judicially created rights like the right to abortion into preferred constitutional rights, while disfavoring many of the rights actually enumerated in the Constitution."

Justice Alito began his dissenting opinion by contending at length that the current challenge to the Texas legislation was barred by prior litigation. He next attacked the grounds set forth by the majority to support its conclusion that the legislation unconstitutionally placed an undue burden on a woman's right to choose an abortion. To begin with, he pointed out that *Gonzales v. Carhart* required that a petitioner challenging a restriction on abortion had to demonstrate that a "large fraction" of Texas women would be impacted by those restrictions. But the petitioners here only relied upon "two crude inferences" in their challenge to the Texas legislation. First, they pointed to the number of abortion clinics that closed after the legislation was enacted. Justice Alito contended this was insufficient proof of undue burden since there was no evidence of exactly why each of the closed clinics chose to shut down. Second, the petitioners pointed to the reduced number of abortions. With respect to this point, Justice Alito contended there were at least four factors that might explain the reduction in the number of Texas abortions, including a general reduction nationwide during the same period.

Justice Alito also emphasized that "Precise findings" had to be made by the trier of fact because "The key issue . . . is not the number or percentage of clinics affected, but the effect of the closures on women seeking abortions, *i.e.*, on the capacity and geographic distribution of clinics used by those women." On that issue, there was no evidence advanced regarding the actual capacities to perform abortions of those clinics which remained open. Indeed, Justice Alito pointed to a chart submitted by the petitioners, which he attached to the final page of his opinion, which suggested that the total actual capacities of the remaining abortion clinics were sufficient to perform the same number of abortions that were performed in Texas in 2002, prior to the implementation of the challenged legislation.

The dissenters also addressed a number of other points relied upon by majority. First, with respect to travel times to abortion clinics, they pointed out that the *Planned Parenthood* opinion did not find it impermissible that, as a result of the restrictions at issue in that case, 42 percent of Pennsylvania women would be required to travel between one and three hours to the nearest abortion clinic. Moreover, as indicated as appropriate in *Gonzales v. Carhart*, any particular woman who did suffer severe inconvenience from the need to travel a long distance was free to make an as-applied challenge to the law. Second, since the Texas statute had a severability provision, the requirement that doctors in abortion clinics have admitting privileges in hospitals should have been left into place for those clinics that remained open. Similarly, with respect to the requirements regarding surgical centers, those should have been evaluated requirement by requirement, rather than having been entirely rejected as a matter of course.

The dissenters also pointed to the fact that the Philadelphia Grand Jury investigating the Kermit Gosnell infanticides suggested that Pennsylvania adopt a law similar to that later adopted by Texas regulating abortion clinics, contending this provided additional support for enactment of the Texas legislation.

The *Whole Woman's Health* majority imposed a notable change in emphasis in the Supreme Court's abortion jurisprudence. In two important ways, it shifted the focus from the approach taken in *Gonzales v. Carhart.* First, the majority opinion repeatedly referred to the need for the trier of fact to weigh the burdens imposed upon access to abortion against the benefits flowing from the regulations in question. This, in turn, would require detailed findings of fact, and those supporting the regulations would need to present detailed evidence regarding the specific benefits of the law, including identifying deaths and serious injuries to women undergoing abortions in the affected clinics that would be remedied by the law. Such detailed evidence would be particularly important because the majority opinion puts two thumbs on the scale against upholding any abortion regulation of the type involved in *Whole Woman's Health.* Thus, the majority emphasized the safety of abortion compared to other procedures and dismissed reference to the Gosnell case as justifying the Texas law.

A second significant change related to the level of deference that should be afforded state legislation. *Gonzales v. Carhart* held that fact-finding is subject to a deferential standard, indicating that "Where it has a rational basis to act, and it does not impose an undue burden, the State may use its regulatory power to bar certain procedures and substitute others, all in furtherance of its legitimate interests in regulating the medical profession in order to promote respect for life, including life of the unborn." By contrast, the *Whole Woman's Health* majority substituted a burdens-versus-benefit analysis, cautioning that it "is wrong to equate the judicial review applicable to the regulation of a constitutionally protected personal liberty with the less strict review applicable where, for example, economic legislation is at issue."

The benefits-versus-burdens test of *Whole Woman's Health* experienced a shortened life span four years later when the court decided *June Medical Services L.L.C. v. Russo* (2020). That case involved a challenge to a Louisiana law that was "almost word-for-word identical" to the Texas law struck down in *Whole Woman's Health.* While the Louisiana law was also struck down, only four members of the court, in a plurality opinion by Justice Breyer, followed the benefits-versus-burdens test of the prior decision. The decisive vote on that issue was that of Chief Justice Roberts. He ruled in a concurring opinion that respect for precedent required that the Louisiana law be struck down because "*Stare decisis* instructs us to treat all cases alike," but that the test enunciated in *Whole Woman's Health* was incorrect, having departed from past precedent. In the view of the chief justice, applying such a test "would require us to act as legislators, not judges, and would result in nothing other than an 'unanalyzed exercise of judicial will' in the guise of a 'neutral utilitarian calculus.'" Citing the *Gonzales* decision, he pointed out that the "traditional rule" was that "State and federal legislatures [have] wide discretion to pass legislation in areas where there is medical and scientific uncertainty." Chief Justice Roberts also analyzed the controlling decision of *Planned Parenthood v. Casey* at length. He concluded, quoting the *Casey* opinion, that so long as the State had a "legitimate purpose" in enacting abortion-related legislation and that legislation was "reasonably related to that goal," "the only question for a court is whether a law has the 'effect of placing a substantial obstacle in the path of a woman seeking an abortion of a nonviable fetus.'"

Justices Thomas, Alito, Gorsuch, and Kavanaugh each filed a dissenting opinion, contesting both the plurality opinion of Justice Breyer and parts of the concurring opinion of Chief Justice Roberts.

Initially, Justice Thomas would have denied standing to the private party doctors and clinics. On the merits, he noted his opinion that "The Constitution does not constrain the States' ability to regulate or even prohibit abortion" and that the court's "putative right to abortion is a creation that should be undone."

Justice Alito, joined in whole or part by the other dissenting justices, attacked the application of *stare decisis* in Chief Justice Roberts's concurring opinion, as Justice Thomas had also done in his opinion. Justice Alito did, however, agree with the chief justice that the benefits-versus-burdens test should be rejected and that *Whole Woman's Health* should "be overruled in so far as it changed the *Casey* test." Given the agreement on rejecting the benefits-versus-burdens test by five justices, that test was no longer controlling. As such, Justice Alito concluded the case should go back for a new trial utilizing *Casey*'s "substantial obstacle" test, and standing to challenge the law should be denied the abortion clinics and providers.

Justice Gorsuch's dissenting opinion argued the Louisiana case "concerns our willingness to follow the traditional constraints of the judicial process when a case touching on abortion enters the courtroom." He noted support for the *Gonzales* approach, which calls for a "deferential" but "not 'uncritical' standard" of review of a legislature's factual findings regarding the need for the specific type of regulation of abortion covered in the law. Justice Gorsuch then reviewed the evidence presented before the Louisiana legislature, which was considered before enacting the law, and suggested the law was constitutional. He also observed that granting standing to the third-party providers and clinics misapplied the court's standing standards. Next, he argued that any facial challenge to a statute must be presented by a person to whom the statute had been applied, not by providers or clinics. This "as applied" approach will "reduce the risk that a court will 'short circuit the democratic process' by interfering with legislation any more than necessary to remedy a complaining party's injury." Finally, Justice Gorsuch attacked Chief Justice Roberts's concurrence insofar as it found the Louisiana law presented an impermissible substantial obstacle to abortion. He concluded that both the plurality and the concurring opinions brush aside legal rules, leading the court to "a strangely open space, unconstrained by many of the neutral principles that normally govern the judicial process."

Justice Kavanaugh's short dissenting opinion focused on the need for a new trial on the question of whether the Louisiana law imposes an undue burden on women seeking abortions.

With the election of President Trump and the confirmations of Justices Gorsuch and Kavanaugh (and later Justice Barrett), several states were energized to enact new legislation limiting abortion directly or imposing related restrictions on facilities offering abortion or on funding of abortion providers. These new laws had several different approaches. Some prohibited abortions altogether after a fetal heartbeat was detected, while others prohibited abortion after twenty weeks, when a fetus could feel pain, or even earlier. Still other states prohibited specific methods of abortion, or they required women seeking abortions to have an ultrasound before undergoing an abortion. In addition, some states prohibited funding of abortion providers.

In *Box v. Planned Parenthood* (2019), the Supreme Court was asked to adjudicate the constitutionality of two other provisions related to abortion that were imposed by an Indiana law. The first provision excluded fetal remains from the definition of infectious and pathological waste, thus preventing their incineration, and authorized cremation of such remains. The second provision prohibited abortions based on fetal race, sex, or disability. Without hearing oral argument, the court issued a three-page *per curiam* opinion upholding the fetal remains provision but declining to decide the constitutionality of the second provision.

With respect to the fetal remains provision, the court noted that Planned Parenthood had not argued that this provision created an undue burden on a woman's right to obtain an abortion. As such, the proper standard of review was whether that provision was "rationally related to legitimate government interests." The court found that it was, based on a previous ruling that a state has a "legitimate interest in proper disposal of fetal remains." The justices were careful to note they were not making a ruling on whether the fetal remains provision imposed an undue burden on a woman who seeks to obtain an abortion. Dissenting from the court's ruling upholding that provision, Justice Ginsburg expressed the view that heightened review was in order under the undue burden standard, and that she therefore would have declined to hear the case since the outcome might be different if the provision was analyzed under the undue burden standard. Justice Sotomayor independently indicated that she also would have denied the petition for review.

Justice Thomas filed a concurring opinion indicating that he agreed with the court's disposition of both points for review, but he went on to contend that abortions based upon the fetus's sex, race, or disability smacked of eugenics. While he agreed with the court it was premature to decide whether a ban on such selective abortions was constitutional given the absence of other lower court decisions on the issue, he stated that the "Court will soon need to confront the constitutionality of [such laws]." This was because there exists "the potential for abortion to become a tool of eugenic manipulation."

Justice Thomas devoted the bulk of his opinion to a discussion of the history of the eugenics movement, pointing out how its chief proponents favored its use to attain racial goals, aimed particularly at African Americans. He argued that abortions were utilized in the same way, with a disproportionate impact upon African Americans, with abortions among African American women recorded at nearly three and a half times those among white women. Finally, he noted that Planned Parenthood had not challenged the ban on sex-selection abortions in *Planned Parenthood v. Casey*, in which the court first mentioned the undue burden standard.

An interesting and heated exchange between Justices Ginsburg and Thomas in their respective opinions illustrates that the issue of abortion sharply divides members of the court. Thus, in the first footnote to his opinion, Justice Thomas refers to a woman who has an abortion as a mother. In the second footnote of her opinion, Justice Ginsburg characterized Justice Thomas's footnote as displaying "more heat than light," because "a woman who exercises her constitutionally protected right to terminate a pregnancy is not a 'mother.'"

It was against the background of this very muddled, confusing, and heated precedent that the court considered the constitutionality of a Mississippi law that banned most abortions after fifteen weeks of pregnancy. In *Dobbs v. Jackson Women's Health Organization* (2022), six members of the court voted to uphold the Mississippi law, while five members went further and decided that *Roe v. Wade* must be overruled.

In the majority opinion by Justice Alito, the court concluded that "We therefore hold that the Constitution does not confer a right to abortion. Roe and Casey must be overruled, and the authority to regulate abortion must be returned to the people and their elected representatives."

In support of this conclusion, Justice Alito reasoned that "the Constitution makes no reference to abortion, and no such right is implicitly protected by any constitutional provision, including the one on which the defenders of Roe and Casey now chiefly rely—the Due Process Clause of the Fourteenth Amendment." That clause, in the majority's view, "only protects rights not explicitly referenced in the Constitution if such a right is "deeply rooted in this Nation's history and tradition," and is "implicit in the concept of ordered liberty," citing *Washington v. Glucksberg* (1977) (declining to recognize a constitutional right to assisted suicide). *Glucksberg* pointed to a fear that expanding implied rights under "the liberty protected by the Due Process Clause [might] be subtly transferred into the policy preferences of the Members of this Court."

In applying the *Glucksberg* test, the majority pointed out several factors. First, at the time of the adoption of the Fourteenth Amendment, three-quarters of the states made abortion a crime. Second, a detailed review of English and American law showed that abortion was considered a crime historically. Third, even at the time *Roe* was decided, some thirty states still prohibited abortion. Fourth, in the current case, more than one half of the states asked the court to overrule *Roe.* Fifth, the cases on which the defenders of *Roe* relied were fundamentally different, because abortion, unlike the rights recognized in those cases, destroys what the court had called "potential life" in its prior abortion rulings. Based upon these factors, any right to abortion was not "deeply rooted in this Nation's history and tradition," and was not "implicit in the concept of ordered liberty."

Turning to the contention that *stare decisis* required *Roe* to be upheld, the majority rejected that contention based upon analyzing five aspects of the court's opinion in *Roe.* These were "the nature of their errors, the quality of their reasoning, the 'workability' of the rules they imposed on the country, their disruptive effect on other areas of law, and the absence of concrete reliance." Looking at these factors, the court concluded that *Roe* was wrong from the start, employed "reasoning exceptionally weak," and "inflamed debate and deepened division," rather than "bringing about a national settlement of the abortion issue." As to the "undue burden" test, the majority characterized it as unsupported in law or history, lacking any reasonable principle for using viability as *Roe*'s "central holding," sounding more like a legislative determination, and establishing a standard that was too ambiguous to apply objectively.

To claims by the dissenters and legal commentators that the majority opinion threatened other rights, such as those to contraception and same-sex marriage, Justice Alito responded that the opinion does not "cast doubt on precedents that do not concern abortion."

Finally, the majority concluded that going forward, abortion restrictions would be adjudicated on a rational basis standard of review. That standard affords state legislatures' actions a "strong presumption of validity," and would sustain their determination if there was a "rational basis on which the legislature could have thought that it would serve a legitimate state interest."

Chief Justice Roberts wrote a separate opinion, concurring "only" in the judgment upholding the Mississippi law, but opposing overruling *Roe.* On that issue, he wrote that "I would take a more measured course."

With respect to the Mississippi law, its fifteen-week limit for abortions passed constitutional review because the "viability line established by *Roe* and *Casey* . . . never made any sense." The right to choose an abortion "should . . . extend far enough to ensure a reasonable opportunity to choose, but need not extend any further, certainly not all the way to viability." Moreover, there are additional important state interests that are not tied in any way to viability, such as the interests in preventing pain to a fetus or recognizing that certain procedures might affect the "dignity of human life."

Whether to overrule *Roe* presented a separate issue. Since it is "unnecessary to decide the case before us," to reach out and decide the issue violates the doctrine of judicial restraint. Moreover, the issue as to whether there is a constitutional right for a woman to choose to have an abortion is not as clear as either the majority or dissenting opinions believe. Indeed, those opinions "display a relentless freedom from doubt" on that issue, a conclusion that the chief justice cannot share. "I am not sure, for example, that a ban on terminating a pregnancy from the moment of conception must be treated the same under the Constitution as a ban after fifteen weeks."

Justice Thomas wrote a concurring opinion, indicating that he agreed with the majority opinion, but writing separately to attack the doctrine of substantive due process on which *Roe*'s right to choose an abortion was predicated. In his view, the Due Process Clause is limited to *process*, and does not provide an independent basis on which to create new rights. Indeed, he gave a platform for the dissenters to argue that, despite the majority opinion's contention that the decision did not affect anything other than abortion cases, its reasoning could affect other rights recognized under the substantive due process doctrine. Thus, Justice Thomas specifically contended that the court should reconsider its prior precedents creating rights based upon substantive due process, including the cases protecting a right to contraception, a right not to be prosecuted for sodomy, and a right to enter a same-sex marriage. In his view, the court should decide whether other constitutional provisions might protect the rights based in those cases on substantive due process.

The final concurring opinion was written by Justice Kavanaugh. He reiterated many of arguments made by the majority, concluding that the Constitution is neutral on the issue of abortion. With respect to *stare decisis*, he contended that it did not protect *Roe* because the court in that case "erroneously assigned itself authority to decide a critically important moral and policy issue that the Constitution does not grant this Court the authority to decide." He also noted that *Roe* "did not resolve the abortion debate," and that "The national division has not ended."

The most significant aspect of Justice Kavanaugh's concurring opinion is his contention that the majority opinion does not affect the cases highlighted by Justice Thomas. "Overruling *Roe* does *not* mean the overruling of those precedents, and does *not* threaten or cast doubt on those precedents." Moreover, that ruling does not permit, for example, a state to bar one of its residents from traveling to another state to obtain an abortion, nor does it permit a state to punish anyone for taking part in an abortion before the majority opinion takes effect.

Justices Breyer, Sotomayor, and Kagan wrote a joint dissenting opinion. They characterized *Roe* as "Respecting a woman as an autonomous being, and granting her full equality, [which] meant giving her substantial choice over this most personal and most consequential of all life decisions." *Roe* established a "balance" respecting both the rights of states to legislate and the rights of women as free and equal citizens. In their view, the decision of the majority rejected that balance, resulting in "the curtailment of women's rights, and of their status as free and equal citizens." They argued that returning the decision on what restrictions can be imposed upon abortion to the states might result in forcing women to bear children of rape and incest or with "severe physical anomalies." Moreover, some states could choose not to include an exception to protect a woman from "risk of death or physical harm." Other states, moreover, could even block a woman seeking an abortion from traveling to another state to obtain one, or from ordering abortion medications from out-of-state providers.

The dissenters also criticized the majority for focusing on whether reproductive rights were protected in 1868, when the Fourteenth Amendment was ratified. Among other points, the dissenting justices noted that only men could vote in 1868, and that the court itself in subsequent decisions recognized that women must be accorded the same rights as men. Moreover, the meaning of the Constitution may evolve. The Framers of the Constitution in both 1788 and 1868 "did not define rights by reference to the specific practices existing at the time. Instead, the Framers defined rights in general terms, to permit future evolution in their scope and meaning."

The dissent also noted that, contrary to the majority opinion and that of Justice Kavanaugh, concurring, the reasoning of the majority could threaten laws protecting obtaining contraception or entering a same-sex marriage.

Much of the dissenting opinion also relied upon the doctrine of *stare decisis*, and its detailed explication in the *Casey* case. The decision of the majority rejects the holding of *Casey* and that of "more than 20 cases reaffirming or applying the constitutional right to abortion." The majority's reliance upon prior cases that overruled past precedent in other contexts neglects to note the serious differences between those opinions and the current one. In the previous cases there were, for example, "(1) a change in legal doctrine that undermined or made obsolete the earlier decision; (2) a factual change that had the same effect; or (3) an absence of reliance because the earlier decision was less than a decade old." In a detailed analysis, the dissenters contended that none of those factors applied in this case.

The dissent also stressed how women have relied on the availability of abortion to preserve their "plans and expectations," and removal of that access to abortion "diminishes women's opportunities to participate fully and equally in the Nation's political, social, and economic life."

The dissent also rejected the concept that *Roe* somehow usurped the ability of state legislatures to address publicly contested questions. Instead, what is at issue is the protection of a right, and "However divisive, a right is not at the people's mercy."

In the dissenters' view, "The majority has overruled *Roe* and *Casey* for one and only one reason: because it has always despised them, and now it has the votes to discard them. The majority thereby substitutes a rule by judges for the rule of law." They conclude that "With sorrow—for this Court, but more, for the many millions of American women who have today lost a fundamental constitutional protection—we dissent."

Among the many messages that can be gleaned from the *Dobbs* opinion, one that stands out is that elections have consequences. The decision would have been different, and *Roe v. Wade* would have been preserved, if the three justices appointed by President Trump had not taken their seats on the court. Especially significant in this regard was the replacement of the liberal icon Justice Ginsburg by the conservative Justice Barrett. *Roe*, as demonstrated by the decisions summarized above, was always on life support and in danger of being overruled from the very beginning, with many of the decisions decided by a five-to-four vote. Thus, replacing a liberal justice with a conservative justice was all that was needed to overrule *Roe*, as Justice Blackmun, *Roe*'s author, had predicted in his dissenting opinion in *Planned Parenthood v. Casey.*

NOTE

1. The Supreme Court's early decisions on abortion are discussed at length in *Shaping America*, supra, 230–50.

Chapter 12

Limiting Immigration

Restrictions on immigration have been imposed by Congress since the Alien Act of 1798. Under that legislation, and many that followed, Congress has restricted immigration by barring the entry of certain classes of aliens. Legislation enacted in 1875, for example, barred the admission of prostitutes and convicts. That was followed in 1882 by the notorious Chinese Exclusion Act, which was not repealed until 1943. Another, highly criticized, piece of legislation, which was enacted in 1924, imposed quotas based upon national origins, discriminating against those not of northern European ancestry. That law was not repealed until 1965. In 1952, Congress passed the Immigration and Nationality Act, which, with several amendments, remains the controlling law today.

While Congress has the principal role in controlling immigration, broad powers have increasingly been conferred upon the President of United States to bar the admission of certain classes of aliens. While this power has been used forty-two times since 1981, it reached an apogee with the presidencies of Barack Obama and Donald Trump, both of whom implemented restrictions on immigration through unilateral executive orders.

Presidential powers over immigration were conferred by Congress under section 212(f) of the Immigration and Nationality Act. That legislation gives the president power to restrict entry into United States of individuals and classes of individuals who are not citizens. The president may "suspend the entry of . . . any class of aliens" or impose appropriate restrictions if the entry of such individuals "would be detrimental to the interests of the United States."

Are there limits on this presidential power? When are restrictions on immigration imposed by a president not "appropriate"? The Supreme Court confronted this issue in the context of restrictions imposed by President Donald Trump. In doing so, it addressed whether the restrictions violated the Establishment Clause because of the president's comments evincing bias against Muslim immigrants.

In the 2016 presidential race, Donald Trump, the Republican candidate, promised to protect the American people from the entry into this country of illegal immigrants and Islamic terrorists. These promises had a wide appeal, and it helped him win the presidency. He promised to build a wall on the Mexican border ("And Mexico will pay for it!") to keep illegal immigrants from gaining entry. He also promised to take steps to bar the entry of Islamic terrorists. In the first days of his presidency, on January 27, 2017, Trump signed an Executive Order that, among other things, suspended entry of foreign nationals from seven designated countries for ninety days. These were all Middle Eastern or African countries that had previously been identified as posing terrorism dangers. The Executive Order also suspended a refugee admissions program for 120 days and reduced the number of refugees eligible to be admitted to the United States during 2017.

A district court in Hawaii entered a nationwide temporary restraining order enjoining enforcement of key provisions of the Executive Order, and the Ninth Circuit Court of Appeals denied the government's emergency motion to stay that Order. In response, the Trump administration issued a new and revised Executive Order on March 6, 2017. That Order was entitled "Protecting the Nation From Foreign Terrorist Entry into the United States," and it reduced the number of countries listed in the original order from seven to six, with Iraq dropped from the list. Each of the covered states—Iran, Libya, Somalia, Sudan, Syria, and Yemen—was described as "a state sponsor of terrorism, has been significantly compromised by terrorist organizations, or contains active conflict zones." The new Order described the conditions in the six covered countries, indicating that those conditions presented "heightened risks to the security of the United States," and reciting that some of the foreign nationals who had entered the United States through the then-existing immigration system "have proved to be threats to our national security."

The new Executive Order first directed the Secretary of Homeland Security to conduct a global review to ascertain if foreign governments were providing adequate information about their nationals seeking to enter the United States. Second, the entry of all nationals from the six covered countries was suspended for ninety days. Third, all decisions on applications for refugee status, and all travel of refugees to the United States under that program, were suspended for 120 days, during which period the secretary of state was instructed to review the adequacy of the existing refugee admission program. Fourth, the entrance of more than fifty thousand refugees into the United States during 2017 was suspended as "detrimental to the interests of the United States."

The revised Executive Order met the same fate in the lower courts as the original one did. District courts in Hawaii and Maryland enjoined all or parts of the Order. The Fourth Circuit upheld the Maryland court's injunction insofar as it barred the entry of foreign nationals from the six covered countries. It agreed that the district court was correct in concluding that the provision "was motivated principally by a desire to exclude Muslims from United States, not by considerations relating to national security." As such, in the court's opinion, the Executive Order violated the Establishment Clause.

On appeal from the Hawaii district court, the Ninth Circuit upheld the key provisions of the injunction. Unlike the Fourth Circuit, it did not rely on the Establishment Clause, but rather found that portions of the Executive Order "likely exceeded the president's authority" under the immigration laws.

The Government appealed to the Supreme Court, requesting that the court review both decisions on the merits and, during the pendency of its consideration of the appeals, grant stays of the injunctions that had prohibited implementation or enforcement of portions of the revised Executive Order. In response, the Supreme Court granted review in both cases, and directed that the appeals be heard during the first session of the October 2017 term of the Court. With respect to the injunctions, the court granted the Government's application to stay the injunctions as to "foreign nationals who lack any bona fide relationship with a person or entity in the United States." It ruled that "The interest in preserving national security is 'an urgent objective of the highest order,'" and that preventing the Government from enforcing the Executive Order "against foreign nationals unconnected to United States would appreciably injure its interests, without alleviating obvious hardship to anyone else."

With respect to the coverage of the injunctions left in place, the court explained that the injunctions against enforcement of the Executive Order would only cover "foreign nationals who have a credible claim of a bona fide relationship with a person or entity in the United States. All other foreign nationals are subject to the provisions" of the Executive Order. In an effort to avoid controversy as to the application of its ruling, the court noted there must be a "close familial relationship" with an individual, or a "formal, documented, and formed in the ordinary course" relationship with an entity. The court fleshed this out by identifying as protected from enforcement three categories of foreign nationals. Those were students admitted to an American university, workers who accepted offers of employment from American companies, and lecturers invited to address an American audience. Notably, it went on to exclude from protection people with associations with nonprofit groups devoted to immigration where those groups sought to contact foreign nationals and add them to their client lists.

Joined by Justices Alito and Gorsuch, Justice Thomas delivered an opinion dissenting in part, and indicating that the three dissenters "would . . . grant the Government's applications for a stay in their entirety." This was because "Weighing the Government's interest in preserving national security against the hardships caused to respondents by temporary denials of entry into the country, the balance of the equities favors the Government." He criticized the protection the majority afforded to "an unidentified, unnamed group of foreign nationals abroad," noting that "No class has been certified, and neither party asks for the scope of relief that the Court today provides."

Justice Thomas went on to state that the Government "has made a strong showing that it is likely to succeed on the merits—that is, that the judgments below will be reversed." Significantly, the Per Curiam opinion of the court did not expressly state this, but it relied instead on an "equitable balance" of the respective interests and hardships of the parties.

Justice Thomas also predicted that the compromise reached by the majority "will prove unworkable." In his view, "a flood of litigation" would ensue over who qualified as having a "credible claim" to a "bona fide relationship." This prediction soon proved to be accurate, with petitioners going back to the Hawaiian district court seeking a ruling that the Supreme Court opinion protected others whom the Government had refused to recognize as having a credible claim to a bona fide relationship, including grandparents and in-laws. The Hawaii court initially declined to accept jurisdiction, ruling that the request to clarify the group of eligible foreign nationals implicated an interpretation of the Supreme Court's ruling, and therefore the petitioners should present their request to the Supreme Court. On an emergency appeal to the Ninth Circuit, that court declined to accept the appeal, but went on to suggest that the petitioners might reframe their district court request as an application for an injunction, which would be appealable. On remand, the district court granted relief, expanding the categories of individuals which qualified for exemptions.

Ultimately, the Supreme Court declined to decide the underlying merits in the Fourth Circuit case, finding they no longer presented a live case or controversy because the part of the Executive Order challenged in that case (Section 2(c)) "expired by its own terms" on September 24, 2017 (*Trump v. Int'l Refugee Assistance*, No. 16–1436 [Oct. 10, 2017]). While the court's summary disposition noted that "We express no view on the merits," it nevertheless vacated the Fourth Circuit judgment "[f]ollowing our established practice in such cases." Justice Sotomayor alone dissented from the vacating of the judgment, suggesting that the court should have dismissed the petition for review as improvidently granted. The court entered an almost identical Order two weeks later in the Ninth Circuit case, finding that the provisions of the Executive Order challenged in that case (Sections 2(c) and 6) had also expired by their own terms. Justice Sotomayor again dissented (*Trump v. Hawaii*, No. 16–1540 [Oct. 24, 2017]).

When the court finally reached the merits, a third travel ban incorporated in a Proclamation was upheld by a sharply and contentiously divided court in *Trump v. Hawaii* (2018), which was decided on the next to last day of the

Supreme Court's October 2017 term. The Proclamation was designed for "Enhancing Vetting Capabilities and Processes for Detecting Attempted Entry Into the United States by Terrorists or Other Public-Safety Threats." Initially, some forty-seven countries were identified as having deficient systems that presented national security concerns to the United States, or they were at risk of failing to provide sufficient "baseline" information on individuals seeking to enter the United States and to determine if they posed a security threat. After the State Department negotiated with these countries, only eight countries continued to be classified as deficient. Those countries were Chad, Iran, Iraq, Libya, North Korea, Syria, Venezuela, and Yemen. After a further review, Iraq was dropped from the list, and Somalia was added. Entry restrictions of varying types were then placed on nationals of these eight foreign states. Lawful permanent residents of the United States and foreign nationals who had been granted asylum were exempted from these entry restrictions, and a system to seek waivers was established for other foreign nationals. Continuing assessments were ordered, with a report to be given the president every 180 days. After the first such review, Chad was dropped from the list of covered countries.

PLAINTIFFS CHALLENGED THE PROCLAMATION, EXCEPT AS APPLIED TO NORTH KOREA AND VENEZUELA

Writing for a five-member majority, Chief Justice Roberts pointed out the president was acting under a congressional authorization that statutorily permitted him to "suspend the entry of all aliens or any class of aliens" whenever he "finds" that their entry "would be detrimental to the interests of the United States." The majority opinion describes this statutory authorization as one that "exudes deference to the President in every clause," and concludes that the Proclamation falls within its "comprehensive delegation."

Chief Justice Roberts's majority opinion held that the Proclamation passed muster under the controlling statutory delegation for several reasons. First, there was a comprehensive evaluation of every country's compliance with the baseline requirements. Second, extensive findings were set forth as to how the deficiencies in the processes of the countries that did not satisfy the baseline deprived the United States government of "sufficient information to assess the risks" nationals of these countries posed to the United States. Third, the country-specific restrictions were to be reviewed on an ongoing basis and could be lifted when the deficiencies were cured. Finally, a system of waivers had been established.

The majority opinion went on to note that the Proclamation in issue contained more detail than any other prior Order signed by any previous president. For example, President Clinton submitted a one-sentence order imposing restrictions on the Sudan, while President Reagan took only five sentences to curtail the entry of undocumented aliens who were migrating by sea into the southeastern United States.

Chief Justice Roberts rejected the applicability of another immigration statute, which prohibited denying visas based on factors such as nationality, place of birth, or residence. He found this inapplicable to the Proclamation because the statute was limited to the issuance of visas.

The majority opinion also rejected the characterization of the Proclamation as a "Muslim Ban," which was purportedly imposed "for the unconstitutional purpose of excluding Muslims," and as such, allegedly constituted a "religious gerrymander" in violation of the Establishment Clause. The plaintiffs relied on multiple statements made by President Trump, in which he said he was seeking to "ban Muslim immigration." The court held that the issue was not "whether to denounce the statements," but whether the policy implemented in the Proclamation "can reasonably be understood to result from a justification independent of unconstitutional grounds." In making this determination, court review was limited to the lenient standard of whether the action could be justified on a rational basis. The majority held that it could be because there is a "relationship to legitimate state interests" grounded in "national security concerns" to prevent the "entry of nationals who cannot be adequately vetted and inducing other nations to improve their practices."

The majority also relied upon the fact that there were multiple actors, in addition to the president, who were involved in formulating and implementing the Proclamation. These additional actors undertook a "worldwide review process . . . by multiple Cabinet officials and their agencies." Moreover, while it was true that Muslims were the majority in five of the restricted countries, the total population of those countries represented only about 8 percent of the world's Muslim population, and each of the covered Muslim countries had previously been designated by prior administrations, including that of President Obama, "as posing national security risks."

The majority concluded that the plaintiffs had no likelihood of success on the merits, and that the preliminary injunction issued by the lower court constituted an abuse of discretion. Rather than ending the case, the court lifted the injunction and remanded the proceedings to the lower court "for such further proceedings as may be appropriate."

There were two concurring opinions. Justice Kennedy joined fully in the majority opinion, but went on to give a gentle, indirect rebuke to President Trump with a "further observation" regarding the importance of government officials adhering to constitutional guarantees. Justice Thomas also concurred, with a lengthy discussion regarding whether universal injunctions of the type issued by the lower court, binding all people in all jurisdictions, were permissible. He indicated that the court would need to decide this question if courts continued to issue such injunctions, and commented that, in his opinion, "universal injunctions are legally and historically dubious."

There were two dissenting opinions - one by Justice Breyer, joined by Justice Kagan, and a second, authored by Justice Sotomayor, joined by Justice Ginsburg.

Justice Breyer phrased the question presented in the case as whether the Proclamation was "significantly affected by religious animus against Muslims." If it was, in his view, the Proclamation was issued in violation of the immigration statute or the First Amendment. By contrast, if the sole basis for the Proclamation was to protect national security, it was unlikely to violate either.

Justice Breyer suggested the practices under the exemptions and waiver provisions would help to answer what the basis actually was. He concluded that the administration of those provisions supported the conclusion that the responsible officials were "not applying the Proclamation as written." In making this suggestion, Justice Breyer relied upon several facts. First, only two waivers were granted in the first month out of 6,555 eligible applicants. While the government suggested that 430 waivers were granted in the first four months, Justice Breyer believed this was a very minor percentage as well. Second, the numbers of student and nonimmigrant visas granted were significantly lower that under prior practice. Third, and perhaps most significantly, two consular officials, one in New York and the other in Yemen, stated respectively that the waiver provisions were either "window dressing," or were to be granted "only in rare cases of imminent danger." Since these statements were made in other proceedings, and were not subjected to cross-examination, however, Justice Breyer concluded he would send the case back to the lower court for further proceedings. Nevertheless, if he had to decide without further proceedings, he stated that he would rule that there was a sufficient basis to conclude that the Proclamation reflected an anti-religious bias against Muslims, based on President Trump's own statements.

Justice Sotomayor, whose dissenting opinion was joined only by Justice Ginsburg, stated that "a reasonable observer would conclude that the Proclamation was motivated by anti-Muslim bias. That alone suffices to show that plaintiffs are likely to succeed on the merits of their Establishment Clause claim." This was because Supreme Court precedents made it clear that government cannot "favor or disfavor one religion over another." Justice Sotomayor then spent some eight pages of her twenty-eight-page opinion quoting President Trump's negative statements regarding Muslims and his suggestions that the travel ban targeted adherents of that religion. She pointed out that in the court's then-recent decision in the *Masterpiece Cakeshop* case, the court had relied upon far fewer statements to conclude that the religious hostility voiced toward the plaintiff violated the First Amendment.

Justice Sotomayor also criticized the majority for utilizing a "watered-down legal standard." She opined that rational basis review was not appropriate in Establishment Clause cases, which use a heightened standard of review, and she concluded that the waiver provisions were simply a "sham."

Finally, Justice Sotomayor compared the approach of the majority to that of the court in the discredited opinion in *Korematsu v. United States* (1944), a case that the majority in *Trump* stated, "has nothing to do with this case." Moreover, the majority both disavowed, and described *Korematsu* as "gravely wrong the day it was decided, has been overruled in the court of history, and—to be clear—'has no place in law under the Constitution.'" Nevertheless, Justice Sotomayor insisted on characterizing both cases as involving racial or religious animus and stereotyping, the first against those of Japanese descent, and the current case against those practicing the Muslim religion. She concluded her dissenting opinion by criticizing the court for failing "to hold the coordinate branches to account when they defy our most sacred legal commitments."

Observers present in the courtroom when she went over her dissenting opinion reported that Justice Sotomayor delivered her comments in a fury. Her comments were seconded and applauded by many legal commentators and law professors. Even Noah Feldman, a typically measured law professor and social media commentator, stated that Justice Sotomayor "properly invokes the Korematsu case," called the majority opinion "A Decision That Will Live in Infamy," and opined that it might be "the worst decision since . . . Korematsu."[1] Less surprisingly, David Cole, the National Legal Director of the ACLU and a frequent critic of President Trump, charged that "Here, as in *Korematsu*, the president targeted a vast group of people based on prejudice."[2]

Notwithstanding the comments of Professor Feldman and Mr. Cole, the majority opinion is well-grounded and reasonable. Other commentators have properly noted that the majority opinion emphasizes the Office of the Presidency, rather than the particular incumbent president, in order to safeguard presidential freedom and discretion in imposing restrictions on immigration to safeguard national security in the future. Moreover, the major difference between the majority and the dissenters is whether presidential action on immigration must be based *solely* on permissible considerations, or whether any religious bias exhibited by the president is sufficient to strike down an otherwise permissible immigration restriction that is reasonably based on perceived threats to national security. Even if the focus is properly on the beliefs of a particular president, the case for upholding the

Proclamation is particularly strong, given its formulation and implementation not by President Trump, but by multiple other government officials who followed an comprehensive and objectively reasonable process that resulted in restricting entry into the United States only from countries that prior administrations headed by both major political parties had previously classified as posing national security risks to the United States.

NOTES

1. Noah Feldman, "A Decision That Will Live in Infamy," *Bloomberg Opinion/Politics & Policy*, June 26, 2018.
2. David Cole, "The Supreme Court Looks Away," nybooks.com/daily, July18, 2018.

Conclusion

WHITHER GOES THE COURT?

The Supreme Court, throughout its history, and more so in the twenty-first century, has changed its interpretation of several provisions of the Constitution. The court has recently expanded its interpretation of the First and Eighth Amendments, while contracting the interpretation of the scope of congressional power under the Commerce Clause and under the Fourteenth Amendment, particularly in the area of voting rights. It has created new constitutional rights, most significantly by recognizing a constitutional right to a same-sex marriage, while repudiating its prior recognition of a constitutional right to an abortion. The court has also had to deal with changes in technology, particularly as they affect the Fourth Amendment requirement relating to warrants.

Predicting the future course of the Supreme Court on these and other issues is a hazardous undertaking, with so many contingencies that may affect the court. While, as of early 2023, there are six justices who are mainly conservative, and three who are more liberal, political and personnel changes will likely affect this balance. For example, Justice Breyer retired in 2022, and was replaced by Justice Jackson, who is likely to be at least as liberal as he. Moreover, rumors abound that Justice Thomas, who is in his mid-seventies, and Justice Alito, who is over seventy, have been contemplating retirement. The remaining six justices range in age from their forties to their sixties, and they are likely, barring sudden adverse changes in their health, to remain on the court for the foreseeable future.

Political changes may also affect the composition of the court. Some leaders among the Democrats have threatened to expand the court by adding new justices to overcome the current conservative majority, and President Biden appointed a commission to study court reform proposals. That commission reviewed and analyzed a number of possible additional changes that may gain steam given the incendiary reception of the *Dobbs* decision overruling *Roe v. Wade.* In addition, with the replacement of a Republican president with a Democrat, the death or retirement of any of the justices will generate the nomination of a liberal justice. Confirmation of any new justice, however, will be more difficult with a Senate whose membership in 2023 has a Democrat majority of only one.

Nevertheless, to the extent that any changes in the court are only incremental, there are some trends from the court's recent decisions that may illuminate the likely course of future decisions.

FIVE PRINCIPAL TRENDS CAN BE SEEN IN THE RECENT DECISIONS OF THE SUPREME COURT

First, in cases such as *Shelby County, Alabama v. Holder*; *United States v. Bond*; *Murphy v. National Collegiate Athletic Association*; *Gamble v. United States*; and to a very limited degree in *United States v. Windsor* (initially in its "whiffs of federalism," which quickly evaporated in *Obergefell*), and in *Dobbs*, returning the issue of abortion restrictions to the states, the court took steps toward strengthening the concept of federalism, recognizing the sovereignty of the states and their key competence in the areas of voting, reproductive rights, and marriage laws, as well as in policing local crime and permitting sports gambling. In addition, despite the fact that the Individual Mandate imposed under the Affordable Care Act was upheld by one vote in *National Federation*, the conservative justices won two major victories for the New Federalism by placing limits on the power of Congress under the Commerce Clause, and by reinvigorating the role of the States as independent sovereigns by striking down the terms imposed on them by the Medicaid Expansion. Finally, the refusal to address partisan gerrymandering claims in *Rucho v. Common Cause* left the states largely in control of legislative redistricting.

Second, in a series of decisions, the court has strongly defended a broad right of free speech for individuals, corporations, trademark registrants, voters, pro-life groups, nongovernmental organizations, public employees who do not belong to a union, school employees engaging in prayer, and even registered sex offenders. This trend implements the beliefs of the Framers of the Constitution that truth emerges best from the unfettered presentation of conflicting views in the public square. At a time of great polarization in our country, this insight of the Framers assumes particular importance because of significant societal pressures to limit the dissemination of unpopular (or no longer fashionable) views, as well as the initiatives of several universities to proscribe what they consider to be "hate speech" or "racial micro-aggressions." It remains to be seen, however, whether the court will protect free speech in cases where the opponents of same-sex marriage actively protest against its recognition, although the limited decision in *Masterpiece Cakeshop* indicates the court will not countenance any overt, ham-fisted discrimination against those with religious objections to same-sex marriage. Finally, extending these free-speech rights to corporate speakers represents an attempt to level the playing field so that corporations other than those owning media outlets would also be free to actively participate in public political discussion.

Third, several of the current court's earlier decisions manifested a judicial philosophy of minimalism and restraint. This was shown strongly in decisions such as *Northwest Austin Municipal Utility District v. Holder*; *Hollingsworth v. Perry*; *Ricci v. DeStefano*; *Trinity Lutheran*; *Town of Greece*; *Masterpiece Cakeshop*; *American Legion v. American Humanist Ass'n*; *Rucho v. Common Cause*; and *Fulton v. City of Philadelphia.* In most of these cases, the court declined to reach, or to comprehensively resolve, the major constitutional questions presented. Moreover, in the *Northwest Austin* decision, the court afforded Congress the opportunity to first address that issue by enacting new legislation to cure a potential constitutional defect, while in *Rucho v. Common Cause*, the court refused to let itself become the ultimate authority on the drawing of congressional districting maps. The minimalism approach was also pursued in the Supreme Court's first decision in *Fisher v. University of Texas at Austin*, where the court declined to reexamine its decision in *Grutter v. Bollinger* (2003), instead choosing to order the appeals court below to reconsider its decision to uphold the admissions program at issue under the *Grutter* strict scrutiny analysis. By contrast, however, the *Dobbs* and *Obergefell* decisions, as well as the court's decisions on cruel and unusual punishments, reflected a vigorous judicial activism. Such activism is not as unlikely to continue on the liberal side of court because it presently is in a significant minority. Whether the conservatives on the court will continue to be as activist as in *Dobbs* is also questionable because of the significant backlash against the court attributable to its rulings at the end of the 2021–2022 term. Moreover, since Justices Kavanaugh and Barrett have shown reluctance to join their more conservative colleagues in overturning some liberal precedents, this may also result in less activism on the conservative side.

In its earlier decisions, the court also demonstrated a commitment to stare decisis. In *McDonald v. Chicago*, for example, it refused, despite arguments in favor of doing so by both liberal and conservative advocates, to overrule the still controversial eighteenth-century decision in the *Slaughterhouse Cases*, which limited the reach of the Privileges and Immunities Clause. Finally, by construing the Affordable Care Act's penalty on those who failed to obtain health insurance as a tax in *National Federation*, and by saving the Act from "inartful drafting" in *King*, the court extended deference to the legislative branch so as to uphold first the constitutionality, and then the implementation of that statute.

Finally, the court has repeatedly employed the doctrines of standing and justiciability to enable it to avoid deciding constitutional issues. See, for example, *California v. Texas* (2021) (rejecting challenge to the Affordable Care Act based on the plaintiffs' lack of standing); *Trump v. New York* (2020) ("At present, this case is riddled with contingencies and speculation that impede judicial review.")

Fourth, in contrast to some of the earlier decisions just noted, the court demonstrated a continuing judicial activism in its Eighth Amendment jurisprudence on what constitutes "cruel and unusual" punishments, its recognition of a constitutional right to same-sex marriage, and its repudiation of any right to abortion.

With respect to the issue of cruel and unusual punishment, the decision in *Miller v. Alabama* is particularly noteworthy. There, a court majority effectively discarded the first prong of its approach to that question by failing to properly credit the "objective indicia" presented by state legislation upholding life imprisonment without the possibility of parole for juvenile offenders convicted of homicide. Instead, the court relied almost totally on the second prong of the approach it had previously employed, utilizing its own "independent judgment" to decide whether that punishment fit the crime. The court continued this approach in *Hall v. Florida*, in which it principally rested its conclusion that a fixed IQ test for intellectual disability was impermissible on the views of professional associations and on academic studies the majority adopted in an exercise of independent judicial judgment. Finally, in *Glossip v. Gross*, two justices went so far as to call on the full court to determine whether capital punishment itself is a cruel and unusual punishment proscribed by the Eighth Amendment, even though the text of the Fifth Amendment explicitly mentions deprivation of life as a possible penalty.

In holding there was a fundamental, liberty-based, constitutional right to same-sex marriage, the majority opinion in *Obergefell* continued the current of judicial activism demonstrated in the court's Eighth Amendment rulings by discarding both the court's prior careful and limited approach to determining such rights, as well as the popular votes of the people of more than thirty states. Moreover, it completely reversed its approach in *Windsor*, where the law of marriage was said to be virtually the exclusive province of the states. Finally, the majority's approach threatened the free exercise of religion guaranteed by the First Amendment to take action opposing same-sex marriage, stating only that opponents of same-sex marriage had the right to teach and advocate against the redefinition of marriage based on purported new insights and enhanced understandings. The addition of more conservative justices since *Obergefell* will likely lessen this possibility.

Fifth, and finally, the court in its earlier decisions of the twenty-first century exhibited conflicting attitudes toward varying issues of religious freedom. On the one hand, the decisions in *Martinez* and *Obergefell* posed threats to that freedom. *Martinez* marginalized the role of religious institutions on college and law school campuses, and *Obergefell* posed threats to the future free exercise of religion insofar as actions taken to object to same-sex marriage are concerned. Again, the confirmation of Justices Gorsuch, Kavanaugh, and Barrett, as well as several later decisions, particularly in *Kennedy v. Bremerton School District*, suggest that greater deference will be accorded to the free exercise rights of religion in the future.

Moreover, other decisions showed a heightened and continuing concern for protecting religious liberty. *Hosanna-Tabor* and *Our Lady of Guadalupe* insulated religious institutions from employment discrimination claims where a "minister" was the claimant, and the *Town of Greece* and *Kennedy* rulings upheld the right to pray even sectarian prayers at town board meetings and on school property. In addition, *American Legion v. American Humanist Association* permitted a long-standing war memorial erected in the form of a huge cross to remain standing, despite Establishment Clause objections, and *Espinoza v. Montana Department of Revenue* and *Carson v. Makin* protected religious schools from being barred from participating in state programs. Most significantly, in *Trinity Lutheran*, seven justices voted to permit a church under the Free Exercise Clause, for the first time in the court's caselaw, to receive direct governmental aid under a statute which offered generally available benefits, albeit this decision was made in the context of assisting children who played on a church playground, and five justices sought to limit application of the ruling. *Masterpiece Cakeshop* further underlined the court's determination to protect religious liberty from overt hostility to its practitioners.

In addition to these cases favoring religious exercise, *Burwell v. Hobby Lobby Stores, Inc.* and *Holt v. Hobbs* upheld the rights of closely held corporations and Muslim prisoners to the free exercise of their religious beliefs under the Religious Freedom Restoration Act and the Religious Land Use and Institutionalized Persons Act by permitting them respectively to avoid providing their employees with insurance that covered contraceptives that violated the corporations owners' religious beliefs, and to grow a short beard for religious reasons.

Appendix

The Justices

THE CHIEF JUSTICE

In September 2020, John Roberts celebrated his fifteenth anniversary as chief justice of United States. Roberts was educated at Harvard College and Harvard Law School. He initially served in the Reagan White House and subsequently became one of the most well-known appellate advocates in the country. In that capacity, he argued dozens of cases in the Supreme Court and chaired the appellate practice at Hogan and Hartson, a Washington, D.C.–based law firm. Roberts briefly served as a circuit judge on the Court of Appeals for the District of Columbia Circuit before he was nominated first as a justice, and then as chief justice, by President George W. Bush. His nomination as chief justice followed the sudden death from thyroid cancer of Chief Justice William Rehnquist, for whom Roberts had served as a law clerk following his graduation from law school.

While several Democrats feared Roberts would turn out to be a conservative ideologue, he was an impressive witness before the Senate Judiciary Committee, and he was confirmed by a vote of 78 to 22. One memorable quote from his testimony was that he saw the role of the judge as comparable to that of a baseball umpire calling balls and strikes.

In his service on the court, Roberts has more often than not voted with the conservative block, initially consisting of Justices Scalia, Thomas, and Alito (and sometimes Justice Kennedy) in such cases as *Burwell v. Hobby Lobby Stores, Inc.* (2014), which upheld the right of closely held corporations to exercise their religion; *Trump v. Hawaii* (2018), which upheld President Trump's so-called travel ban; and *Town of Greece v. Galloway* (2014), which rejected an Establishment Clause challenge to a town practice that permitted prayer at the beginning of its public meetings.

Despite his generally conservative voting record on the court, including rejecting the claim that there was a constitutional right to same-sex marriage in his dissent in *Obergefell v. Hodges* (2015), Roberts shocked conservatives, and was labeled a traitor by them, for his decisive votes, first to uphold the constitutionality of the Affordable Care Act in *National Federation of Independent Business v. Sebelius* (2012), and next, to rewrite the statute to permit payment of subsidies for the purchase on federal exchanges of health insurance to those unable otherwise to obtain such insurance (*King v. Burwell* [2015]).

Following the confirmations of Justices Gorsuch and Kavanaugh, Roberts was often the swing vote on key five-to-four decisions, and, as discussed in the cases analyzed in this book, he provided the determinative votes in several high-profile cases, voting at times with the court's conservative justices and at other times with the more liberal justices. With the confirmation of Amy Coney Barrett to the court in 2020, the power of the chief justice to determine the outcome in key cases diminished, since there were now five conservative justices other than Roberts, and his vote was no longer as important. This was dramatically demonstrated when those five justices joined to form the majority to strike down *Roe v. Wade* despite Chief Justice Roberts's pleas to deliver a more minimalist decision.

THE ASSOCIATE JUSTICES

Justice Thomas

The longest-serving associate justice is Clarence Thomas, nominated by President George H.W. Bush in 1991, after completing his service on the United States Court of Appeals for the D.C. Circuit for two years. He had previously served as chair of the Equal Employment Opportunity Commission. Justice Thomas is a cum-laude graduate of Holy Cross College, and a graduate of Yale Law School. He was only forty-three years old when nominated.

Justice Thomas is a descendent of slaves and wrote a memoir, *My Grandfather's Son*, in which he recounts his growing up in extreme poverty.[1] He attributes his later success to his grandfather's influence and his Catholic school education. After an extremely acrimonious Senate hearing in which he was accused of sexual harassment by a former employee, he was narrowly confirmed to serve on the Supreme Court by a vote of 52 to 48. He memorably described his treatment at the televised hearings on his nomination, which were chaired by then-senator Joseph Biden, as a "high tech lynching."

Justice Thomas is clearly the most conservative justice on the current court. He is a critic of the regulatory state, and his opinions have attacked and criticized many liberal rulings of the Supreme Court, including several New Deal precedents. He called for the overruling of *Roe v. Wade* for years and joined the majority in *Dobbs v. Jackson Women's Organization*, which did just that. He has consistently opposed affirmative action and has criticized the Takings Clause rulings of the court as violative of property rights. Justice Thomas has also been a consistent defender of federalism, religious liberty, and the right to bear arms, writing several important opinions on the Second Amendment.

Because of these positions, Justice Thomas has consistently been the target of progressives, and over one million people have signed a petition to have him impeached and removed from the Supreme Court.

Justice Alito

In addition to selecting a new chief justice, President Bush was also able to appoint one new associate justice, Samuel Alito of New Jersey. Alito was educated at Princeton University and Yale Law School. In the administration of President Ronald Reagan, he served as an assistant to the solicitor general, and as deputy assistant to the attorney general. Thereafter, he served as the United States attorney for the District of New Jersey, after which he was nominated and confirmed for a seat on the Third Circuit Court of Appeals. He served on that court between 1990 and 2006.

Alito's nomination was more controversial than that of John Roberts, and it generated considerable opposition from liberal Democrats. The Senate nevertheless confirmed him by a vote of 58 to 42, and he was sworn in as an associate justice in January 2006.

As the Democrats who voted against him rightly feared, Alito has become one of the most conservative justices on the Supreme Court. He wrote the highly controversial majority opinion in *Dobbs v. Jackson Women's Health Organization* (2022), which overruled *Roe v.* Wade, and he penned a dissenting opinion in *Obergefell v. Hodges* (2015), opposing the majority's decision to recognize same-sex marriage as a constitutional right.

Alito also authored the majority opinions in favor of both Christian and Muslim religious believers in several significant cases presenting issues of religious freedom, including *Burwell v. Hobby Lobby Stores, Inc.* (2014) and *Holt v. Hobbs* (2015). He also authored the majority opinion in *McDonald v. Chicago* (2010), which ruled that the Second Amendment right to keep and bear arms fully applied to the states. Moreover, in *National Federation of Independent Business v. Sebelius* (2012), he voted with three other dissenting justices who would have declared the Affordable Care Act unconstitutional.

He also wrote a partial dissent joined by Justices Thomas and Gorsuch that would have let the Trump administration enforce the totality of its so-called travel ban during the pendency of its appeal from lower-court rulings enjoining enforcement of the Executive Order imposing the ban, *Trump v. International Refugee Assistance Project* (2017), and he voted to uphold the ban when the court reached the merits (*Trump v. Hawaii* [2018]). Alito also wrote the majority opinion rejecting an Establishment Clause attack on an historic World War I memorial featuring a large cross erected on public grounds (*American Legion v. American Humanist Ass'n* [2019]).

An additional demonstration of Justice Alito's conservatism was provided by his willingness to be the sole dissenter in two First Amendment free speech cases. In *United States v. Stevens* (2010), he voted to uphold the constitutionality of a federal statute criminalizing depictions of animal cruelty, while in *Snyder v. Phelps* (2011), his dissenting opinion outlined why he believed that a civil judgment against protesters who sought to disrupt a military funeral should be upheld.

Justice Sotomayor

President Barack Obama made two appointments to the Supreme Court in his first term. Both new justices were women, and both generally followed the liberal judicial philosophies of those they replaced. Sonia Sotomayor, who replaced David Souter, was the first Hispanic and the third female to serve on the court. She was educated in the Catholic school system for grammar and high school in New York City, and she graduated from Princeton University and Harvard Law School. She is the only justice who served as a trial judge (in the Southern District of New York), and she also served thereafter on the Second Circuit Court of Appeals. President Obama was the third president to appoint Judge Sotomayor to a judicial post. With her appointment, an unprecedented six Catholic justices comprised two-thirds of the court, beginning in 2009.

Justice Sotomayor was fifty-four at the time of her 2009 appointment. She was confirmed on a mainly party-line vote of 68 to 31 by a Senate controlled by the Democratic Party majority. During her confirmation, two areas of controversy emerged, one based on a lecture she had given in 2001, and the other rooted in a comment made by President Obama before her appointment regarding the qualities he would seek in a prospective Supreme Court nominee. In her lecture Sotomayor expressed the hope, regarding the impact of ethnic background on judicial decision-making, that a "wise Latina woman" would "reach a better conclusion than a white male." The separate controversy tied to President Obama stemmed from his announcement that would seek to appoint judges with "empathy," that is, judges who would be "identifying with people's hopes and struggles as an essential ingredient for arriving at just decisions." Both comments raised issues of whether Sotomayor would "follow the law" or would instead inappropriately favor the poor and racial and ethnic minorities in her decisions. The prospective justice testified in her confirmation hearing that she would follow the law.

In her years of service on the court, Justice Sotomayor joined Justice Ruth Bader Ginsburg as the most liberal justice on the court. In *Pitre v. Cain* (2010), for example, Sotomayor was the only justice who dissented from a denial of certiorari in a case involving allegedly cruel treatment of a prison inmate. The inmate claimed that he was subjected to hard labor as a punishment when he refused to take his AIDS medication. Justice Sotomayor's opinion suggested this stated a claim under the Eighth Amendment as infliction of a cruel and unusual punishment. In addition, in the highly publicized decisions on the constitutionality of the Affordable Care Act, only she and Justice Ginsburg dissented from the holding in *National Federation of Independent Business v. Sebelius* (2012) that the terms imposed on the states for expansion of Medicaid under the Act were unconstitutional. Again, in *Trinity Lutheran Church v. Comer* (2017), only she and Justice Ginsburg voted to uphold the constitutionality of a Missouri constitutional amendment which barred religious institutions from receiving generally available benefits for resurfacing playgrounds. Justice Sotomayor also joined in Justice Ginsburg's dissenting opinion in *Burwell v. Hobby Lobby Stores, Inc.* (2014), with both rejecting the claim that closely held corporations were entitled to exercise their religion (within the meaning of the Religious Freedom Restoration Act) by refusing to offer certain contraceptives mandated by the Affordable Care Act to their employees. In *Trump v. Hawaii* (2018), Justice Sotomayor characterized the court's decision to uphold President Trump's administration's travel ban as worse than the infamous decision in *Korematsu v. United States* (1944), a completely discredited opinion which the majority opinion in *Trump* expressly repudiated. Once more only one (Justice Ginsburg) of the four dissenting justices joined her opinion. In addition, in *American Legion v. American Humanist Ass'n* (2019), Justice Sotomayor joined Justice Ginsburg in dissenting from the majority's decision upholding the constitutionality of the continued presence on public grounds of a war memorial featuring a large cross.

Justice Sotomayor also authored two (what critics could label as "empathetic") dissents in cases involving race and police conduct. First, in a dissenting opinion (once again only joined by Justice Ginsburg) in *Schuette v. Coalition to Defend Affirmative Action* (2013), she proclaimed that "Race matters," and that a voter-approved constitutional amendment in Michigan that prohibited state universities from considering race in their admissions process was itself unconstitutional. Second, in *Utah v. Strieff* (2016), again joined, but only in part, by Justice Ginsburg, Justice Sotomayor dissented from a decision permitting search of a vehicle stopped for failure to pay a traffic ticket, where the search was ruled by the majority to initially have been illegal, but nevertheless permissible as incident to an arrest where the arresting officer later discovered an outstanding arrest warrant. At the conclusion of her dissenting opinion, "Writing only for myself," she set forth a lengthy list of indignities visited on people of all races and nationalities during police stops. She claimed that the majority opinion "tells everyone, white and black, guilty and innocent, that a officer can verify your legal status at any time. . . . It implies that you are not a citizen of a democracy but the subject of a carceral state, just waiting to be cataloged." Indeed, in the justice's view, these citizens "are the canaries in the coal mine whose deaths, civil and literal, warn us that no one can breathe in this atmosphere. . . . Until their voices matter too, our justice system will continue to be anything but."

Justice Kagan

The second appointment to the Supreme Court made by President Obama was Elena Kagan. Justice Kagan replaced Justice John Paul Stevens in 2010, and she was confirmed by a vote, again mainly on party lines, of 63 to 37.

Kagan was only fifty at the time of her nomination, then the youngest member of the Supreme Court. She is also the only justice now on the court who had no previous judicial experience. Like Justice Sotomayor, she is from New York City, and she attended Princeton and Harvard Law School, after which she served as a law clerk to Justice Thurgood Marshall. Kagan taught at the University of Chicago and Harvard Law Schools, with service in President Bill Clinton's White House as a domestic policy advisor between her years of law school teaching. Prior to her Supreme Court appointment, Kagan served as solicitor general of the United States in 2009 and 2010.

With Justice Kagan's confirmation, the religious makeup of the Supreme Court became six Catholics and three Jews. For the first time in history, there were no Protestants on the court, a situation that would change in 2017, when Justice Neil Gorsuch, a Protestant, joined the court.

Justice Kagan is aptly celebrated for her excellent writing style, with opinions that are well reasoned and presented with vigor, humor, and memorable phrasing. She has also emerged as the liberal wing's voice in some of the most hotly contested cases. For example, she authored the dissenting opinion in *Rucho v. Common Cause* (2019), the partisan gerrymandering case discussed later, reading her impassioned opinion from the bench.

Although she often votes with the court's more liberal justices, Justice Kagan has proven to be a more moderate member of the Supreme Court's liberal wing than Justice Sotomayor or Justice Ginsburg. In the *Sebelius* case, for example, she joined with six other justices to hold that the terms mandated on the states for the expansion of Medicaid under the Affordable Health Care Act were unconstitutional, a ruling from which Justices Sotomayor and Ginsburg both dissented. Justice Kagan also joined the majority in two cases presenting First Amendment issues relating to religion. These were *Trinity Lutheran*, holding that the denial of generally available benefits to a church under a state law that funded safety renovations of playgrounds violated the Free Exercise Clause of the First Amendment, and *American Legion v. American Humanist Ass'n*, which permitted state authorities to maintain a large cross, despite Establishment Clause objections. In addition, Justice Kagan joined with three of the court's conservatives and Justice Breyer in *Hollingsworth v. Perry* to deny standing to the proponents of California's Proposition 8 (which voted down same-sex marriage in that state) to appeal the Ninth Circuit's ruling that the action was unconstitutional. This approach permitted the court to avoid a ruling (if only for a brief time) on the broader question of whether a popular vote could bar the availability of same-sex marriage, and was thus an example of judicial minimalism, as opposed to judicial activism. Justices Ginsburg and Sotomayor, by contrast, would have found standing to appeal and would have reached the merits of the case. Finally, in the controversial *Masterpiece Cakeshop* case, Justice Kagan provided one of the seven votes to reverse the penalties imposed on the baker who refused to design a cake for a same-sex wedding based on his religious beliefs. She agreed that the Colorado commission which imposed the penalties evinced an unconstitutional hostility to the baker's religious beliefs.

An additional Supreme Court vacancy was created in February 2016, with the sudden death of Justice Antonin Scalia, a conservative stalwart on the court. President Obama nominated Merrick Garland of the United States Court of Appeals for the District of Columbia to fill this vacancy, but the Republican Senate majority refused to hold hearings on the nomination, citing the pendency of the upcoming presidential election in November 2016. They argued that the new president, Republican or Democrat, should be permitted to select the individual to be nominated, rather than to permit a lame-duck president to do so. Judge Garland's nomination to the Supreme Court was not acted upon, and it expired in January 2017. The denial of a seat on the Supreme Court to Judge Garland aroused a storm of protest that has not abated but has only intensified with the subsequent nominations of Justices Gorsuch, Kavanaugh, and Barrett by the Republican president Donald Trump. Thereafter, Judge Garland was appointed attorney general by President Joseph Biden.

Justice Gorsuch

During the 2016 presidential campaign, the Republican candidate, Donald J. Trump, with the assistance of the Heritage Foundation and the Federalist

Society, released two lists, totaling twenty-one individual judges, whom he identified as the universe of judges from which he would choose his Supreme Court nominee if elected president. After Trump won the presidency, he nominated one of those on the lists, Neil Gorsuch of the United States Court of Appeals for the Tenth Circuit, to fill the Scalia vacancy. Judge Gorsuch was forty-nine years old when nominated, and he is a graduate of Columbia University and Harvard Law School. He also has a doctorate in philosophy from Oxford University, having studied under John Finnis, a conservative Catholic legal philosopher. Gorsuch is a member of the Anglican Communion, and he is the first Protestant on the Supreme Court since the retirement of Justice John Paul Stevens. He is also noted as a colorful writer and a textualist who focuses upon the plain language of statutory texts, rather than on broader policy questions implicated in the interpretation of a statute.

Democrats mounted a fierce campaign against the Gorsuch nomination. Much of the opposition centered on fears by advocates of abortion rights regarding Gorsuch's perceived position in opposition to *Roe v. Wade*'s holding that there was a constitutional right to abortion. Although Gorsuch had never written against abortion in his judicial opinions or in his other writings, the opposition focused on his 2006 book, *The Future of Euthanasia and Assisted Suicide.* That book opposed legalization of both practices, based upon a natural law view, in his words, which was "premised on the idea that all human beings are intrinsically valuable." Based in part on these views of the nominee, Planned Parenthood, NARAL, and other progressive groups ran ads against confirming Gorsuch in multiple media outlets, including Twitter and other internet sites. The fears of the opponents to Gorsuch's nomination proved to be correct when he joined the majority opinion in *Dobbs*, overruling *Roe v. Wade.*

Opponents also emphasized Gorsuch's opinions in favor of religious liberty and of corporate interests. As a last salvo, they accused him of plagiarizing some excerpts from other authors in both his book and in another article he wrote. Finally, there was a feeling among his opponents that the Supreme Court seat he was assuming was "stolen" from Judge Garland, and Gorsuch was thus a tainted candidate put up for the court by Republicans who had improperly denied Garland a hearing on his nomination for the court by President Obama.

All this resulted in Democrats orchestrating the first filibuster ever of a Supreme Court nominee. Despite the filibuster, Gorsuch was confirmed by a vote of 54 to 45 on April 7, 2017. His confirmation was only obtained after a cloture vote, and the Republican majority then voted to allow the Gorsuch nomination to be approved by a majority vote. On the two votes to end debate, all fifty-two Republican senators voted to close debate, with only three Democrats supporting ending the debate. By contrast, on the vote to keep the sixty-vote threshold, all Democrats voted unsuccessfully to do so. On the final confirmation vote, fifty-one Republicans and three Democrats voted to confirm Judge Gorsuch, with one Republican senator absent because of illness.

Justice Gorsuch upheld his reputation as a textualist in the tradition of Justice Scalia in his first opinion for the court. *Henson v. Santander Consumer USA Inc.* (2017) presented the question as to whether a bank that acquired a debt from another qualified as a "debt collector" under the Fair Debt Collections Practices Act when it sought to collect that debt. In his opinion for a unanimous Court, Gorsuch concluded that it did not. First, he looked at the statutory text, pointing out that it referred to a person who collected debts "owed . . . another," and "by its plain terms this language seems to focus our attention on third party collection agents working for a debt owner—not on a debt owner seeking to collect debts for itself." Second, he noted the "larger statutory landscape" supported the same reading, referring in another subsection to a creditor as someone "to whom a debt is owed." Finally, Gorsuch rejected an appeal to policy, writing that "it is never our job to rewrite a constitutionally valid statutory text under the banner of speculation about what Congress might have done had it faced a question that, on everyone's account, it never faced."

Gorsuch also demonstrated his writing skill, including an ability to write alliterative prose, in his first opinion. His opening lines read "Disruptive dinnertime calls, downright deceit, and more besides drew Congress's eye to the debt collection industry. From that scrutiny emerged the Fair Debt Collection Practices Act."

In his first months on the court, Justice Gorsuch proved to be a reliable and aggressive conservative in his votes on cases. Moreover, he and Justice Thomas formed a conservative voting block of two in several early cases, mirroring the alliance of Justices Ginsburg and Sotomayor on the liberal side of the court. Indeed, Gorsuch voted with Thomas in all the cases on which he sat in his first Term on the court. Thus, for example, Justice Gorsuch was the only justice to join Justice Thomas in dissenting from the court's refusal to grant review in a case which presented the question whether the Second Amendment protects the right to carry firearms in public for self-defense (*Peruta v. California* [June 26, 2017]). The same two justices joined a concurring opinion in *Trinity Lutheran* written by Justice Gorsuch, objecting to a footnote in the majority opinion that sought to limit the impact of its ruling. Justice Gorsuch was again the only justice joining the concurring opinion of Justice Thomas in *Weaver v. Massachusetts* (2017). In that case, they dissented from the majority's assumption that closing a court room during jury selection violated the Sixth Amendment. In *Pavan v. Smith* (June 26, 2017), Justice Gorsuch was joined by both Justice Thomas and Justice

Alito in his opinion dissenting from a summary reversal that struck down an Arkansas law that only permitted a same-sex birth mother's name to be listed on a birth certificate, while at the same time requiring that the spouse's name also be listed where the couples were of different sexes. In addition, in a decision on an application to stay lower court rulings enjoining the Trump administration's so-called "travel ban," Justices Gorsuch, Thomas, and Alito dissented in part from the majority opinion in *Trump v. International Refugee Assistance Project* (2017), which partially denied the stay. The dissenting justices, in an opinion by Justice Thomas, indicated that they would have upheld the entire travel ban during the pendency of a decision on the merits during the next court Term. And when the merits of the travel ban were finally reached, Justice Gorsuch provided the fifth vote to uphold the ban in *Trump v. Hawaii*.

In his second term on the court, Justice Gorsuch began to author more majority opinions, and was selected by the chief justice to write the opinion of the court in five of the seventeen five-to-four decisions in that term, more than any other justice. On occasion in his second and third terms, moreover, he joined with some of the more liberal justices, particularly on criminal justice issues. For example, in *United States v. Haymond* (2019), he announced the judgment of the court, and wrote an opinion joined by Justices Ginsburg, Sotomayor, and Kagan, contending that the Fifth and Sixth Amendment's guarantee of trial by jury was violated by a federal law permitting a judge, without a jury, to order a registered sex offender back to prison if the judge finds that the defendant violated the terms of his supervised release. In one other example, Justice Gorsuch, joined only by Justice Sotomayor, dissented from the court's denial of review in *Hester v. United States* (2019). In that case, the Ninth Circuit had ruled that when a restitution order is entered in a criminal case, the facts supporting that order can be found by a judge rather than by a jury. The dissenters indicated that that issue was worthy of Supreme Court review because of the increasing issuance of restitution orders in federal criminal sentencing, and the dissenters' view that the Ninth Circuit ruling "seems doubtful." Notably, Justice Gorsuch adhered to his originalist approach by stating that the government's defense of the ruling below was "difficult to reconcile with the Constitution's original meaning." Justice Gorsuch also joined with Justice Sotomayor on Sixth and Eighth Amendment decisions supporting the positions of criminal defendants on issues of forensic analysis and civil forfeiture.

Justice Gorsuch has been a consistent and vocal proponent of religious liberty rights. He joined a dissenting opinion by Justice Alito in *Foster v. City of Philadelphia* (2021), which called for the overruling of *Employment Division v. Smith* (1990). The *Smith* opinion, written by Justice Scalia, held that the First Amendment did not protect religious believers who refused to obey a neutral law of general applicability. He has also been a dissenter in several cases denying stays of orders upholding state laws which mandated the taking of COVID-19 vaccines by individuals who had sincere religious beliefs preventing them from taking the available vaccines. See, for example, Dr. A v. Hochul, No. 21A145 (Dec. 13, 2021).

When Justice Gorsuch assumed his seat on the Supreme Court, a majority of the court had turned over in less than twelve years. Three justices—Chief Justice Roberts and Associate Justices Alito and Gorsuch—were appointed by Republican presidents, and two justices—Associate Justices Sotomayor and Kagan—by Democratic presidents.

Justice Kavanaugh

On June 27, 2018, the last day of the Supreme Court Term, Justice Anthony Kennedy notified President Donald Trump that he was ending his regular active service as an associate justice, but he would continue to serve in a senior status. He had served for forty-three years as a federal judge, thirty of which were on the Supreme Court. On July 9, 2018, President Trump nominated Judge Brett Kavanaugh of the United States Court of Appeals for the District of Columbia to replace Justice Kennedy.

Judge Kavanaugh is a graduate of Yale College and Yale Law School, and has taught at Harvard, Yale, and Georgetown Law Schools. He was fifty-three years old at the time of his nomination, and he had served on the D.C. Court of Appeals for twelve years, authoring approximately three hundred opinions, many of which involved questions of administrative law.

After law school, Kavanaugh clerked for two federal appellate judges, then went on to clerk for Justice Kennedy after one year in the office of Solicitor General Kenneth Starr. Remarkably, both he and Justice Gorsuch served as law clerks to Justice Kennedy at the same time. Kavanaugh then joined Starr in his work as the Independent Counsel investigating President Clinton, and worked on the so-called Starr Report, which set forth eleven grounds for Clinton's impeachment.

Thereafter, Kavanaugh was first a partner at Kirkland and Ellis, and then served in the White House under President George W. Bush for five years as counsel and staff secretary to the president. When Bush nominated Kavanaugh to the D.C. Circuit in 2003, the Senate stalled his nomination based on Democratic claims that he was too partisan. He was finally confirmed by the Senate in 2006 by a vote of 57 to 36.

Kavanaugh was the fifth Catholic then serving on the court. He is active in his faith, acting as a lector at his parish church and serving meals for Catholic Charities. He also coached the girls' championship basketball team at his local Catholic parish. He and his wife, Ashley, are the parents of two daughters.

Kavanaugh's opinions on the D.C. Circuit showed some adherence to principles of textualism and originalism. He also voted in favor of religious objectors to the HHS Contraception Mandate; in favor of expansive Second Amendment rights; and in favor of the government's power to detain enemy combatants. In a 2017 speech at Notre Dame Law School, he echoed Chief Justice Roberts's view of "the judge as umpire," and suggested that in construing ambiguous statutes, "judges should strive to find the best reading of the statute, based on the words, context, and appropriate semantic canons of construction." He also has suggested a limited use of legislative history to interpret statutes.

Hearings before the Senate Judiciary Committee on Kavanaugh's nomination were the most chaotic and contentious in the court's history. Organized opposition by angry Democrats and progressive groups, including women's pro-choice organizations, succeeded in disrupting the hearings. Women dressed in the red robes and white bonnets from *The Handmaid's Tale* assembled in the corridors in opposition to what they perceived as Kavanaugh's opposition to women's reproductive rights. Inside the hearings, numerous protesters made loud, disrupting comments. In the course of four days of hearings, 227 individuals were arrested, seventy on the first day. They shouted out "Vote No," and characterized Kavanaugh as illegitimate and as a judge who would protect President Trump from criminal charges and impeachment. A women's group proudly announced that they had been recruiting protesters with the express purpose of disrupting the hearings. Some of those protesters were photographed or observed accepting cash after they were expelled from the hearing room.

Democrats on the Judiciary Committee repeatedly called for adjourning the hearings until thousands of additional documents in the National Archives relating to Kavanaugh's service in the White House under President George W Bush were released. They also protested that forty thousand documents had been dumped on them the night before the hearing, and that over one hundred thousand documents had been marked *Committee Confidential* or withheld entirely. The motions to adjourn were ruled out of order by Senator Grassley, the committee chairman.

Questioning during the hearings by the Democratic minority focused repeatedly on abortion and on President Trump's alleged exposure to criminal proceedings and impeachment. On abortion, Senator Durbin charged that Kavanaugh wanted to change "life and death values" because "he sees things differently." Senator Hirono went even further, claiming that the nominee "really want[s] to limit a woman's reproductive rights." Senator Feinstein and many others repeatedly questioned Kavanagh on his view of the precedential status of *Roe v. Wade*. Kavanaugh described the holding of *Roe* as being "a woman has a constitutional right to obtain an abortion before viability subject to reasonable regulation by the state up to the point where that regulation constitutes an undue burden on the woman's right to obtain an abortion." He replied that *Roe* was "settled law," was "an important precedent that has been reaffirmed many times," and was "entitled [to] respect under *stare decisis*." He also described *Planned Parenthood v. Casey* as a "precedent on precedent." These responses did not stop further skeptical questioning. Senator Durbin, for example, claimed that President Trump's "people" were sure that Kavanaugh would vote to overrule *Roe*. And, indeed, he did so in the *Dobbs* case, joining Justice Alito's majority opinion.

With respect to President Trump, Senator Hirono charged that Kavanaugh was selected by right-wing groups to protect President Trump from criminal charges. Senator Coons questioned whether the nominee believed that the president could remove the special counsel investigating Russian influence in the presidential election of 2016, and whether the president could be sued or prosecuted, and if so, whether he could be during his presidency or only thereafter. Senator Blumenthal characterized the president as an "unindicted coconspirator," and called Kavanaugh "a loyal soldier" to the far right. Senator Klobuchar also focused on "seismic shifts in our democracy," seeing foreign adversary interference in Trump's election. She saw Kavanaugh's nomination as stemming from her view that he had the "most expansive view of presidential power imaginable." Kavanaugh declined to answer several of these questions, as well as whether a president could be required to respond to a subpoena or could pardon himself.

Another recurring area of questioning related to the perception that Kavanaugh was a slave of big business. Senator Whitehouse accused him of being a "political operative" who made fifty speeches to the Federalist Society as "an audition" for a spot on the court to serve the interests of big business and "dark money." Senator (and later vice president) Kamala Harris accused him of being "a politician in robes."

Several senators also accused Kavanaugh as being hostile to affirmative action, civil rights, and same-sex marriage. He was also questioned on health-care issues, including interpretation of Obamacare, and on environmental issues, and was assailed as too friendly to gun rights.

A final area of incendiary questioning was led by Senator Leahy, who accused Kavanagh of lying at his previous confirmation hearings for a spot on the D.C. Circuit. At issue was whether Kavanagh had received certain documents stolen from Democratic senators that revealed what they would question prior Republican nominees on in confirmation hearings. Leahy called this theft a "digital Watergate." Kavanaugh denied receiving any such documents, while Leahy produced certain documents he claimed showed that Kavanaugh had received some of those stolen documents. A progressive group used this and related exchanges to file a criminal charge against Kavanaugh with the D.C. Circuit. Ironically, the charges were presented to Chief Judge Merrick Garland, whose provisional Supreme Court seat was allegedly "stolen" by Judge Gorsuch.

Following the conclusion of the formal hearings, Senate Democrats submitted 1,278 written questions to Kavanaugh, all of which he answered. The questions tallied almost four times the previous high of 324 for Justice Gorsuch.

At this point, it seemed that Judge Kavanaugh was certain to be confirmed. But, just at this very same point, a very heavy shoe dropped. Senator Dianne Feinstein, a Democrat from California, released a letter she had received six weeks previously from Doctor Christine Blasey Ford. Dr. Ford claimed that a drunken Judge Kavanaugh had sexually assaulted her in his high school years, pushing her into a bedroom, throwing her on a bed, and groping her before he was knocked off the bed by a friend who also jumped on the bed. This ignited a firestorm of protest against Kavanaugh, who was assailed as a rapist, although Dr. Ford had never claimed the assault eventuated in rape.

Other accusations soon followed. One woman, a college classmate, claimed Kavanaugh had waved his private parts in her face at a party. A third woman, who was represented by the same lawyer who was suing President Trump for allegedly sexually assaulting a porn star, claimed that Kavanaugh was involved in a ring that arranged for gang rapes of women.

Following these allegations, another Senate Judiciary Committee hearing was scheduled, but only after several lengthy delays occasioned by Dr. Ford's attorneys attempting to set specific ground rules for the hearing. They demanded, for example, that Judge Kavanaugh not be in the room while Dr. Ford testified, and that Judge Kavanaugh testify first. They prevailed on the first, but not on the second, point.

At the hearing, Dr. Ford repeated her claims in a composed matter, while Judge Kavanaugh vehemently denied the allegations, and lashed out at the Senate Democrats, characterizing their actions as a deliberate, coordinated effort to stop his confirmation because of his conservative views. He angrily proclaimed that he would not withdraw. His performance at this hearing led to several organizations, universities, law schools, and publications that had previously supported him withdrawing their support, on the grounds that he had not displayed the appropriate judicial temperament in that testimony. In addition, the American Bar Association announced it would reexamine its previous determination that he was well qualified.

The Democrats repeatedly called for an FBI investigation into the allegations of sexual misconduct against Judge Kavanaugh. Senator Jeff Flake, an

Arizona Republican, conditioned his vote to advance Kavanaugh's nomination on the FBI opening a one-week investigation into those allegations. Without Flake's vote, the nomination would not have been forwarded to the Senate.

The FBI then conducted an investigation into the claims of both Dr. Ford and Judge Kavanaugh's college classmate, but not into the gang-rape allegations. After interviewing nine witnesses, the FBI was unable to confirm either of the allegations.

On October 6, Judge Kavanaugh penned an op-ed in the *Wall Street Journal* entitled "I Am An Independent, Impartial Judge." He noted that his second testimony "reflected my overwhelming frustration at being wrongly accused, without corroboration, of horrible conduct completely contrary to my record and character," and he admitted that he "might have been too emotional at times." He also wrote that "my tone was sharp, and I said a few things I should not have said."

Judge Kavanaugh's nomination then went to the floor of the Senate for a final vote. Angry and noisy protesters continuously disrupted the proceedings until they were ushered out of the room by security. On the next day, October 8, 2018, the nomination was confirmed by a 50 to 48 vote, which would have been 51 to 49, but to accommodate a Republican senator who wanted to attend his daughter's wedding, Senator Lisa Murkowski of Alaska, the sole Republican opposed to Judge Kavanaugh, voted "present" to allow the senator to attend the wedding without changing the margin of victory. Judge Kavanaugh's nomination was approved on nearly a totally partisan vote, with all the Democrats except Senator Manchin of West Virginia voting against him, while all the Republicans except Senator Murkowski supported him. His margin of victory was the narrowest since Justice Stanley Matthews was confirmed (on his second nomination) by a vote of 24 to 23.

Joining in the *Dobbs* majority opinion overruling *Roe v. Wade* might have been Justice Kavanaugh's most controversial vote, and Senators Collins and Manchin, who voted to confirm him, essentially accused him of lying to them about his views on *Roe* and *Casey*. Without their votes, the vote on his nomination would have been 50 to 50, with Vice President Michael Pence breaking the resulting tie.

In other areas, Justice Kavanaugh gave two early indications of his strong support for what he termed "religious equality" in a Statement respecting the denial of review in *Morris County Board of Chosen Freeholders v. Freedom From Religion Foundation* (2019), and in a concurring opinion in *Murphy v. Collier* (2019), on the grant of an application for a stay by a death row inmate facing imminent execution. The *Morris County* case involved the denial of a historic preservation grant to a religious building. Joined by Justices Alito and Gorsuch, Justice Kavanaugh wrote that the decision of the

New Jersey Supreme Court "is in serious tension with this Court's religious equality precedents." While he agreed that, on technical grounds, the case was not appropriate for review, he nevertheless went on to state that his view was that "prohibiting historic preservation grants to religious organizations simply because the organizations are religious would raise serious questions under this Court's precedents and the Constitution's fundamental guarantee of equality."

The *Murphy* case also presented issues of unequal treatment. Murphy was a Buddhist who requested the presence of his spiritual adviser to accompany him in the execution chamber during the execution. Justice Kavanaugh pointed out that Christian and Muslim inmates were accorded this accommodation, while members of other religions were not. He stated that "The government may not discriminate against religion generally or against particular religious denominations," and that Texas therefore must allow all inmates to have a religious advisor present in the execution room, or allow all to have such an advisor present only in the viewing room. "What the State may not do, in my view, is allow Christian or Muslim inmates but not Buddhist inmates to have a religious adviser of their religion in the execution room."

In another religious freedom case discussed below in the review of Justice Barrett, he joined Barrett's concurring opinion in *Foster v. City of Philadelphia* (2021), declining to join Justice Alito's dissenting opinion calling for the overruling of *Employment Division v. Smith* (1990).

In his first actual opinion on the merits, Justice Kavanaugh wrote for a unanimous court in *Henry Schein, Inc. v. Archer & White Sales, Inc.* (2019), a case that involved the interpretation of the Federal Arbitration Act. Under the court's precedent, the question of whether a particular arbitration agreement covers a specific dispute is left to the arbitrator to decide. Some courts, however, had ruled that a court may decide the arbitrability question if the argument that the arbitration agreement applied to a particular dispute was "wholly groundless." The question presented in the *Schein* case was whether that exception was consistent with the Federal Arbitration Act. The court held it was not.

Much as Justice Gorsuch had done in his first opinion, Justice Kavanaugh relied heavily upon the statutory text, noting that it did not contain such an exception, and that the court "may not engraft our own exceptions onto the statutory text." These rulings by the two most recently appointed justices suggest the statutory text will continue to be the principal focus of any dispute involving interpretation of the statute, with policy arguments not likely to affect the result where they conflict with the text of the statute.

In a mild surprise, Justice Kavanaugh and Justice Gorsuch voted differently in a number of cases, most often in cases that did not present a constitutional question. In each of these cases, one of them voted with the more liberal justices, and against the other four more conservative justices. Indeed, in the 2018–2019 term, they voted differently in nineteen cases. One such example occurred in the case of *Apple Inc. v. Pepper* (2019), an antitrust case in which Justice Kavanaugh wrote the majority opinion, with the four other more conservative justices dissenting in an opinion written by Justice Gorsuch.

In the 2020–2021 term, Justice Kavanaugh emerged as a critical vote in close cases. He voted in the majority more than any other member of the court in that term. His vote, particularly in cases not involving a constitutional question, was not predictably conservative.

Justice Barrett

On October 26, 2020, Judge Amy Coney Barrett of the Seventh Circuit Court of Appeals was confirmed as an associate justice of the Supreme Court by a vote of 52 to 48. The Senate vote reflected steep and vocal disagreement along party lines, with every Democrat voting against Judge Barrett's confirmation and all Republicans, except Susan Collins of Maine, voting for her confirmation. Republicans were criticized for hypocrisy given their position for not confirming Judge Garland to the Supreme Court in a presidential election year.

Judge Barrett, who was forty-eight years old at the time of her nomination by President Trump, is the youngest member of the Supreme Court. She had a sterling academic record at Rhodes College and Notre Dame Law School, graduating first in her class and summa cum laude from the latter institution. She is the only member of the current Supreme Court who did not attend Harvard or Yale Law School. The American Bar Association gave her a well-qualified rating, and she is also a member of the prestigious American Law Institute. She and her husband have seven children, two of whom were adopted from Haiti, and one of whom is a special needs child.

After graduating from Notre Dame, Justice Barrett clerked for Justice Scalia in the 1998–1999 court term, joining a Washington, D.C. law firm thereafter. She then joined the faculty of the Notre Dame Law School, and served as a professor of law there until her appointment to the Seventh Circuit in 2017. She was confirmed to that position by a vote 55 to 43, with three Democrats voting to confirm her to that position. Those hearings are best remembered for extensive questioning by Democratic senators on her religious beliefs, and particularly for her membership in an evangelical, charismatic Christian association, People of Praise, whose female members' opponents were analogized to the subservient women in Margaret Atwood's dystopic novel, *The Handmaid's Tale*. Senator Dianne Feinstein paid particular attention in her questioning of Judge Barrett to her Catholic faith, concluding that "The [Catholic] dogma lives loudly within you."

The proceedings on Judge Barrett's confirmation were conducted, with a few exceptions, in a much more civil tone than those for Justices Gorsuch and Kavanaugh. The Republicans stressed her commitment to the rule of law, and her ability to judge cases as an originalist, respecting the text and the original public meaning of constitutional and statutory provisions, rather than imposing her policy preferences on the litigants before her. They cited her opening remarks at the hearing, during which Judge Barrett stated that courts must enforce "the rule of law," and that "courts are not designed to solve every problem or right every wrong in our public life." Those policy judgments, she commented, are committed instead to the "political branches" under our system of government.

The Democrats emphasized two objections to confirming Judge Barrett. To begin with, they pointed out that an attack on the Affordable Care Act would be argued in the Supreme Court in early November, shortly after her anticipated confirmation, and that she had been critical, in an law review article, of Chief Justice Roberts for upholding that legislation by pushing it "beyond its plausible meaning to save the statute." The Democrats repeatedly dramatized the issue by invoking the real-world experiences of specific individuals suffering from serious medical ailments and their need for the insurance provided to them under the Affordable Care Act. When all the Democratic senators boycotted the final vote on Judge Barrett's confirmation, many of them left life-sized pictures of these individuals in their chairs in the hearing room. The Democrats' fears proved baseless, as Justice Barrett joined with six other colleagues to reject the challenge to the Affordable Care Act that was advanced in *California v. Texas* (2021), albeit on the grounds that all the challengers, Texas and more than twelve other states, joined by two individuals, lacked standing.

The second major objection advanced by the Democrats to reject Judge Barrett focused indirectly on her religious beliefs, particularly as they may have impacted her view of *Roe v. Wade.* She testified that she did not consider *Roe* to be a "super precedent," "But that does not mean it should be overruled." She also refused to opine as to whether *Roe* was correctly decided. Democratic senators repeatedly pointed to a pro-life ad in a local newspaper which she and many others signed. That ad referred, on a separate, unsigned page to the "barbaric legacy" of *Roe v. Wade.* Their questioning also referenced a Notre Dame commentary that referred to the ruling in that case as "infamous." In the end, she also, along with Justices Gorsuch and Kavanaugh, voted to overrule *Roe* in the *Dobbs* case.

Given her clerkship and respect for Justice Scalia, Judge Barrett was also accused of being a clone for that justice. She replied that if she were confirmed, "you will be getting a Justice Barrett, not a Justice Scalia."

Justice Barrett was questioned on many other issues. Because President Trump repeatedly stated that he wished to have a ninth justice appointed before the election, she was questioned as to whether she would recuse herself if there were an election challenge by President Trump, as well as whether the president could pardon himself. She responded that if there were an election dispute, she would look to the cases interpreting the recusal statute and confer with her colleagues on that issue. She was also asked to opine on whether prior decisions regarding the availability of contraceptives, the legality of gay marriage, and other issues were correctly decided. She declined to give an opinion on any of these issues.

Justice Barrett was also criticized for dissenting from an opinion that upheld a statutory ban on felons owning guns. In her dissenting opinion from the Seventh Circuit ruling, she indicated that a nonviolent felon should not forfeit his Second Amendment right to apply for a gun license.

Justice Barrett was also questioned on voting laws, the Emoluments Clause, and standing issues. As many of the prior justices had done, she declined to express an opinion on any of these issues. When questioned regarding climate change, she replied that "I am not a scientist," that her views were "not relevant," and that she had "no informed opinion."

When she joined the court, Justice Barrett had an immediate impact in cases in which houses of worship challenged COVID-19–related restrictions on their conduct of religious services. These cases arose on the court's so-called shadow docket, which involve emergency appeals seeking injunctive relief against a lower court's decision. These appeals are decided quickly without full briefing or oral argument. In discussing the court's decisions in these cases in a 2020 address to the Federalist Society, Justice Alito stated that "The pandemic has resulted in previously unimaginable restrictions on individual liberty."

Before Justice Barrett's confirmation, Justice Ginsburg had joined a ruling (entered without an opinion) that denied an appeal from an order upholding restrictions on religious services which were imposed by California. In a concurring opinion, Chief Justice Roberts wrote that it was appropriate in cases involving a pandemic to defer to the expertise of governmental authorities. *South Bay United Pentecostal Church v. Newsom* (2020). The court similarly declined to block capacity limits in Nevada and Illinois. After the death of Justice Ginsburg, the court reversed course, striking down several restrictions imposed by state authorities on religious institutions. It did so on the grounds that the regulations in question singled out houses of worship for "especially harsh treatment." These decisions, in which Justice Barrett joined, held that such disparate treatment violated the First Amendment, making judicial deference to the government inappropriate. See, for example, *Roman Catholic Diocese of Brooklyn v. Cuomo* (2020) (decided 5 to 4).

Justice Barrett wrote an opinion in only one of these cases. At issue in a second appeal by the South Bay United Pentecostal Church in 2021 were three restrictions: a ban on indoor worship in Tier 1 counties; a state-wide ban on singing or chanting during such worship services; and a statewide 25 percent capacity limit on indoor worship. A six-member majority of the court struck down the Tier 1 ban on indoor worship, while a different six-member majority declined to block the state-wide ban on singing and chanting. In addition, eight of the nine justices declined to interfere with the 25 percent statewide limit on indoor services. The court left open the possibility that new evidence could be adduced by the church that the state was not applying either the percentage capacity limitations or the ban on singing and chanting in a generally applicable manner. Justice Barrett wrote a one-paragraph concurring opinion, joined by Justice Kavanaugh, limited to the issue of singing and chanting. She indicated that the church had failed to carry the burden of establishing entitlement to relief from that ban, but it was free to provide further evidence that the ban was not generally applicable. She declined to join the Statement of Justice Gorsuch, joined by Justices Thomas and Alito, which argued that a total ban on singing and chanting was not "narrowly tailored to [the state's] legitimate public health concerns."

In two subsequent decisions on the shadow docket, however, she declined to join Justices Gorsuch, Alito, and Thomas who would have granted injunctive relief in cases from Maine and New York which refused to allow religious exemptions to mandatory COVID-19 vaccinations. See, for example, *Dr. A v. Hochul* (Dec. 13, 2021). Once again, Justice Kavanaugh took the same position.

Justice Barrett's first merits opinion came in *United States Fish and Wildlife Service v. Sierra Club, Inc.* (2021). The case involved interpretation of the Freedom of Information Act, specifically whether draft biological opinions analyzing a proposed rule, making of the Environmental Protection Agency were protected from disclosure by the deliberative process privilege. In an opinion for seven members of the court, Justice Barrett wrote that the drafts were privileged because they reflected a preliminary review, and not a final decision, regarding the proposed EPA rule. They were "both predecisional and deliberative." Perhaps most notable about the decision was that Justices Breyer and Soyomayor dissented, in a six-page dissenting opinion written by Justice Breyer. This is unusual when a new justice writes her first opinion, since such opinions are usually delivered on behalf of a unanimous court.

As has been the case with Justice Kavanaugh, Justice Barrett has not been a predictably conservative vote on the court. She has, at times, joined with more liberal judges in separate opinions. In addition, she has sometimes differed from some of her conservative colleagues, even in cases involving constitutional adjudications, including the pandemic ban on religious services discussed above. Most notable was her separate concurring opinion in *Fulton v. City of Philadelphia* (2021), in which she (along with Justice Kavanaugh) declined to join three conservative justices who called for the overruling of *Employment Division v. Smith* (1990), which had held that religious believers could not justify noncompliance with a neutral law of general applicability even where they had a bona fide religious objection to doing so. Both *Fulton* and *Smith* are discussed in chapter 2.

Justice Barrett is also proving to be an independent voice on the court. One example of this is the fact that she wrote three dissenting opinions in close cases that were decided at the end of the courts' term.

Justice Jackson

Upholding his campaign promise to nominate an African American woman to serve on the Supreme Court, President Joseph Biden nominated Ketanji Brown Jackson on February 25, 2022. She is a magna-cum-laude graduate of Harvard-Radcliffe College and a cum-laude graduate of Harvard Law School, where she was an editor of the *Harvard Law Review.* Justice Jackson was fifty-one years old at the time of her nomination to the Supreme Court. She is married to a general surgeon and has two daughters.

Justice Jackson served as a district judge in the District of Columbia from 2013 to 2021 before being confirmed as a judge on the United States Court of Appeals for the District of Columbia Circuit less than a year before her Supreme Court nomination. She served as Justice Breyer's law clerk on the Supreme Court during the Supreme Court 1999–2000 term, and he administered her oath of office when she was appointed to the district court. She also served as a public defender, and was an associate with several well-regarded law firms, before joining the large law firm of Morrison & Foerster LLP, where she practiced appellate litigation.

In swearing her in to the district court, Justice Breyer said that "She sees things from different points of view, and she sees somebody else's point of view and understands it."

While her judicial record is sparse, her three most noteworthy district court opinions all involved ruling against the Trump administration on cases involving fast-track deportations, grants for teenage pregnancy prevention, and immunity for a former White House Counsel from providing congressional testimony regarding President Trump's alleged efforts to obstruct an investigation into Russian interference with the presidential election. Her most notable quote came in the last of these three opinions, where she wrote that "Presidents are not kings. They do not have subjects, bound by loyalty or blood, whose destiny they are entitled to control."

Her stance on abortion favors the pro-choice position. For example, in 2001, she signed on to an amicus brief supporting a Massachusetts law creating a "buffer zone" to bar the public from approaching abortion clinics. Two of the clients on whose behalf the brief was filed were the Abortion Access Project of Massachusetts, and NARAL Pro-Choice America. While she served for a year on the board of a private Christian school whose statement of faith opposed both abortion and same-sex marriage, she nevertheless testified in a Senate hearing on her confirmation to the court of appeals that she was not aware of that statement, and she did not necessarily agree with all the statements of the boards on which she served. She went on to explain that "I do believe in religious liberty," which she characterized as a "foundational tenet of our entire government."

In the Senate Hearings on her nomination, Justice Brown somewhat surprisingly depicted herself in terms that resonated with originalism. She testified that she focused on the text of a provision and its original public meaning, stating that "I am focusing on original public meaning because I'm constrained to interpret the text." When questioned regarding her overall judicial philosophy, she testified that she has no such overarching philosophy but believed that judges should not use their policy preferences in judging, but that she should instead "stay in my own lane."

The Republican opposition to Justice Jackson focused on two specific areas. First, they criticized her sentencing of several defendants who downloaded videos of child abuse or were otherwise engaged in pedophilia, since the terms she imposed fell below the federal sentencing guidelines. She was defended by academics and others contending that many judges in similar cases also departed from the sentencing guidelines, and she noted additionally that a sentencing judge must adjudicate each case on its particular facts.

The second and also heated exchanges probed her stance on the controversial issue of teaching critical race theory ("CRT") to young students. Senator Ted Cruz displayed a series of books from the library of a grammar school on whose board she served which presented that theory in books that were targeted to younger children. Justice Jackson testified that she was not an expert on CRT and that, in any event, she did not use it in her judging. She explained that she had not ever relied upon the theory in her judging, was not an expert on it, and had not studied it, although she was aware of it. She also testified that she did not know that the books Senator Cruz brought with him were in the school's library.

Justice Jackson was also questioned about her representation of Guantánamo Bay prisoners as a public defender, as well as signing on to a brief which accused President George W. Bush of war crimes. She claimed to have no memory of the brief and testified that she had no intent to disparage former President Bush.

Justice Jackson also declined to express an opinion on court expansion, although she did have a private view on it. She expressly refused to rule out the concept of expanding the number of Supreme Court justices.

On questions relating to abortion and gender identity, she stated that she was not a biologist and did not know whether a child can live outside the womb at twenty-eight weeks, and she could not define what constitutes a "woman." When Senator Blackburn pointed out that the brief in which she had joined in the abortion buffer zone case started by describing protesters at abortion clinics as "a hostile, noisy crowd of 'in-your-face' protesters," she responded that the quote was directed at protesters on both the pro-life and pro-choice sides.

With respect to Supreme Court precedent, she stated when questioned regarding the status of *Roe v. Wade* and the *Heller* precedents that "All precedents of the Supreme Court have to be respected."

Justice Jackson was confirmed by a vote of 53 to 47. Unlike Justice Barrett, who did not receive one vote from a Democratic senator, three Republican senators (Collins, Murkowski, and Romney) voted to confirm Jackson's nomination. She assumed her seat on the court after Justice Breyer retired at the end of June 2022.

From her beginning on the court, she has been very vocal in oral arguments, and has indicated a belief that a colorblind approach is not appropriate under the Fourteenth Amendment, a key issue for the adjudication of affirmative action and voting cases.

PUBLIC PERCEPTION OF THE SUPREME COURT

Until recently, public opinion regarding the Supreme Court generally had been positive during the twenty-one years the Gallup Poll and other organizations have sampled opinion on the court.

For example, a survey by the Pew Research Center in August 2106, shortly before the court's new term opened with one judicial vacancy, showed a favorable view of the court by the public. Some 60 percent had a favorable view, which Pew noted to be "in line with the generally positive opinions found before 2015." Only 32 percent had an unfavorable view of the court in August. Pew also recorded "a significant partisan gap" in the views of the court, with 73 percent of Democrats having a favorable opinion, compared to 57 percent of Republicans.

Pew attributed the overall rise in the popularity of the court to the fact that there were "fewer high-profile decisions" in 2016, noting that the atypically large number of unfavorable views in 2015 could be attributed to "the court's upholding of the Affordable Care Act and legalization of same-sex marriage."

A July 2019 Pew Research Center Survey reported a 62 percent approval rate for the Supreme Court. The most notable finding was that of a "Partisan gap," which was "among the widest in two decades." While approximately 75 percent of Republicans and Republican-leading independents had a favorable opinion of the court, only 49 percent of Democrats and Democratic leaners did, representing a 26-point gap. The gap was most noticeable among liberal Democrats, only 40 percent of whom approved of the court, compared to a 57 percent favorable view of the court by conservative and moderate Democrats.

The depths of this partisan gap were shown with particular force in a brief filed in the Supreme Court by five Democratic senators of the party's progressive wing, signed by Senator Sheldon Whitehouse of Rhode Island. The case questioned the constitutionality of a New York law banning the transport of gun owners' handguns outside their homes even if they were locked and unloaded. Although the Supreme Court had accepted the case for review, New York made subsequent changes to the law which lessened the restrictions on transportation. The Democratic senators urged the court to dismiss the appeal, relying heavily upon a Quinnipiac poll reporting that 55 percent of the respondents thought that the Supreme Court was "motivated by politics," and that 51 percent favored that the court be restructured to minimize the influence of politics. These senators warned the Supreme Court that it must dismiss the appeal to "stem the growing public belief that its decisions are 'motivated mainly by politics.'" The brief cited seventy-eight five-to-four or five-to-three opinions delivered in the twelve-year period between 2005 and 2017, contending that seventy-three of these decisions favored "interests important to the big funders, corporate influencers, and political base of the Republican Party." In an incendiary and unprecedented conclusion, these senators proclaimed that: "The Supreme Court is not well. And the people know it. Perhaps the court can heal itself before the public demands it be restructured in order to reduce the influence of politics. Particularly on the urgent issue of gun control, the nation desperately needs it to heal."

While the Supreme Court ultimately dismissed the appeal, Justice Alito characterized the senators' brief in an October 2020 Address to the Federalist Society as "an affront to the Constitution and the rule of law" because it was an inappropriate attempt "to influence our decision by anything other than legal argumentation. That sort of thing has often happened in countries governed by power, not law."

The generally positive view of the court by members of the general public took a radical turn in September of 2021, when the Gallup organization reported that the approval of the Supreme Court had fallen to 40 percent, which was the lowest rating since Gallup starting surveying public opinion on the court twenty-one years earlier, and nine points lower that had been reported in July of the same year. This Gallup poll was taken right after the court refused to void a Texas abortion law which radically shortened the time in which a woman could obtain an abortion. That decision was the subject of disapproval by 54 percent of the adults who were surveyed by Monmouth University in September 2021.

Gallup also reported that 37 percent, a new high, considered the court to be too conservative, although 40 percent still viewed it as "about right" in its ideology. Moreover, majorities of all Republicans, Democrats, and independents registered their disapproval of the court.

Attacks on the Supreme Court reached a fever pitch soon after with the unauthorized leaking in February 2022 of a draft majority opinion by Justice Alito in *Dobbs v. Jackson Women's Health Organization*. That draft opinion would have overruled *Roe v. Wade*, and the final opinion did so. Almost immediately, two radical pro-abortion organizations threatened to burn down the Supreme Court and assassinate the conservative justices. Protesters appeared at the homes of these justices with one protester from California traveling to Justice Kavanaugh's home with a bag full of weapons and ammunition with the admitted intent to kill the justice. He was arrested in the vicinity by police and charged with attempted murder. Many states have, or promised to enact, legislation that would make abortion freely available in their states should *Roe v. Wade* be overruled. Moreover, government officials in several big cities and elsewhere vowed that they would not enforce any decision that limited abortion rights.

A Gallup Poll in June 2022 reported that confidence in the Supreme Court had fallen to 25 percent, five points lower than the previous low. That poll predated the final opinion in *Dobbs*, as well as later decisions on public carry of firearms and the right of a college football coach to pray on the field at the end of games. Finally, after those decisions were released, the Pew Research Center reported in September 2022 that 49 percent of those it surveyed had an unfavorable view of the Supreme Court, with 48 percent reporting a favorable view. Significantly, the partisan gap between Republicans and Democrats reached 45 percent, which Pew noted was "wider by far than at any point in 35 years of polling on the court.." Only 28 percent of Democrats had a favorable view of the court, compared to 73 percent of Republicans.

NOTE

1. Clarence Thomas, *My Grandfather's Son: A Memoir* (New York: Harper, 2007).

Bibliography

BOOKS AND ARTICLES

Abrams, Floyd, *The Soul of the First Amendment* (New Haven: Yale University Press, 2017).

Adler, Jonathan H.,"Judicial Minimalism, The Mandate, and Mr. Roberts," ssrn.com/abstract=2169933.

Avstreih, Melissa, "The Cash Behind the Super PACs," *Bloomberg Businessweek*, July 23–July 29, 2012.

Barrett, Paul M., "Opening Remarks: John Roberts, CEO, *Bloomberg Businessweek*, July 9-July15, 2012.

Blackman, Josh, "Obergefell and Tradition," joshblackman.com/blog, April 13, 2017.

Cole, David, "The Supreme Court Looks Away," nybooks.com/daily, July 18, 2018.

Desmond, Joan Frawley, "San Francisco High-School Teachers Approve Contract, Amid Ongoing Tensions," *National Catholic Reporter*, August 23, 2015.

Dworkin, Ronald, "A Bigger Victory Than We Knew," *New York Review of Books*, August 16, 2012.

Feldman, Noah, "A Decision That Will Live in Infamy," *Bloomberg, Opinion/Politics and Public Policy*, June 26, 2018.

Garnett, Richard, "2012 Supreme Court Roundup," *First Things*, No. 227, October 2012.

Goldstein, Tom, "Analysis: Supreme Court Invalidates Section 5's Coverage Scheme," SCOTUSblog Commentary, June 22, 2009.

Hamburger, Philip, *Separation of Church and State* (Cambridge: Harvard University Press, 2002).

Kroll, Andy, "The Supreme Court Just Gutted Another Campaign Finance Law. Here's What Happened," *Mother Jones*, April 2, 2014.

Levy, Robert A. and Mellor, William, *The Dirty Dozen: How Twelve Supreme Court Cases Radically Expanded Government and Eroded Freedom* (New York: Sentinel, 2008).

Liptak, Adam, "Court's Free-Speech Expansion Has Far-Reaching Consequences," *New York Times*, August 17, 2015.

Liptak, Adam, "How Conservatives Weaponized the First Amendment," *New York Times*, June 30, 2018.

Mannino, Edward F., *Shaping America: The Supreme Court and American Society* (Columbia: University of South Carolina Press, 2009).

Mannino, Edward F., *The Roberts Court and Terrorism: A Citizen's Guide* (Amazon Kindle, 2016).

Mannino, Edward F., "The Sinking Wall of Separation: The Supreme Court and the Establishment Clause 1947– 2005," *American Experiment Religious Freedom* (Portland: University of Portland Press, 2008).

McConnell, Michael, "A Free Speech Year at the Court," *First Things*, No. 216, October 2011.

Movsesian, Mark, "*Masterpiece Cakeshop* and the Future of Religious Freedom," 42 *Harvard Journal of Law & Public Policy* 711, Summer 2019.

O'Donnell, Patrick, "Cleveland Diocese Adds Detailed 'Morality Clause' to High School Teachers, Too," *Plain Dealer,* April 8, 2015.

Parker, Ashley, "Outside Money Drives a Deluge of Political Ads," *New York Times*, July 17, 2014.

Phillips, Jack, "Jack Phillips: Can I Just Be a Cake Artist Again?" *Denver Post*, OpEd, March 8, 2019.

Pinckney, Darryl, "Young Barry Wins," *New York Review of Books*, August 16, 2012.

Pullman, Joy, "After More Evidence of Its Anti-Christian animus, Colorado Commission Suspends Harassment of Cake Baker," thefederalist.com, March 6, 2019.

Ruger, Todd, "Alito Defends 'Citizens' in Speech to Federalist Society." *The BLT: The Blog of Legal Times*, November 16, 2012.

Thomas, Clarence, *My Grandfather's Son: A Memoir* (New York: Harper, 2007).

Turley, Jonathan, "The Trouble with the 'Dignity' of Same-Sex Marriage," *Washington Post*, July 2, 2015.

Waggoner, Kristen, "Jack Phillips Wins Again," nationalreview.com/benchmemos, March 11, 2019.

Cases

Abington School District v. Schempp, 374 U.S. 203 (1963)

Abood v. Detroit Bd. of Ed., 431 U.S. 209 (1977)

Abrams v. United States, 250 U.S. 616 (1919)

Agency for International Development v. Alliance for Open Society International, Inc., 570 U.S.—(2013)

American Legion v. American Humanist Ass'n, 588 U.S.—(2019)

American Tradition Partnership, Inc. v. Bullock, 567 U.S. 516 (2012)

Americans for Prosperity Foundation v. Bonta, 594 U.S.—(2021)

Apple Inc. v. Pepper, 587 U.S.—(2019)

Atkins v. Virginia, 536 U.S. 304 (2002)

Baker v. Nelson, 409 U.S. 810 (1972)

Barr v. American Association of Political Consultants, Inc., 591 U.S.—(2020)

Box v. Indiana, 587 U.S.—(2019)
Brandenburg v. Ohio, 395 U.S. 444 (1969)
Brnovich v. Democratic National Committee, 594 U.S.—(2021)
Brown v. Board of Education, 347 U.S. 483 (1954)
Brown v. Entertainment Merchants Ass'n, 564 U.S. 786 (2011)
Bond v. United States, 572 U.S.—(2014)
Buckley v. Valeo, 424 U.S. 1 (1976)
Burwell v. Hobby Lobby Stores, Inc., 573 U.S.—(2014)
Business Leaders in Christ v. The University of Iowa, C.A. No. 17-cv-00080-SMR-SBJ (S.D. Iowa, January 23, 2018).
Byrd v. United States, 584 U.S.—(2018)
Cady v. Dombrowski, 413 U.S. 433 (1973)
Caetano v. Massachusetts, 577 U.S.—(2016)
California v. Texas, 593 U.S.—(2021)
Caniglia v. Strom, 593 U.S.—(2021)
Carpenter v. United States, 585 U.S.—(2018)
Carson v. Makin, 596 U.S.—(2002)
Cedar Point Nursery v. Hassid, 594 U.S.—(2021)
Christian Legal Society v. Martinez, 561 U.S. 661 (2010)
Citizens United v. Federal Election Commission, 558 U.S. 310 (2010)
City of Austin v. Reagan National Advertising of Austin, LLC, 596 U.S.—(2022)
Civil Rights Cases, 109 U.S. 3 (1883)
Collins v. Virginia, 584 U.S.—(2018)
Commonwealth of Pennsylvania v. Batts, No.45 MAP 2016 (Pa. Sup. Ct. June 26, 2017)
Cooper v. Aaron, 358 U.S. 1 (1958)
County of Allegheny v. ACLU, 492 U.S. 573 (1989)
Crawford v. Marion County Election Board, 553 U.S. 181 (2008)
Dennis v. United States, 341 U.S. 494 (1951)
District of Columbia v. Heller, 554 U.S. 570 (2008)
Dobbs v. Jackson Women's Health Organization, 596 U.S.—(2022)
Doe v. Bolton, 410 U.S. 179 (1973)
Dr. A. v. Hochul, 595 U.S.—(Dec. 13, 2021)
Edwards v. Aguillard, 482 U.S. 578 (1987)
Employment Division v. Smith, 494 U.S. 872 (1990)
Engel v. Vitale, 370 U.S. 421 (1962)
Epperson v. Arkansas, 393 U.S. 97 (1968)
Espinoza v. Montana Department of Revenue, 591 U.S.—(2020)
Everson v. Board of Education, 330 U.S. 1 (1947)
Expressions Hair Design v. Schneiderman, 581 U.S.—(2017)
Fisher v. University of Texas at Austin, 570 U.S.—(2013)
Fisher v. University of Texas at Austin, 579 U.S.—(2016)
Fulton v. City of Philadelphia, 593 U.S.—(2021)
Furman v. Georgia, 408 U.S. 238 (1972)
Gee v. Planned Parenthood Gulf Coast, Inc., No. 17–1492, (Dec. 10, 2018)

Gibbons v. Ogden, 22 U.S. (9 Wheat.) 1 (1824)
Gonsales v. Raich, 545 U.S. 1 (2005)
Gonzales v. Carhart, 550 U.S. 124 (2007)
Glossip v. Gross, 576 U.S.—(2015)
Graham v. Florida, 560 U.S. 48 (2010)
Gregg v. Georgia, 428 U.S. 153 (1976)
Gratz v. Bollinger, 539 U.S. 244 (2003)
Grutter v. Bollinger, 539 U.S. 306 (2003)
Hall v. Florida, 572 U.S.—(2014)
Hammer v, Dagenhart, 247 U.S. 251 (1918)
Heart of Atlanta Motel, Inc. v. United States, 379 U.S. 241 (1964)
Henderson v. United States, 339 U.S. 816 (1950)
Henry Schein, Inc. v. Archer & White Sales, Inc., 586 U.S.—(2019)
Henson v. Santander Consumer USA Inc., 582 U.S.—(2017)
Hester v. United States, No. 17–9082 (January 7, 2019)
Hill v. Colorado, 530 U.S. 703 (2000)
Holder v. Humanitarian Law Project, 561 U.S. 1 (2010)
Hollingsworth v. Perry, 570 U.S. 693 (2013)
Holt v. Hobbs, 574 U.S.—(2015)
Hosanna-Tabor Evangelical Lutheran Church & School v. EEOC, 565 U.S. 171 (2012)
Iancu v. Brunetti, 588 U.S.—(2019)
Jones v. Mississippi, 593 U.S.—(2021)
June Medical Services L.L.C. v. Gee, No. 18A774, 586 U.S.—(Feb. 7, 2019)
June Medical Services L.L.C. v. Russo, 591 U.S.—(2020)
Janus v. American Federation of State, County, & Municipal Employees, 585 U.S.—(2018)
Katz v. United States, 389 U.S. 347 (1967)
Katzenbach v. McClung, 379 U.S. 294 (1964)
In re Kemmler, 136 U.S. 436 (1890)
Kennedy v. Bremerton School District, 597 U.S.—(2022)
King v. Burwell, 576 U.S.—(2015)
Korematsu v. United States, 323 U.S. 214 (1944)
Lange v. California, 594 U.S.—(2021)
Lee v. Weisman, 505 U.S. 577 (1992)
Lemon v. Kurtzman, 403 U.S. 602 (1971)
Little Sisters of the Poor Saints Peter and Paul Home v. Pennsylvania, 591 U.S.—(2020)
Loving v. Virginia, 388 U.S. 1 (1967)
Lucas v. South Carolina Coastal Council, 505 U.S. 1003 (1992)
Mahanoy Area School District v. B.L., 594 U.S.—(2021)
Masterpiece Cakeshop, Ltd. v. Colorado Civil Rights Commission, 584 U.S.—(2018)
Matal v. Tam, 582 U.S.—(2017)
McCollum v. Board of Education, 333 U.S. 203 (1948)
McCullen v. Coakley, 573 U.S.—(2014)

McCutcheon v. Federal Election Commission, 572 U.S. 185 (2014)
McDonald v. Chicago, 561 U.S. 742 (2010)
McLaurin v. Oklahoma State Regents, 339 U.S. 637 (1950)
Meyer v. Nebraska, 262 U.S. 390 (1923)
Milliken v. Bradley, 418 U.S. 717 (1974)
Miller v. Alabama, 567 U.S. 460 (2012)
Minersville School District v. Gobitis, 310 U.S. 586 (1940)
Mitchell v. Helms, 530 U.S. 793 (2000)
Mitchell v. Wisconsin, 588 U.S.—(2019)
Montgomery v. Louisiana, 577 U.S.—(2016)
Moore v. Illinois, 55 U.S. (14 How.) 13 (1852)
Morris County Board of Chosen Freeholders v. Freedom From Religion Foundation, 586 U.S.—(March 4, 2019)
Murphy v. National Collegiate Athletic Association, 584 U.S.—(2018)
National Institute of Family & Life Advocates v. Becerra, 585 U.S.—(2018)
National Federation of Independent Business v. Sebelius, 567 U.S. 519 (2012)
New York State Rifle & Pistol Association, Inc. v. City of New York, No. 18–280, 590 U.S.—(April 27, 2020)
New York Rifle & Pistol Association v. Corlett, No. 20–843 (April 26, 2021)
New York State Rifle & Pistol Association v Bruen, 597 U.S.—(2022)
New York Times Co. v. Sullivan, 376 U.S. 254 (1964)
NLRB v. Jones & Laughlin Steel Corp., 301 U.S. 1 (1937)
Northwest Austin Municipal Utility District Number One v. Holder, 557 U.S. 193 (2009)
Obergefell v. Hodges, 576 U.S.—(2015)
Olmstead v. United States, 277 U.S. 438 (1928)
Our Lady of Guadalupe School v. Morrissey-Berri, 591 U.S.—(2020)
Packingham v. North Carolina, 582 U.S.—(2017)
Parents Involved in Community Schools v. Seattle School District No. 1, 551 U.S.—(2007)
Pavan v Smith, 582 U.S.—(2017)
Penn Central Transportation Co. v. New York City, 438 U.S. 104 (1978)
Peruta v. California, 582 U.S.—(2017)
Pitre v. Cain, 562 U.S. 992 (2010)
Planned Parenthood v. Casey, 505 U.S. 833 (1992)
Plessy v. Ferguson, 163 U.S. 537 (1896)
Reed v. Town of Gilbert, 576 U.S.—(2015)
Regents of the University of California v. Bakke, 438 U.S. 265 (1978)
Reynolds v. United States, 98 U.S. 145 (1879)
Ricci v. DeStefano, 557 U.S. 557 (2009)
Riley v. California, 573 U.S.—(2014)
Roe v. Wade, 410 U.S. 113 (1973)
Rogers v. Grewal, 590 U.S.—(2020)
Roman Catholic Diocese of Brooklyn v. Cuomo, 592 U.S.—(2020)
Rucho v. Common Cause, 588 U.S.—(2019)

Santa Fe Independent School District v. Doe, 530 U.S. 290 (2000)
Schechter Poultry Corp. v. United States, 295 U.S. 495 (1935)
Henry Schein, Inc. v. United States, 586 U.S.—(2019)
Schenck v. United States, 249 U.S. 47 (1919)
Schuette v. Coalition to Defend Affirmative Action, 572 U.S. 291 (2014)
Scott v. Sandford, 19 How. (16 U.S.) 393 (1857)
Shelby County, Alabama v. Holder, 570 U.S. 529 (2013)
Shelley v. Kramer, 334 U.S. 1 (1948)
Sherbert v. Verner, 374 U.S. 398 (1963)
Shurtleff v. City of Boston, 596 U.S.—(2022)
Slaughterhouse Cases, 16 Wall. (83 U.S.) 36 (1873)
Silvester v. Becerra, 583 U.S.—(2018)
Snyder v. Phelps, 562 U.S. 443 (2011)
Sorrell v. IMS Health, 564 U.S. 552 (2011)
South Bay United Pentecostal Church v. Newsom, 590 U.S.—(2020) and 592 U.S.—(2021)
South Carolina v. Katzenbach, 383 U.S. 301 (1966)
Stenberg v. Carhart, 530 U.S. 914 (2000)
Storman's, Inc. v. Weisman, No. 15–862, 579 U.S.—(June 28, 2016)
Swann v. Charlotte-Mecklenburg County Board, 402 U.S. 1 (1971)
Sweatt v. Painter, 339 U.S. 629 (1950)
Tanzin v. Tanvir, 592 U.S.—(2020)
Timbs v. Indiana, 586 U.S.—(2019)
Tinker v. Des Moines Independent Community School District, 393 U.S. 503 (1969)
Torres v. Madrid, 592 U.S.—(2021)
Town of Greece v. Galloway, 572 U.S. 565 (2014)
Trinity Lutheran Church v. Comer, 582 U.S.—(2017)
Trop v. Dulles, 356 U.S. 86 (1958)
Trump v. Hawaii, 585 U.S.—(2018)
Trump v. International Refugee Assistance Project, 582 U.S.—(2017) and 583 U.S.—(2017)
Trump v. New York, 592 U.S.—(2020)
United States v. Alvarez, 567 U.S. 709 (2012)
United States v. Butler, 297 U.S. 1 (1936)
United States v. Cruikshank, 92 U.S. 542 (1876)
United States v. Darby, 312 U.S. 100 (1941)
United States v. E.C. Knight Co., 156 U.S. 1 (1895)
United States v. Haymond, 588 U.S.—(2019)
United States v. Jones, 565 U.S. 400 (2012)
United States v. Karo, 468 U.S. 705 (1984)
United States v. Knotts, 460 U.S. 276 (1983)
United States v. Lanza, 260 U.S. 377 (1922)
United States v. Lopez, 514 U.S. 549 (1995)
United States v. Miller, 307 U.S. 174 (1939)
United States v. Morrison, 529 U.S. 598 (2000)

United States v. Reese, 92 U.S. 214 (1876)
United States v. Stevens, 559 U.S. 460 (2010)
United States v. Windsor, 570 U.S. 744 (2013)
United States Fish and Wildlife Service v. Sierra Club, Inc., 592 U.S.—(2021)
Utah v. Strieff, 579 U.S.—(2016)
Walker v. Texas Div., Sons of Confederate Veterans, Inc, 576 U.S.—(2015)
Weaver v. Massachusetts, 582 U.S.—(2017)
Webster v. Reproductive Health Services, 492 U.S. 490 (1989)
Weems v. United States, 217 U.S. 349 (1910)
West Virginia State Board of Education v. Barnette, 319 U.S. 624 (1943)
Wickard v. Filburn, 317 U.S. 111 (1942)
Whole Woman's Health v. Hellerstedt, 579 U.S.—(2016)
Williams-Yulee v. Florida Bar, 575 U.S.—(2015)
Yates v. United States, 354 U.S. 298 (1957)
Yick Wo v. Hopkins, 118 U.S. 356 (1886)
State of Wisconsin v. Yoder, 406 U.S. 205 (1972)
Zablocki v. Redhail, 434 U.S. 374 (1979)
Zelman v. Simmons-Harris, 536 U.S. 639 (2002)
Zorach v. Clauson, 343 U.S. 306 (1952)
Zubik v. Burwell, 578 U.S.—(2016)

Index

About the Author

Edward F. Mannino is a lawyer and historian. He is a member of the Supreme Court Bar, and he has taught courses on the Supreme Court and on American Law at the University of Pennsylvania and at Chestnut Hill College. This is his third book on the Supreme Court, following *Shaping America: The Supreme Court and American Society* (University of South Carolina Press, 2009) and *The Roberts Court and Terrorism: A Citizen's Guide* (Amazon Kindle, 2016). He lectures and writes on the Supreme Court and other topics. He has also written books on legal, business, and religious history.

An active trial lawyer for over forty years, Mannino was named as one of the "Nation's Top Litigators" by the *National Law Journal.* He was listed for many years in *The Best Lawyers in America* and in *America's Leading Lawyers for Business* for Business and Commercial Litigation, and for Securities Litigation. He is an Elected Life Member of the American Law Institute, a Knight of Malta, and a member of the Organization of American Historians and the Fellowship of Catholic Scholars. Mannino has served as a member of the Board of Overseers of the University of Pennsylvania School of Arts and Sciences, and as a Commonwealth Trustee of Temple University. He was named to the Temple position by Governor Robert P. Casey of Pennsylvania and confirmed by the Pennsylvania Senate.

Mannino is married to Antoinette K. O'Connell, a former Wall Street training executive. They live in Gwynedd Valley, Pennsylvania.

www.ingramcontent.com/pod-product-compliance
Ingram Content Group UK Ltd.
Pitfield, Milton Keynes, MK11 3LW, UK
UKHW040857081026
15587UKWH00016B/747

9 781666 938302